Political Questions/Judicial Answers

❖

Political Questions/
Judicial Answers

DOES THE RULE OF LAW APPLY
TO FOREIGN AFFAIRS?

✢

THOMAS M. FRANCK

PRINCETON UNIVERSITY PRESS

PRINCETON, NEW JERSEY

Library of Congress Cataloging-in-Publication Data

Franck, Thomas M.
    Political questions/ judicial answers : does the rule of law apply
to foreign affairs? / Thomas M. Franck.
        p. cm.
Includes index.
ISBN 0-691-09241-9
    1. United States—Foreign relations. 2. Political questions and
judicial power—United States. 3. Judicial review—United States.
4. Courts—United States. 5. Separation of powers—United States.
6. United States—National security—Law and legislation.
I. Title.
KF4651.F73   1992
342.73'044—dc20   92-4218
[347.30244]   CIP

This book has been composed in Linotron Palatino

Princeton University Press books are
printed on acid-free paper, and meet the guidelines
for permanence and durability of the Committee
on Production Guidelines for Book Longevity
of the Council on Library Resources

Printed in the United States of America

1 3 5 7 9 10 8 6 4 2

FOR ILSE FRANCK

✤

❖ Contents ❖

CONTENTS

❖ *Acknowledgments* ❖

Funding for this study was generously provided by the Filomen D'Agostino and Max E. Greenberg Research Fund of New York University School of Law, which, guided by its diligent faculty committee, has transformed the climate for serious writing at my home institution.

When setting forth, it seemed useful to compare the practice of U.S. courts in cases with serious foreign-policy implications with the work of the German Constitutional Court. The U.S. and German federal constitutions are very similar, which makes comparison of the respective judicial practices both feasible and enlightening. The Max-Planck Institute of International and Public Law (MPI) invited me to work in that eminent institution, and its directors—especially Dr. Rudolf Bernhardt and Dr. Jochen Abr. Frowein—were constantly helpful and encouraging. So were other members of the scintillating faculty: Dr. Juliane Kokott, Dr. Georg Nolte, Prof. Karl Doehring, and Dr. Torsten Stein. Special thanks are due to MPI's wonderfully knowledgeable head librarian, Dr. Joachim Schwietzke.

During the New York phase of my research I was fortunate to be assisted by several outstanding NYU law students, including Deborah Niedermeyer, Michael S. Nelson, J. Russell Bulkeley, Julie L. Novkov, Dennis Sughrue, and Kieran J. Fallon.

As always, my warmest thanks go to my administrative assistant, Rochelle Fenchel, who in the course of this writing has made the transition from a word star to being word (and otherwise) perfect.

New York
July 1991

Political Questions/Judicial Answers

❖

Introduction

By the constitution of the United States, the President is
invested with certain important political powers, in the
exercise of which he is to use his own discretion, and
is accountable only to his country in his political
character and to his own conscience. . . .
The application of this remark will be perceived by adverting
to the act of congress for establishing the department of
foreign affairs. . . . The acts of such an officer, as an
officer, can never be examinable by the courts.
—Chief Justice John Marshall, *Marbury v. Madison (1803)*

WITH THAT seemingly offhand remark, Chief Justice Marshall introduced into American jurisprudence a theory that continues to affect profoundly the way power is exercised in the United States. Whatever Marshall's intent in these paragraphs, the effect was to initiate a constitutional theory, still asserted by many lawyers and judges, that foreign affairs are *different* from all other matters of state in some crucial fashion. From this is sometimes derived the conclusion, one with which Marshall might well have disagreed,[1] that the conduct of foreign affairs by the political agencies should be immune to judicial scrutiny. What a paradoxical by-product of the very decision that made judicial review the touchstone of the American system of government! How odd that Marshall should have sounded this uncertain note with the same breath as *Marbury's*[2] clarion call to judicial activism.

In *The Federalist No. 78*, Alexander Hamilton had foreseen this activist role. He had designated the judiciary as the guarantor of the new Constitution, "the best expedient which can be devised in any government, to secure a steady, upright and impartial administration of the laws."[3] Moreover, in a system of deliberately divided and limited power the judiciary, the "least dangerous" branch, must be vested with the authority "to declare all acts contrary to the manifest

3

tenor of the constitution void. Without this, all the reservations of particular rights or privileges would amount to nothing."[4]

Marbury is justly celebrated for establishing the authority of the federal judiciary as umpire of a new system of divided authority and as guardian of an unprecedented process in which political power is not merely divided and distributed but also limited. Yet, incongruously, the chief justice seems to accord a deference to executive officials engaged in the conduct of foreign affairs that effectively exempts them from the normal judicial umpiring process. As for foreign affairs, the chief justice may be understood to have said, the judiciary's guardianship of the limits of political power are suspended.

These thoughts are but sketched in Marshall's divertissement to the majestic theme of *Marbury*. No effort is made to explain *why* foreign affairs should be placed beyond the reach of judicial review. Nor is it self-evident what is meant by placing foreign-affairs "acts" outside the ambit of what is "examinable by the courts." In practice, however, some courts have taken the theory of inviolability to mean that judges must refrain from examining either the legality or even the constitutionality of actions taken by the president and his subordinates once it has been asserted that they acted in the name of foreign policy or national security. According to this line of reasoning, courts may not inquire whether soldiers are being sent lawfully into combat or whether members of Congress have been deprived of their constitutional role in the decision to go to war. Aliens arbitrarily excluded or deported from the United States on executive fiat in the name of national security may not look to judges for help; neither are businesspeople whose assets are requisitioned to advance foreign-policy purposes. In this view, levying taxes or disposing of government property without congressional authority is not open to challenge in courts of law if the avowed purpose is to promote international policies. Carried to its logical extreme, this doctrine holds that the political authorities are suit-proof as long as they purport to act in pursuance of their "foreign-affairs" power.

Fortunately, the courts' abdication usually has not gone this far—not quite. But some decisions, including pithy paragraphs in several Supreme Court opinions we shall be examining, come uncomfortably close. One central theme of this study is that the abdicationist tendency, primarily expounded in what has become known as the "political-question doctrine," is not only not required by but wholly incompatible with American constitutional theory. What is the point of a carefully calibrated system of divided and limited power if those who exercise authority can secure an automatic exemption from its strictures merely by playing the foreign-affairs trump?

Lawyers and judges who defend the doctrine, however, usually do so less by pleading theoretical justification than by arguing practical necessity or "prudential considerations." They insist that because of the very nature of "foreign affairs," the nation must operate with a single voice—by which they mean the president's—and that only the executive branch has the information and expert experience necessary to make informed choices in matters crucial to national security. Or they argue that the controversies bearing on foreign affairs raise issues regarding which no legal standards are applicable or involve policy choices that are too political, complex, or specialized for resolution by courts. It is another theme of this book that these arguments, persuasive to many courts, are both alien to the U.S. system and unfounded.

In a system of divided powers, there cannot be a "single voice," as there is in the British parliamentary system, that concentrates all authority in the executive (so long as it commands the allegiance of the Commons) and in which no written constitution limits the political writ. In such a system, the role of courts is bound to be different and less. In our system, however, courts may and do speak in dissonant tones, even sometimes in questions affecting "foreign affairs." Indeed, it may be argued that in our system *only* courts can end disputation, thereby helping the nation to find its single voice.

This does not mean, however, that American courts have, or should have, license to make foreign policy. When courts speak in cases and thereby incidentally affect some aspect of foreign relations, they do not make foreign policy. They make judicial policy. What may at first appear a mere semantic quibble is an important distinction that this study will seek to elucidate. The frequent failure of the judicial and political branches to make that distinction has contributed to the conceptual chaos that surrounds judicial treatment of cases with foreign-affairs implications.

For example, when a U.S. court is faced with a divorce decree issued by the authorities of the Lithuanian Soviet Socialist Republic, the argument whether to give judicial effect to that decree tends to slip into the courtroom as a debate about whether the Soviet authorities' decree should be "recognized." The court is likely to be told that in a question of recognition, it must not contradict the voice of the State Department, which has not accepted the bona fides of the Soviet regime to speak for Lithuania. That argument, however, is spurious. It confuses the judicial with the diplomatic process. If the court decides to treat the Lithuanian divorce as valid, it is not "recognizing" the issuing government. Only the State Department recognizes governments or withholds recognition. Whether to give effect to a Lithuanian divorce in private litigation in our system should be the outcome of a judicial process that decides a justiciable matter on the evidence before it. The resultant judicial decision does not extend diplomatic recognition but does acknowledge an authority's domestic lawmaking competence. This judicial function is both separate and of an entirely different kind from the executive's prerogative to determine which foreign governments to recognize. The executive's decision turns on many factors other than whether the regime exercises authority over its population, being colored by such questions as how the government came to power, how it respects its nation's commitments, whether it abides by international law, whether it respects human rights. These are considerations that have little to do with whether divorces granted by its magistrates are entitled to judicial notice in a New York court. Even foreign governments, let alone our own, can be expected to respect that difference.

Indeed, this study will show that in several important foreign-affairs areas of adjudication—cases concerning title to property expropriated by foreign governments and cases in which foreign governments claim immunity from judicial process—the U.S. political branches have actually taken the initiative to ask the courts to stop abdicating and start adjudicating precisely in order to remove the foreign-policy implications from the outcome of these disputes by having them decided by the judicial process. As for recognition, the State Department has recently taken the position that it will normally refrain from recognizing regimes precisely to give itself greater flexibility to conduct pragmatic foreign relations.[5] If that decision is carried out in practice, it will be further encouragement to judges to perform their judicial tasks without constantly looking over their shoulders to those in another branch engaged in a different, political, pursuit.

If the "single-voice" polemic is misleading, so is the argument that judges are untrained to handle cases with foreign implications.

Judges are much better suited than is sometimes alleged to make decisions incidentally affecting foreign relations and national security. It is the business of the courts to understand any issue of fact or law, aided by exposure to the relevant evidence. Contrary to popular myth, the evidenciary matrix of foreign-relations cases is neither more difficult to present nor harder to understand than other technical data. This study will seek to demonstrate this point by examining the many complex foreign-affairs cases judges have handled successfully. It will also look at the experience of the German Constitutional Court, which has rejected the political-question doctrine explicitly. Special judicial procedures may be needed to illuminate judges and protect secrets, but this is also true of other kinds of litigation—for example, suits involving trade secrets or criminal actions in which sources or witnesses require special protection. Moreover, as the study will demonstrate, procedures are available to balance the special needs of confidentiality with other legitimate interests.

In sum, what this study tries to show is that there are no valid reasons—constitutional, prudential, technical, or policy-driven—for treating foreign-relations cases differently from any others. If there is a genuine, that is, a "ripe" dispute between parties with standing, courts can and should always offer the parties due process of law. In defending that proposition, this study will also seek to refine and explicate it; for example, by examining the experience of German courts in fashioning applicable rules of evidence and standards for reviewing foreign-affairs cases in which judicial deference may sometimes be appropriate to give the political branches the discretion authorized by laws or a constitution and to take into account any expert knowledge of the government's foreign-affairs specialists.

The German courts' experience demonstrates that it is possible to do this without judicial abdication. The German experience is also valuable in demonstrating to those who need reassurance that rejection of the political-question doctrine does not lead to wholesale judicial interference with the political branches' discretion to set and execute foreign policy or protect national security.

In proposing that the U.S. federal courts stop abdicating in foreign-affairs cases, this study does not propose a radical renunciation of a magisterial jurisprudence grown from the seeds of foreign-affairs dicta sown in *Marbury v. Madison*. Rather, it will become apparent that despite the didactic rhetoric of some abdicationist judges, there is no consistent jurisprudence but only a welter of contradictory cases and that the state of the law governing the judicial role in foreign-affairs cases is essentially incoherent. The American courts' tendency to abdicate in matters of foreign affairs is not only wrongly conceived but has been applied only fitfully and erratically.

Barring the way to reform is not a firm if pernicious principle of abdication but a state of jurisprudential chaos. For example, two hundred years after confederation we still do not know whether the president may terminate treaties on his own initiative or must obtain the consent of the Senate or Congress. The courts have been unable to tell us. That is less the consequence of a deliberate doctrine of abstention than the product of judicial fragmentation and doctrinal disagreement that renders judges unable to speak coherently to policymakers. Some judges practice abdication; others do not. Still more proclaim their continence but do not practice it. Some courts interpret the political-question doctrine as requiring them only not to question the political branches' right to make policy within their allotted area of jurisdiction, but others see the doctrine as granting those political branches the right to define conclusively their jurisdiction. Often a court will treat the political-question doctrine as applicable to a case for reasons that fail to distinguish it from similar litigation in which judges felt entitled to decide without deferring to the doctrine. In still other instances, judges have simply ignored the doctrine, passing it in silence while slouching to a decision.

Such incoherence should not be surprising. In seeking to demarcate an entire class of disputes, foreign affairs, as exempt from judicial review, the political-question doctrine and its conceptual penumbra has brought not order, the nation speaking with a "single voice," but doctrinal cacophony. This is to be expected of a notion that so ferociously wars against the basic organizing principle, the peculiar genius, of the American system of government under law. Judicial deference ignores the evident truth that in our system a law that is not enforceable by adjudicatory process is no law at all. A foreign policy exempt from judicial review is tantamount to governance by men and women emancipated from the bonds of law.

It is the argument of this study that "foreign affairs" does not need, and dare not be entrusted with, such a special jurisprudential dispensation. The category itself is highly suspect. Foreign affairs have become inextricably interwoven with the fabric of American life and ought to be treated holistically, especially by the only disinterested party, the judiciary. Every action taken in the name of foreign policy, defense strategy, or national security has a broad range of consequences that are not necessarily limited to, or felt by, the Departments of State and Defense, the CIA, or the National Security Council. Even the White House is rarely an impartial arbiter between the advocates of national security and competing interests. In this century, presidents have tended to emphasize the paramountcy of national security over competing national values. This may be a defensible value judgment, but it disqualifies the presidency from claiming to be the final arbiter of those values enshrined in the nation's basic charter. If competing constitutionally or legally protected interests of private citizens, businesses, and legislators are to be accorded their fair weight, it is in the courts that credible weighing must occur.

In any event, Marshall's "foreign-affairs" category no longer describes a much more complex reality. At the end of the twentieth century, in a world so interdependent that the flow of persons, goods, and ideas between states is almost as ordinary as between states of our Union, no "affair" is any longer exclusively denominable as "foreign." Every "foreign" initiative, every foreign expenditure of lives and treasure, has significant domestic repercussions. The elements of these mixed domestic-foreign affairs often cannot be disentangled even in theory, let alone in practice. Whatever the global conditions in which Chief Justice Marshall wrote, there is now scarcely such a thing as a discrete "foreign-affairs" enterprise, certainly not one so distinct as to warrant an entire, radically different jurisprudence of its own.

The current state of jurisprudential incoherence presents both a problem and an opportunity. After two centuries, there is still no single, clear judicial guidance in the matter. It is time, surely, to examine the history, theory, and practice that have shaped the way we treat foreign affairs in our courts and to explicate a principled role for the courts that comports with the nation's highest purposes.

How Abdication Crept into the
Judicial Repertory

THE FAUSTIAN PACT

THERE ARE hundreds of cases today in which federal courts face "political questions." Stalwart federal judges think nothing of deciding such hot-potato issues as the constitutionality of the lines on maps demarking congressional[1] or school districts,[2] the hiring practices of fire departments,[3] or standards for admission to medical schools.[4] Yet these same jurists tend to turn coy when challenged to decide whether a military conflict, such as the one in Vietnam, ultimately involving the expenditure of tens of thousands of lives and hundreds of billions of dollars, is lawful when waged by the president on his sole authority without a formal congressional declaration of war *strictu sensu* in accordance with article 1, section 8(11) of the Constitution.[5] With a few exceptions,[6] the courts have simply refused to answer that question, with grave results for the public's perception of the war's—and perhaps the courts'—legitimacy. Lower-court judges dodged the issue as too "political,"[7] and the Supreme Court succeeded in avoiding it largely by hiding behind refusals to grant certiorari.[8]

This is distinctly dispiriting. Ever since *Marbury*, when the judiciary gave itself the general intendance of the rules of the game—in Chief Justice Marshall's words, the duty definitively to "say what the law is"[9]—the United States has found itself with the world's most powerful judiciary. Matters that in other democracies such as Britain or France would clearly be far beyond the reach of judicial scrutiny are regulated by U.S. judges without any sense of overreaching. Such intensely controversial political initiatives as school desegregation,[10] regulation of pornography[11], abortion,[12] punishment of private homosexual acts,[13] and the death penalty[14] have been faced by the federal judiciary, interpreting the Constitution with an alacrity unknown in the courtrooms of other nations. The American system of governance under law has thus come to rely heavily on the expectation that the judiciary will umpire. The public in America expects that the legitimacy of almost any exercise of political power can be tested by referring it to the validating authority of the judiciary.

That makes all the more incongruous a long-standing reluctance of U.S. judges to decide an entire category of serious disputes in which the legitimacy of an exercise of political power is questioned. The category, foreign affairs, involves extraordinarily high stakes, but the reasons for its exemption from judicial review are far from self-evident.

The origins of this abdicationist phenomenon can be understood only in terms of the judicial politics of the Supreme Court's earliest years. Marshall's readiness to bargain away some ill-defined degree of judicial review over foreign affairs had been foreshadowed in some earlier political views he expressed while a member of the House of Representatives. There, in opposing a resolution seeking to criticize President Adams for intervening with a federal judge to secure the repatriation of a British sailor to stand trial for a murder committed on a British ship, he had argued that "the President is the sole organ of the nation in its external relations, and its sole representative with foreign nations."[15] It is tempting to attribute this pro-presidential sentiment to Marshall's high-federalist politics honed by the experience of seeing the nation hobbled in its fight for independence by lack of a strong central executive authority.

That, however, cannot be the whole story, for Marshall also seemed genuinely inclined to extend similar deference in foreign affairs to other loci of political power. He appeared convinced that there is something about "foreign affairs" that renders them particularly impervious to judicial inquiry. In 1831, for example, the Cherokee tribe sought the federal courts' protection against alleged unilateral violations of its treaty rights by the state of Georgia. Marshall replied: "The propriety of such an interposition by the court may be well questioned. It savours too much of the exercise of political power to be within the proper province of the judicial department."[16] Justice Johnson, concurring, was prepared to go further. "What these people may have a right to claim of the executive power is one thing: whether we are to be the instruments to compel another branch of the government to make good the stipulations of treaties, is a very different question." "Courts of justice," he continued, "are properly excluded from all considerations of policy, and therefore are very unfit instruments to control the action of that branch of the government; which may often be compelled by the highest considerations or public policy to withhold even the exercise of a positive duty."[17]

Article 4, clause 2, of the Constitution says that treaties are the supreme law of the land. How could the Court avoid interpreting a treaty when a litigant had asserted injury as a result of its violation by a state government? Johnson tried to answer that question by reference to the persuasive force of a British precedent, the *Nabob of Arcot* case, a British decision of the 1790s holding that "as between sovereigns, breaches of treaty were not breaches of contract cognizable in a court of justice" and that "for their political acts states were not amenable to tribunals of justice."[18]

Is such a uniquely British precedent a sufficient basis for overriding a constitutional stricture and importing into American jurisprudence a monarchial notion of indivisible power over foreign affairs? Did the Revolution really mean to let a writ *non procedendo ad assissam rege inconsulto* continue to operate in the Republic's courts as if the king's council still had the power to command his judges to refrain from cases touching upon his prerogatives? Against all the evidence and common sense, Justice Johnson seemed to believe that a rule of judicial reticence steeped in the ethos of monarchial (or later, parliamentary) absolutism and undivided legislative-executive power could be harnessed quite comfortably to a system of divided power in which the "supremacy" of treaty law had been written into the Constitution. He could hold that belief only by ignoring altogether the constitutional ratification debates so recently held in state legislatures,[19] where the treaty clause had been defended as an instrument designed to bar the previously prevalent practice of states' negating the federal government's solemn agreements.[20]

What we have here is a sort of Faustian pact between the courts and the political organs. The use of British case law to plant the political-question doctrine on American soil may be seen as an expedient by a fragile federal judiciary bent first on establishing its supremacy in domestic matters and thus looking for a convenient, relatively inexpensive "giveback" to throw to the political branches and the states. Had the abdicationist theory not survived so long beyond the days of judicial frailty, and were its consequences to contemporary American governance not so serious in terms of lives and resources, the opportunistic adoption by the new Republic's judges of a quaint British tradition of judicial deference to royal inviolability might be tolerated as no more than an amusing anachronism. In practice, however, its consequences have proven dangerously inconsistent with the very nature and functioning of the Republic, giving encouragement and legitimacy to the rise of the imperial presidency.

More than a hundred years ago, in *U.S. v. Lee*,[21] the Supreme Court seemed to steel itself for a final repudiation of those incongruous British notions that had infiltrated American jurisprudence. In some of the Court's most magisterial prose, Justice Miller wrote that "it is difficult to see on what solid foundation of principle the [executive's] exemption from liability to suit rests." He conjectured that publicists had falsely persuaded courts "that the supreme power in every State, wherever it may reside, shall not be compelled, by process of courts of its own creation, to defend itself from assaults in those courts."[22] Caustically, Miller tackled the appropriateness of citing for this proposition cases from Britain where "the monarch is looked upon with too much reverence to be subjected to the demands of the law as ordinary persons are, and the king-loving nation would be shocked at the spectacle of their Queen being turned out of her pleasure-garden by a writ of ejectment against the gardener."[23] But America, he said, is not Britain. "Under our system the *people*, who are there called *subjects*, are the sovereign. . . .The citizen here knows no person, however near to those in power, or however powerful himself, to whom he need yield the rights which the law secures to him when it is well administered." He should be able "in one of the courts of competent jurisdiction" to employ "the means which the law gives him for the protection and enforcement of that right."[24]

Brave words, these, from a judge defending the rights of the heirs of a Confederate general against a government that had sought to confiscate his estate to establish a national cemetery. In America, no exercise of political power is wholly above the law, and in consequence, no act by Congress or president is beyond judicial review. Nevertheless, even Miller's resonance carried only as far as the water's edge. Although foreign affairs had nothing to do with this litigation, he seemed irresistibly drawn to the "giveback" tradition. In both "the English courts and ours," he said, "it has been uniformly held that . . . questions . . . which . . . might involve war or peace, must be primarily dealt with by those departments of the government which had the power to adjust them by negotiation, or to enforce the rights of the citizen by war. In such cases the judicial department of this government follows the action of the political branch, and will not embarrass the latter by assuming an antagonistic jurisdiction."[25]

Once again, the British monarchial practice, although held inapplicable to defining the immunities of government in domestic exercises of power, was confirmed as perfectly appropriate to the conduct of U.S. foreign affairs. There is a direct line from this sort of gratuitous giveback to a federal court's recent conclusion that it could not examine the legality of former Panamanian dictator Manuel Noriega's kidnapping in Panama by U.S. military forces because the political-question doctrine "precludes courts from resolving issues more properly committed to the political branches" and would constitute "judicial interference in the conduct of foreign policy."[26]

Why are foreign affairs different? Many judges, like many citizens, seem persuaded that "it's a jungle out there" and that the conduct of foreign relations therefore requires Americans to tolerate a degree of concentrated power that would be wholly unacceptable domestically. After all, they may think, few other governments in competing for power and influence with America must endure the handicap of judicially enforced limits on their discretion.

This view is expressed most eloquently in the Supreme Court's 1936 decision in *United States v. Curtiss-Wright Export Corporation.*[27] The opinion, written by Justice George Sutherland, contains the most expansive dicta written by the Court on presidential power over foreign affairs, intended to free him of all constraints. Typically, the case actually raised only a very narrow issue of congressional, rather than presidential power. Congress had authorized the president to prohibit U.S. arms sales to nations involved in the Chaco war if he believed such an embargo would "contribute to the reestablishment of peace."[28] The Court was challenged to say whether that rather broad delegation by Congress violated the constitutionally ordained separation of powers. Had Congress, in other words, attempted to breach the ship of state's watertight compartments by delegating what amounted to "legislative" power to the executive branch? Quite reasonably, the Court thought not. However, in seeking to explain why the president should be allowed to exercise such unconstrained regulatory authority, Sutherland not only cobbled together a sweeping doctrine allowing broader delegations in the foreign-relations field than the Court at the time would have tolerated in domestic matters, but he also invented an exclusive presidential franchise to conduct foreign relations beyond the control of either Congress or the courts. Sutherland rooted this franchise in the interstices of the Constitution and the nature of the statehood the United States inherited from Britain.

"Not only . . . is the federal power over external affairs in origin and essential character different from that over internal affairs," the justice wrote, "but participation in the exercise of the power is significantly limited. In this vast external realm, with its important, complicated, delicate and manifold problems, the President alone has the power to speak or listen as a representative of the nation. . . . It is important to bear in mind that we are here dealing . . . with . . . the very delicate, plenary and exclusive power of the President as the sole organ of the federal government in the field of international relations."[29] Like Marshall, Sutherland was using dicta to introduce into the Court's jurisprudence pro-presidential views that he had earlier developed in Congress,[30] and in this he was successful, as courts began to cite *Curtiss-Wright* for the proposition that external affairs are exclusively a presidential prerogative. Indeed, nowadays few students of the law remember that *Curtiss-Wright* was a case upholding the authority of Congress to legislate a foreign arms embargo and to delegate its timing and execution to the president, not one in which the exclusive "prerogative" powers of the president to run foreign affairs was sustained against congressional encroachment. The "doctrine" for which the case is usually cited is in Sutherland's dicta but has nothing to do with the issues presented by the case.

That doctrine also has no perceivable connection with the Constitution. Are foreign affairs somehow fundamentally different from all other areas of power? Are they inherently incapable of being divided among president, Congress, and courts like all other authority? Are they exempt from the carefully crafted scheme created by the drafters of the Constitution to obviate the oligarchic tendencies so evident in eighteenth-century Britain and France, tendencies against which the entire American revolutionary enterprise had been conceived?

Even a cursory reading of the black letters of the Constitution reveals the contrary intent. The drafters deliberately did not create, let alone assign exclusively to the president, authority over a "field of foreign relations." No such "field" is designated. Rather, wary of precisely such monarchial concentration of power, they enumerated several lesser powers and distributed them between the executive, legislative, and judicial branches, specifically allocating an important role to Congress or the Senate (sometimes authorized to act alone, in other instances only in conjunction with the executive) in such matters as foreign commerce; declaring war; raising, commanding, and funding the armed forces; spending on foreign affairs; appointment of ambassadors; and consent to treaties.[31] To the judiciary they left the resolution of disputes without any specific subject-matter exceptions. On the contrary, in article 3, sections 2 and 3, they invented special accelerated procedures for litigating one kind of foreign-relations issue: cases involving foreign governments and their ambassadors. Moreover, Hamilton made no exceptions whatever when he wrote, "A constitution is in fact, and must be, regarded by the judges as a fundamental law. It therefore belongs to them to ascertain its meaning."[32] The founders' argument for judicial review proceeds on the straightforward assumption that the Constitution's distribution and limitation of political power can be accomplished only by the "courts of justice" stopping political "encroachments" on "the bulwarks of a limited constitution."[33]

The history-defying sweep and reach of *Curtiss-Wright*—or rather, its dicta—are breathtaking. It virtually purports to take out of the foreign-relations business both Congress and the courts, leaving an effectively uncontrollable presidency. While the *Curtiss-Wright* court's inflated language, seemingly bent on abdicating judicial responsibility to "say what the law is" in the entire foreign-relations field, cannot be regarded as part of the actual *decision* of the case, its mellifluous certitude has nevertheless secured a far greater deference to its abdicationist philosophy, especially from lower courts, than is normally accorded such expansive excursions into matters peripheral to the facts of a case. While this is no doubt partly due to literary audacity, it is also evident that Sutherland's words succeeded in capturing a widely shared public preference for rallying around the president in the face of foreign threats. Many Americans, although perhaps fewer now than in 1936, may still believe that not only politics but also the writ of the law should stop at the water's edge.

Unlike lower courts, the Supreme Court today tends to avoid endorsing Sutherland's dictum specifically. But the spirit survives. One current manifestation of this water's-edge constitutionalism may be observed in the Court's 1990 decision in *U.S. v. Verdugo-Urquidez* in which the majority held that the Fourth Amendment's prohibition on unchecked presidential power to search and seize does not apply to warrantless searches conducted by U.S. agents abroad.[34] Sutherland's *Curtiss-Wright* dicta, however, went even further than *Verdugo-Urquidez* in seeming to make unreviewable any executive conduct of foreign relations, wherever its effects are manifest. "It is quite apparent," the justice said in a memorable dictum since quoted in numerous decisions handed down by other judges, "that if, in the maintenance of our international relations, embarrassment—perhaps serious embarrassment—is to be avoided and success for our aims achieved, congressional legislation which is to be made effective through negotiation and inquiry within the international field must often accord to the President a degree of discretion and freedom from statutory restriction which would not be admissible were domestic affairs involved."[35] In other words, not only does the president have wide, judicially unreviewable discretion, but that discretion should not—perhaps even may not—be constrained by the exercise of Congress's general legislative authority.

Why should this be so? What reasoning could justify such an extraordinary departure, not only from the text but also from the essential architecture of a Constitution that features both divided and overlapping allocation of power among the parts of a trifurcated governmental entity? Sutherland sought to answer this by hypothesizing that foreign relations are by their very nature different from other exercises of authority. In this view, only the president, as opposed to the legislator or judge, "has the better opportunity of knowing the conditions which prevail in foreign countries. . . . He has his confidential sources of information. He has his agents in the form of diplomatic, consular and other officials. Secrecy in respect of information gathered by them may be highly necessary, and the premature disclosure of it productive of harmful results."[36]

Sutherland concluded in *Curtiss-Wright* that the Constitution simply does not apply to foreign affairs. His radical assumption is that the rule "that the federal government can exercise no powers except those specifically enumerated in the Constitution, and such implied powers as are necessary and proper to carry into effect the enumerated powers, is categorically true only in respect of our internal affairs." As for external affairs, a different principle must apply, the

17

one inherited from monarchial Britain: "A political society cannot endure without a supreme will somewhere. Sovereignty is never held in suspense. When, therefore, the external sovereignty of Great Britain in respect of the colonies ceased, it immediately passed to the Union. . . . It results that the investment of the federal government with the powers of external sovereignty did not depend upon the affirmative grants of the Constitution."[37]

The radical notion, first mooted in a dictum in *Marbury*, that the political discretion of the president in foreign affairs is neither circumscribed by the Constitution nor reviewable by the courts was thus refined and reenforced by Sutherland's dictum in *Curtiss-Wright*. In neither instance was the question of presidential supremacy over foreign affairs presented to the Court by the facts of the case. The doctrine rests on pure dicta.

No less a source than Chief Justice Marshall warned against taking such utterances too seriously. In *Cohens v. Virginia*,[38] he wrote, "It is a maxim not to be disregarded, that general expressions, in every opinion, are to be taken in connection with the case in which those expressions are used. If they go beyond the case, they may be respected, but ought not to control the judgment in a subsequent suit when the very point is presented for decision. The reason for this maxim is obvious. The question actually before the Court is investigated with care, and considered in its full extent. Other principles which may serve to illustrate it, are considered in their relation to the case decided, but their possible bearing on all other cases is seldom completely investigated. In the case of *Marbury v. Madison*," Marshall added with characteristic candor, the "Court decided, and we think very properly, that the legislature could not give original jurisdiction in such a case. But, in the reasoning of the Court in support of this decision, some expressions are used which go far beyond it."[39]

All too evidently, however, Marshall's cautious advice has been but imperfectly followed. Much of the vitality of the political-question doctrine in foreign-relations cases derives from the automaticity with which judges have fallen in line with sweeping pronouncements favoring judicial abdication in cases that had nothing to do with foreign-affairs (like *Marbury*) or in which the prerogative foreign-policy powers of the president were not at issue (like *Curtiss-Wright*). Another example is the 1939 decision in *Coleman v. Miller*[40] where the Supreme Court asserted that "many illustrations" for the proposition that "essentially political" questions are "not justiciable" were to be found "in the field of our conduct of foreign relations."[41] Yet *Coleman*, all too typically, had nothing to do with foreign affairs, being concerned exclusively with the propriety of Kansas's process for disposing of a federal constitutional amendment. The Supreme Court's 1962 decision in *Baker v. Carr*[42] is another example of a case in which jurisdiction over foreign-relations issues featured prominently in the judgment even though the issue concerned a purely domestic matter, the apportionment of Tennessee's state legislative districts. The occasion moved Justice Brennan to attempt a comprehensive ordering of policy questions that are beyond judicial purview, and in oft-quoted dicta he concluded that foreign-relations issues are among these when, as is "frequently" the case, they "turn on standards that defy judicial application, or involve the exercise of a discretion demonstrably committed to the executive or legislature" or when "questions uniquely demand single-voiced statement[s] of the Government's views."[43]

It is particularly odd that several of the most redolent dicta seemingly making the political question doctrine mandatory in foreign-relations cases are not merely substantively irrelevant to the cases in which they originate but that those cases often repeal the application of the political-question doctrine to various other, domestic issues. This reflects the continued efficacy of the Faustian pact struck in *Marbury*, the giveback practice of judges who enlarge their jurisdiction over domestic political conflicts but then seek to pacify the enraged political beast by making a grand gesture of jettisoning judicial review of disputes touching foreign affairs. *Baker v. Carr* is an excellent example. There, the Supreme Court found that the political-question doctrine did not prevent it from overturning the Tennessee legislature's apportionment of legislative districts, thereby significantly enlarging the judiciary's supervisory powers, narrowing the constraints of the political-question doctrine, and overturning its prior rule in *Colegrove v. Green*[44] that had made such matters nonjusticiable. At the same time, while vastly expanding the courts' domestic powers, the judges reinforced their commitment to abdication in foreign affairs.

As a result of such tactics, the political-question doctrine's domestic use has been virtually eradicated in recent years even as its applicability to foreign affairs has been reinforced by the courts. This has widened the gulf and accentuated the paradox between judicial treatment of foreign and domestic issues. As the ambit of judicial review has been expanded, review of foreign affairs has been abjured as if in expiation. The doctrine, which once applied to many areas of governance, now applies almost exclusively to foreign-affairs and national-security cases. Its use to insulate the autonomy of the legislative process in *Luther v. Borden*[45] was cut back drastically in *Powell v. McCormack*.[46] In *Barnes v. Kline*,[47] to cite another example of the doctrine's recession, the D.C. Circuit Court decided a dispute between the White House and thirty-three members of Congress whether the president could exercise a "pocket veto" when the congressional adjournment constitutionally required for the exercise of that power was merely an intersessional one sine die. Referring to the judicial-deference and separation-of-powers doctrines, the Court, citing *Marbury*, said: "[W]hen a proper dispute arises concerning the respective constitutional functions of the various branches of the government, '[i]t is emphatically the province and duty of the judicial department to say what the law is.' Courts may not avoid resolving genuine cases or controversies—those 'of a type which are traditionally justiciable'—simply because one or both parties are coordinate branches."[48] The time and occasion for the courts to act is when Congress and the president have "reach[ed] a constitutional impasse."[49]

In 1990, the Court held that it was no political question whether a law passed by both houses of Congress and signed by the president had originated in the wrong chamber.[50] Thus, although there are still a few recherché instances of its more general application,[51] *Baker v. Carr* and its progeny[52] have had the incidental effect of revoking most of the political-question doctrine's fiat *except* in the foreign-relations field. Consequently, the doctrine's primary object nowadays is to protect a sole and unchecked presidential power in that single area. Persons stopped from seeking judicial redress by the political-question doctrine currently tend to be citizens refusing service in an undeclared war, aliens seeking relief from a deportation order, and members of Congress wishing to participate in war-peace decisions allegedly allotted to them by the Constitution. It is instructive in this respect to compare the judges' willingness to adjudicate the *Barnes* case with refusals to do so in the recent *Lowry* case involving a challenge by members of Congress to presidential use of force in the (Iran v. Iraq) Persian Gulf War.[53]

Double-Entry Bookkeeping

Why abdication in foreign-affairs cases—a legal concept evidently at odds with the constitutional text and the purpose of the revolutionary enterprise—should continue to prosper can be understood only in terms of its judicial pedigree. The tradition of abdication has been built, bit by bit, on the straw foundations of dicta imported from the British monarchial system, deployed in cases where it was irrelevant to the matters being litigated, and thus was introduced into American law essentially without benefit of genuine adversary process, let alone profound jurisprudential reflection. Indeed, judicial abdication in foreign-affairs cases has entered the jurisprudence primarily through rhetorical extravagance in cases with little or no foreign content rather than by a juridical practice of rigid abstinence in real foreign-affairs disputes. In particular, abstinence (as is often true of protestations of abstemiousness) is far more vehemently asserted than practiced. Many of the oft-cited precedents are less examples of abdication than double-entry bookkeeping by the judiciary. Judges have purported to defer to the president even when they actually did not.

In particular, there are numerous instances in which judges have used the political question as little more than makeweight embroidery, purporting to deny themselves the right to decide but then, unwilling to rely exclusively on the doctrine, deciding nevertheless on the merits. This forked endorsement of abstention has been facilitated by the fact that when the Court does deal with the merits of a case, even while denying its authority or intent to take jurisdiction, it has generally found in favor of the challenged exercise of executive and/or legislative power. Understandably, the political branches have been disinclined, when they have won, to cavil at the niceties of judicial reasoning. Nevertheless, these cases should be seen in retrospect as instances in which the Court while saying one thing did quite another. They can be read to support a future reevaluation and reversal of the political-question doctrine.

This forked approach is evident in several Supreme Court cases, and the abstentionist language in these has been seized upon by lower-court judges to reinforce their own abdicationist tendencies rather than being recognized as no more than peripheral rhetoric.

This confusion is as old as the political question doctrine itself. Chief Justice Marshall himself showed the way in *Foster v. Neilson* (1829).[54] That case concerned the interpretation of the Treaty of Paris of 1803 by which the United States acquired lands east of the Mississippi that had earlier been ceded by Spain to France. The issue was whether these lands included an area in which petitioner had title claims deriving from a Spanish Crown grant made after the cession to France. Marshall admitted that the text of the Spanish cession was unclear but said, "However this may be, it is, we think, incontestable, that the American construction of the article, if not entirely free from question, is supported by arguments of great strength."[55] At this point he might have examined those arguments and with or without giving them presumptive evidentiary preference, found for the political branches' interpretation. Instead he took a different conceptual route: "We think then, however individual judges might construe the treaty of St. Ildefonso, it is the province of the Court to conform its decisions to the will of the legislature, if that will has been clearly expressed."[56]

The will of the legislature in this instance was contained in several acts of Congress of 1803 and 1804 providing for the governance of the newly acquired territories and defining their areas.[57] These laws also voided all land grants made by the Spanish Crown after 1803. In 1812 Congress passed a further statute that "describe[d] lines which comprehend the land in controversy" and made them part of the state of Louisiana.[58] "In a controversy between two nations concerning [a] national boundary," Marshall stated, "it is scarcely possible that the courts of either should refuse to abide by the measures adopted by its own government. There being no common tribunal to decide between them, each determines for itself," and "[t]he judiciary is not that department of the government, to which the assertion of its interests against foreign powers is confided." Rather, "its duty commonly is to decide upon individual rights, according to those principles which the political departments of the nation have established."[59]

That would seem to be the end of the matter. Nevertheless, having firmly established the principle that courts are without power to construe the meaning of the treaties, statutes, and asserted interests in question, Marshall went on for twelve more excruciatingly detailed pages of evidentiary deduction to do precisely that, holding that certain key phrases in an agreement must be given their "plain meaning" and that the parties cannot be taken to have had them "inserted carelessly." He conjectured on intent, weighed alternative meanings in one agreement by reference to context, and did what courts ordinarily do when they have jurisdiction rather than when they have found an issue nonjusticiable.[60]

The *Prize Cases*[61] similarly illustrate this tendency. There, Justice Grier said that the question whether the president decides to treat a civil conflict as a belligerency permitting him to seize vessels of neutrals trading with the enemy is one in which the courts "must be governed by the decisions and acts of the political department."[62] But having said that such military-hostilities cases must be left by the judges to the politicians, he nevertheless proceeded to examine quite thoroughly the government's disputed actions, applying the law to the facts as in any other case. This enabled him to conclude that the president had not really acted alone. "If it were necessary to the technical existence of a war, that it should have a legislative sanction, we find it in almost every act passed at the extraordinary session of the Legislature of 1861, which was wholly employed in enacting laws to enable the Government to prosecute the war with vigor and efficiency. And finally, in 1861, we find Congress *'ex majore cautela'* and in anticipation of such astute objections, passing an act 'approving, legalizing, and making valid all the acts, proclamations, and orders of the President, etc., as if they had been *issued and done under the previous express authority* and direction of the Congress of the United States.' "[63] It thus appears that Grier had not genuinely convinced himself that the legality of these presidential actions could or should be immune to judicial review.

Such decisions by the Supreme Court feature extravagant outbursts of judicial modesty marked by assertions of incompetence to decide issues of global gravamen. A few pages later, however, the same judge uses traditional legal reasoning to decide the very issue declared to be beyond his competence. Another example of such judicial double-entry bookkeeping is found in the Court's 1902 decision in *Terlinden v. Ames*,[64] a case in which extradition was being sought under an 1852 treaty between Prussia and the United States. Terlinden, wanted for forgery in Germany, argued that the treaty had lapsed as a result of the 1871 transformation of Prussia and neighboring states into the German Empire. The U.S. government, seeking to extradite, argued that the agreement with Prussia remained in effect.

"We concur in the view," said the Court, "that the question whether power remains in a foreign State to carry out its treaty obligations is in its nature political and not judicial, and that the courts ought not to interfere with the conclusions of the political department in that regard."[65] Nevertheless, the Court examined in detail the relevant international law of treaties and state succession as well as the history and constitution of the German Empire,[66] and it made its findings accordingly: "We do not find in this [German imperial] constitution any provision which in itself operated to abrogate existing treaties or to affect the status of the Kingdom of Prussia in that regard."[67] Thus the Court itself ("we") determined the continuing treaty capacity of Prussia. As to whether, despite that residual capacity, the parties had terminated the treaty, the Court again exercised its judgment by examining, not deferring to, government conduct. "[W]e think that on the question whether this treaty has ever been terminated, governmental action in respect to it must be regarded as of controlling importance."[68] With that, the judges proceeded to examine evidence of the conduct of the parties (not merely what the government's lawyers said but how the governments had acted) and to reach the conclusion that both parties had in practice continued to regard the agreement as valid.[69]

The government's attorneys had urged the Court simply to adopt a formulation found in a note accompanying the State Department's compilation of treaties and conventions of 1889, which maintained that if both governments claimed the treaty to be in effect, it must be taken to be so. "Such a question," they had argued, "is, after all, purely a political one."[70] That view would have left the Court no choice but to decide the case on the basis of the pleadings of one of the interested parties. Instead, the Court actually treated the ongoing pattern of government conduct as relevant evidence of the applicable international law, much as state practice is a source of international law in the International Court of Justice.[71]

In this radically modified version of the political-question doctrine, it is patterns of state conduct, not a self-interested statement of the law made by the state in its pleadings, that is considered (respectfully but not uncritically) by the Court as a source of relevant evidence. Moreover, the Court decides what probative weight to give such evidence and adds it to other evidence and additional demonstrated facts to make its own determination. It does not refuse to decide.

Thus what at first looks like an abdication of jurisdiction turns out to be a taking of jurisdiction, and what is claimed to be a denial of justiciability is in the event an ordinary adjudication in which the Court plays its usual role, albeit with some deference to the evidence adduced by government experts.

This modified approach was illustrated once again in the 1947 case of *Clark v. Allen*[72] in which the Court's nearly unanimous[73] opinion was written by Justice William O. Douglas. The litigation concerned the estate of a California resident who had died during the Second World War, bequeathing everything to nationals and residents of Germany who could not inherit in wartime. Thus, the parties to the ensuing litigation were the U.S. Alien Property Custodian, acting under the Trading with the Enemy Act, and the deceased's Californian heirs-at-law, who were entitled to share the estate if the will was declared invalid. The custodian sought to assert rights based on the Treaty of Friendship, Commerce and Consular Rights of 1925,[74] which entitled German heirs of property in the United States to inherit real property, sell it, and withdraw the proceeds on terms identical to those applicable to U.S. nationals. The custodian,[75] whose right to the property derived from the title of the putative German heirs, argued that the 1925 treaty was still in effect and had not been abrogated by the outbreak of war; the California heirs-at-law asserted the opposite position.

Douglas's opinion paid lip service to the political-question doctrine, piously intoning that "the question whether a state is in a position to perform its treaty obligations is essentially a political question."[76] By this, however, Douglas decidedly did *not* mean that the Court would refuse to decide, or would accept without further investigation the unsupported assertion of the executive branch in a case in which it was a party at interest. Rather, the Court embarked on its own assessment of the question of the treaty's current status, an investigation in which the *conduct* of the political branches—whether consistent or inconsistent with the treaty's (or even part of the treaty's) having survived the declaration of war—is relevant evidence. Certainly the fact that the attorney general had asserted the treaty's continuing validity in arguing the case was not binding on the Court or even particularly persuasive. Instead, the Court looked at the history of the State Department's attitude in the matter of treaty survival, finding that it had asserted one position during World

25

War I and taken a contrary posture in World War II.[77] Douglas carefully canvassed the treaty text for evidence of the parties' intentions.[78] Finding "no reliable evidence of the intention of the high contracting parties outside the words of the . . . treaty" and that the instrument itself yielded "no plain indication that it is to become inoperative in whole or in part on the outbreak of war,"[79] he restated his view that it is the Court that must determine "whether the provision under which rights are asserted is incompatible with national policy in time of war," in this instance even after the surrender of Germany but before a formal peace. Douglas concluded: "[w]e find no evidence that the political departments have considered the collapse and surrender of Germany as putting an end to such provisions."[80]

Once again, the key words are "we find." The evident thrust of Douglas's reasoning is to ensure full judicial review of the attorney general's self-interested assertion that the treaty had remained in effect rather than to implement any self-denying practice of judicial abstinence. The Court examined the assertion of the law advanced by the attorney general in the light of other, more independent sources: prior positions on the matter declared by the State Department, the text of the treaty, evidence of the stated intention of the parties to the agreement, and evidence of the conduct of those parties toward each other during belligerency and thereafter. In this instance, these did sustain the attorney general's claim, but that result was not reached by judicial abdication. The Court plainly fulfilled its role of declaring what the law is, even while genuflecting perfunctorily to a political-question doctrine that it should nevertheless be seen as ignoring or reinterpreting into at most a nonconclusive minor rule of evidence. A computer check, however, will turn up this case, and others, as an example of the Supreme Court's adherence to the political-question doctrine.[81]

As in the Supreme Court, the circuit courts too sometimes proclaim their adherence to the political-question doctrine but then adjudicate other procedural aspects, or even the merits, of a case. In a 1940 decision,[82] for example, the D.C. Circuit Court decided that the issue, the lawfulness of an appointment of a resident commissioner of the Commonwealth of the Philippines to the United States, was nonjusticiable under the doctrine. To this end, the court indulged in the baleful practice of resuscitating obscurely irrelevant British precedents, in this instance *The Duke of York's Claim to the Crown*[83] in which judges had cautioned that they "durst not enter into eny communication thereof, for it perteyned to the Lordes of the Kyngs blode."[84] Yet the court apparently "durst" after all, for it then went on to decide that the appointment had been exercised within the discretion granted by relevant U.S. and Philippine legislation and was in conformity with international and U.S. constitutional law.[85] Similarly, in the *Holtzman* litigation testing the legality and constitutionality of U.S. bombing of Cambodia during the Vietnam War,[86] the Second Circuit first decided that plaintiff had raised a nonjusticiable political question[87] but then went on to say: "We cannot resist . . . " examining congressional appropriations that would legitimate the president's actions, "[a]ssuming arguendo that . . . we were obliged to find some participation by Congress."[88] For good measure, the judges also found the plaintiffs to lack standing.[89]

The same forked abdication was evident when the D.C. Circuit refused to hear a recent suit by twenty-nine members of Congress challenging the U.S. military presence in El Salvador.[90] After invoking the political-question doctrine, the judges nevertheless went on to exercise their "equitable discretion" to deny relief on the further ground that the issue was unripe for adjudication because Congress as a whole had not asserted its interest.[91] Judge Bork based a concurring opinion exclusively on the plaintiffs' lack of standing.[92] In a 1985 case, the Seventh Circuit classified "immigration matters" as "so exclusively entrusted to the political branches of government as to be largely immune from judicial inquiry or interference."[93] Nevertheless, the judges also determined the merits after examining and interpreting the relevant legislative texts, their history, and evidence of the intent of the legislators.[94] Indeed, the court tried to devise an appropriate standard for judicial review where abuse of discretion or "a wholesale, carefully orchestrated, program of constitutional violations is alleged."[95]

In a recent Fourth Circuit case,[96] plaintiffs, relatives of persons missing in Vietnam, sought a mandamus to compel the president to intensify efforts on behalf of their kin in accordance with the Hostage Act of 1982.[97] The court dutifully intoned that "conduct of foreign policy" is "an area traditionally reserved to the political branches and removed from judicial review."[98] However, the judges went on to examine the duty imposed on the president by the statute and determined that he had wide discretion in its discharge. However, they also noted that where a law creates a duty on the part of president to make inquiries, the court would have the power to order such an inquiry had he failed to do so.[99] Double-locking the door, the court also found that the plaintiffs lacked standing to enforce the act.[100]

In *Belk v. U.S.*,[101] the Federal Circuit was faced with a claim that the political branches had acted unconstitutionally in agreeing with Iran to extinguish the claims former hostages of the Iranians might have had against their captors. The judges held that the issues raised were barred by the political-question doctrine[102] but also that the discretion to negotiate claims settlements by executive agreement has long been recognized as a constitutionally sanctioned prerogative of the president.[103] The jurisprudential effect of this forked decision is to leave unclear whether the courts will take jurisdiction in such cases, examining and determining the extent of presidential prerogatives and discretion, or whether they wash their hands of the duty "to say what the law is" whenever the foreign-policy talisman is invoked.

As long as this central question remains unclarified, because different courts have decided differently and because the same courts have used self-contradictory reasoning, ludicrous results are likely to ensue in the name of abstinence. A good example is the recent case[104] in which the First Circuit was asked by a former government official to hold various present and past senior officials of the State Department and the CIA to have acted in violation of the RICO antiracketeering law.[105] The allegations ranged from refusing to follow plaintiff's advice in matters pertaining to the Middle East to engaging in racketeering with the government of Israel by those making U.S. policy. Once again the court asserted its lack of jurisdiction on the ground that the plaintiff "cannot use RICO to seek judicial redress for such a political question."[106] However, it also decided against plaintiff for failure to exhaust his administrative remedies.[107]

This latter ground surely presupposes that there are administrative remedies to be pursued, and the court examines the Administrative Procedure Act to show that this is so.[108] If such remedies were pursued, however, would the court review the administration's decision in accordance with the standard established in that law?[109] Or is the plaintiff being sent on a fool's errand that would end with another determination that his case is nonjusticiable per se? What makes this case particularly poignant is that the plaintiff had alleged that he had been "discredit[ed] . . . as a national security risk," that his business interests had been deliberately destroyed, that he had been the object of "libel, slander, character assassination, the publication of false charges, and attempted murder . . . " and had been caused "to live below the poverty level."[110] That these allegations may sound improbable in no way mitigates the seriousness of a decision (if such it was) that plaintiff's complaints (the validity of which must be assumed for purposes of determining justiciability) are beyond remedial scrutiny by a court of law in the United States. Apparently, it is not only hard cases but also fantastic ones that tend to make bad law.

A further, particularly telling example of double-entry bookkeeping is afforded by a 1989 case before the D.C. Circuit in which plaintiffs, residents of the Marshall Islands in the former Pacific Trust Territory, claimed damages for injuries sustained by U.S. nuclear tests conducted on their islands.[111] The court devotes seven closely reasoned pages to examining relevant laws and the intent of Congress to conclude that various agreements and laws creating the independent status of the Marshall Islands have withdrawn the jurisdiction of U.S. federal courts to determine such claims from residents of its former dependencies.[112] The decision then continues: "While, of course, our conclusion that the Compact Act incorporating the international agreements expressly stripped the courts of jurisdiction is sufficient to dispose of this appeal, even if we err in our interpretation of that Act, I would not reach the merits but would conclude that the District Court was without jurisdiction over this matter of international relations by reason of the political question doctrine. The law has recognized since 1803 that certain political decisions are by their nature committed to the political branches to the exclusion of the judiciary."[113]

The detailed examination of these double-entry cases is justified by the problem they create for those seeking to understand and reform the jurisprudential chaos surrounding the role of the judiciary in foreign-relations cases. On their face, these cases seem to support a doctrine of judicial abdication and strict adherence by judges to the political-question doctrine. A computer search turns up these and many other cases as examples of the doctrine's application. But the cases illustrate nothing of the sort; rather, they show judges judging, determining the outcome of a litigation normally, on the evidence. The political-question doctrine serves as no more than a grace note, but one contradicted by the actual disposition of the case.

Why do courts say one thing while doing another? Judges seem always to be talking about foreign-policy questions as beyond judicial review but then reviewing the legality of the "political policies" in question. In such fundamental self-contradiction, the *Prize Cases* correctly pressage the tenor of much subsequent jurisprudence. The decisions feature extravagant outbursts of judicial modesty marked by assertions of incompetence to decide issues of global import. A few pages later, however, the same judges use traditional legal reasoning to decide the very issues declared beyond their competence.

Perhaps what is really happening is that the judges themselves are torn: In foreign-relations and national-security cases, they want the government generally to have its way, but they do not wish to be seen as its subservient collaborators. Thus they ensure that the government always wins but without appearing to decide in its favor on the merits. If that is the purpose, it is not what has been achieved. Rather, the jurisprudence has a powerful whiff of hypocrisy: Judges say they will abstain but fail to do so; judges proclaim the separation of powers but almost always decide in favor of the government in a process where the players—the government and those challenging its actions—appear not to be playing on a level field.

Two Principled Theories
of Constitutionalism

ABDICATIONISM is generally defended by judges who practice it as a recognition that the courts are but one of three coequal branches of government. Professor Alexander Bickel, describing and lauding the judiciary's "passive virtues,"[1] has identified its two conceptual components: constitutionally mandated limits and self-imposed prudential limits.[2]

The constitutionally mandated limit on adjudication is either of very little or very great importance, depending on how it is construed. On the one hand, the limit may mean no more than this: If in the Court's opinion either the presidency or Congress has acted within its constitutionally allotted ambit of political discretion, the Court will not replace the political judgment of a coordinate branch with its own preferences. No judge, and no scholar of note, has ever expressed disagreement with such a self-evident proposition. It surely requires no *doctrine* of its own. On the other hand, the limit may mean much more: If in the opinion of one of the political branches that branch is authorized by the Constitution to take an action, the Court will not substitute its view of whether such action is constitutionally authorized for that of the political branch. In other words, the courts should not substitute their interpretation of the Constitution's allocation of powers to a political branch for the latter's understanding of that allocation. Each branch should be free to set the limits of its powers by expressing its essentially unreviewable understanding of the Constitution's parameters and acting thereon without fear of judicial contradiction.

This far more expansive formulation of the political-question doctrine and its adoption by some judges has always been exceedingly controversial. The consequence of the lesser version is to subject the actions of the president and Congress to judicial review (albeit not to foreign-policy review). The effect of the greater version is to place acts of the political branches beyond the reach of the courts' umpiring function. To put it even more directly: The effect of the first version is to subject the political branches to law—including, of course, the law of the Constitution—while the effect of the second is to exonerate them from the control of law.

The expansive version of the doctrine of abstention has its origins in British constitutional practice. The rationale for that practice is well described by the great British jurist William Blackstone in his *Commentaries* of 1765, with which the early American jurists were quite familiar. "With regard to foreign concerns," he wrote, "the king is the delegate or representative of his people. It is impossible that the individuals of a state, in their collective capacity, can transact the affairs of that state with another community equally numerous as themselves. Unanimity must be wanting to their measures, and strength to the execution of their counsels. In the king therefore, as in a centre, all the rays of his people are united, and formed by that union, a consistency, splendor and power, that make him feared and respected by foreign potentates; who would scruple to enter into any engagement that must afterwards be revised and ratified by a popular assembly. What is done by the royal authority, with regard to foreign powers, is the act of the whole nation."[3] What the king does in the realm of foreign affairs cannot be contradicted by either the legislature or the courts.[4]

But the Revolution and its aftermath specifically sought to break with such monarchial custom. Alexander Hamilton, despite his advocacy of a strong central executive authority, wrote in *Federalist No. 75* in 1788: "The history of human conduct does not warrant that exalted opinion of human virtue which would make it wise in a nation to commit interests of so delicate and momentous a kind as those which concern its intercourse with the rest of the world to the sole disposal of a magistrate, created and circumstanced, as would be a president of the United States."[5] Equally, the Revolution and the drafting of the federal Constitution were motivated by rejection of unrestricted *parliamentary* supremacy. In Professor David Richards's summary: "Americans rapidly came to see British insistence on the principle of parliamentary sovereignty not as a constitutional or moral argument at all, but as a bare assertion of factionalized self-aggrandizing power masquerading as an elevated impartiality in the balanced assessment of evolving historical practice for the greater good of all. American 'common sense' concluded that the British did not take seriously the arguments that Americans had made, often at great and learned length, about violations of their constitutional and moral rights; furthermore, they interpreted the British appeal to parliamentary sovereignty as an insult to everything Americans took constitutional argument to be." They concluded that the vaunted British constitution "was no 'fixed Constitution' at all."[6]

Nevertheless, American judges have had difficulty in making a clean break with this aspect of our legal heritage. The notion that the presidency—or the president and Congress—constitutes the king-in-Parliament's heir in wielding undivided and unreviewable foreign affairs authority remains in the consciousness and rhetoric of many judges even when they stop short of carrying out the full implications of their pronouncements. In the *Prize Cases*, for example, the Supreme Court was invited to find that President Lincoln had exceeded his constitutional powers in seizing neutral vessels trading with the Confederacy without having obtained a congressional declaration of war. Such seizures are normally an incident of war or belligerency. Must not Congress first declare that such war exists? Justice Grier, as we have seen, found ample basis for establishing that the legislature had given its assent in kind. Nevertheless, he also expressed support for an expansive doctrine of nonreviewability. "Whether the President in fulfilling his duties, as Commander-in-Chief, in suppressing an insurrection, has met with such armed hostile resistence, and a civil war of such alarming proportions as will compel him to accord to them the character of belligerents," he wrote for the Court, "is a question to be decided *by him*, and this court must be governed by the decisions and acts of the political department of the Government to which this power was entrusted."[7]

"Governed by"? With that statement, the Supreme Court seemed to take the broader view of the constitutional basis for its abdication. In such matters, Grier implied, the government's views are dispositive, even when the constitutionality of its conduct is at issue.

In a vociferous dissent, Justice Nelson wrote, "No doubt this is a war . . . of the most extensive and threatening dimensions and effects, but . . . [that] has no relevancy or weight when the question is what constitutes war in a legal sense, in the sense of the law of nations, and of the Constitution of the United States? For it must be a war in this sense to attach to it all the consequences that belong to belligerent rights. . . . For we find . . . that to constitute a civil war in the sense in which we are speaking . . . it must be recognized or declared by the sovereign power . . . [which] by our Constitution is lodged in the Congress."[8] He went on to make a scathing comparison between the king of England's absolute right to make civil war against the American colonies and the power of the president, for whom "no such power existed."[9] The duty of the courts to abstain, he added, does not extend to a war improperly declared, adding that only "when such a war is recognized or declared to exist by the war-making power, *but not otherwise*, it is the duty of the Courts to follow the decision of the political power of the Government."[10]

The distinction between the two theories of constitutionalism appears even more starkly in the Supreme Court's 1950 disposition of *Johnson v. Eisentrager*.[11] There the petitioners were German nationals who had been captured by American forces in China. They were charged with violating the laws of war and were tried and convicted in China by an American military commission. The offense consisted of continuing to engage in military activity against the United States after Germany's unconditional surrender. At the time of their appeal to the Supreme Court, they were serving their sentence in the American zone of Germany.

The petitioners' plea before the Supreme Court raised constitutional issues about the circumstances of their trial and the jurisdiction of the tribunal that had convicted them. This is the sort of issue courts normally review. Even the jurisdiction of the military tribunal that tried General Yamashita for war crimes in the Philippines was ultimately reviewed by the Supreme Court.[12] Justice Robert Jackson's judgment, however, purports to stop far short of determining the constitutional and legal basis for the military commission's jurisdiction over the petitioners. "Certainly it is not the function of the Judiciary," he wrote, citing *Curtiss-Wright*, "to entertain private litigation—even by a citizen—which challenges the legality, the wisdom, or the propriety of the Commander-in-Chief in sending our armed forces abroad or to any particular region."[13] Wisdom and propriety, yes, but legality? The Court, Jackson insisted, must refuse to decide any issue that "involves a challenge to conduct of diplomatic and foreign affairs, for which the President is exclusively responsible."[14]

That, in starkest form, is the expansive version of the constitutional basis for judicial abdication. Foreign affairs are the exclusive preserve of the president. Whether an action taken by the president falls within that exclusive preserve, even alleged denials of due process in a criminal proceeding, is not subject to judicial review. Each branch, in effect, is free to interpret the limits of its own jurisdiction. That is the necessary corollary of their coequality.

Justice Hugo Black wrote the dissent for himself and Justices Douglas and Burton, calling the Jackson decision "a broad and dangerous principle."[15] He added that the issue was simply whether "the judiciary has power in habeas corpus proceedings to test the legality of criminal sentences imposed by the executive through military tribunals. . . . Perhaps, as some nations believe, there is merit in leaving the administration of criminal laws to executive and military agencies completely free from judicial scrutiny. Our Constitution has emphatically expressed a contrary policy."[16]

Eisentrager marks a high point—or an aberrational example—of the working of the broadest version of constitutional abdicationism. It has not stood the test of time well. The power of military justice over *American* civilians abroad was finally restricted in 1957 in *Reid v. Covert*,[17] a case in which the Court was not persuaded, either by statute or by an executive agreement with Great Britain, to hold such military jurisdiction constitutional. The Supreme Court not only rejected any notion that this matter was nonjusticiable but also definitively "recognized the supremacy of the Constitution over a treaty"[18] and then vacated the conviction.

Nevertheless, the more expansive view of the constitutional limitation on judicial review has never entirely abandoned the field, although it has probably lost its capacity to determine the outcome of cases in some federal jurisdictions and even when invoked is more likely to serve solely as a makeweight item in double-entry bookkeeping. However, it retains considerable potential for conceptual mischief, and there continues to be ample confusion between the two constitutionally based concepts of judicial restraint, particularly in foreign-policy cases. This has not been dissipated by the Supreme Court's one deliberate effort systematically to clarify the matter. In *Baker v. Carr*, writing for the majority, Justice William Brennan said that the Court must refuse to decide cases that "involve the exercise of a discretion demonstrably committed to the executive or legislature."[19] But to whom must the commitment be demonstrable? To the Supreme Court? Or only to an executive or Congress self-judging the scope of its constitutional authority? In an extended essay on the political-question doctrine, the *Baker* Court, perhaps the last one in recent times to have the intellectual cohesion necessary to clarify the doctrinal position, did not give a dispositive answer. Predictably, the question (demonstrable to whom?) has returned to haunt the Supreme Court.

In the *Goldwater* case,[20] the demonstrable-to-whom? question remained painfully unresolved because of what by 1979 had become the Court's deep division on precisely this issue. Senator Barry Goldwater and several other members of Congress had brought an action against President Carter to compel him not to carry out his stated intention to terminate a mutual-defense treaty with Taiwan until receiving either the consent of the Senate or legislated authority from Congress. Goldwater had argued that as the Constitution in article 2, section 2(2), requires the advice and consent of two-thirds of the Senate to make a treaty, it followed that something more than a solitary exercise of presidential discretion must be required to terminate it. Alternatively, it was contended that since the Constitution declares a treaty to be the "supreme law of the land,"[21] it must be repealed like a law, by act of Congress.

In a system that accepted the notion that the Supreme Court should umpire all disputes over the allocation of power between branches of the government, it would be difficult to think of an issue more facially suitable to judicial determination. The dispute pertained to a fundamental question of governance, one likely to arise repeatedly and thus to bedevil interbranch as well as international relations until finally resolved one way or the other, a finality only the Supreme Court could achieve. Moreover, *Goldwater* raised a question posing a choice among a limited number of well-defined options and offered the Court an opportunity to base such choice on constitutional text, general evidence of the framers' intent, and an extensive repertory of practice. And while the functional issues raised by the case were no doubt delicate and important, they could be addressed without specialized foreign-policy expertise or secret information.

Despite these favorable portends, the Court deliberately failed to decide, leaving the issue to rankle and bedevil some future presidency. Moreover, Chief Justice Burger and three justices—Rehnquist, Stewart, and Stevens—explicitly said that their refusal to decide was constitutionally required since the case raised a political question, one committed exclusively to the coequal political branches.[22] Four justices—Blackmun, Brennan, Powell, and White—disagreed, although they further disagreed among themselves whether the case was moot (Powell),[23] ought to be set down for further argument on justiciability as well as the merits (Blackmun and White),[24] or should simply be resolved on the merits in favor of the president (Brennan).[25] One justice, Marshall, offered no view but merely concurred in the result,[26] which was to uphold the decision (in favor of the president) but not the reasoning of the circuit court,[27] which, like the district court (which had decided for Goldwater),[28] had thought the case perfectly justiciable. So much for clarity.

Justice Rehnquist, writing for the four justices relying on the political-question doctrine, argued that the issue was inappropriate to judicial resolution "because it involves the authority of the President in the conduct of our country's foreign relations."[29] The effect of that view is to leave the president entirely free to determine the scope of his "foreign-relations" powers. Justice Brennan, at the other end of the spectrum, wrote that Justice Rehnquist "profoundly misapprehends the political-question principle as it applies to matters of foreign relations."[30] Quoting his opinion in *Baker v. Carr*, Brennan noted that the doctrine applies only when "judgment has been 'constitutionally committed' " to a political branch of government. He now sought to clarify the unanswered question left pending in *Baker*—as determined by whom? "But the doctrine does not pertain", Brennan wrote, "when a court is faced with the *antecedent* question whether a particular branch has been constitutionally designated as the repository of political decisionmaking power."[31] It was too late, however, to gather a majority of supporters among his brethren for that limited version of the doctrine.

Thus the issue in *Goldwater*—how are treaties terminated?—was left unresolved, as was the scope of the issue of the Court's powers of judicial review in foreign affairs. In the circumstances, the effect was to let the president terminate the treaty with Taiwan on his sole authority, but only one justice (Brennan) was forthright enough to interpret the Constitution explicitly to give him that right. We cannot today, two hundred years after the Constitution was ratified, say with certainty how the nation extricates itself from treaties. Perhaps more important, we still cannot say definitively whether in our system of governance it is the courts that determine whether the president, in matters affecting foreign affairs, has acted within the ambit of discretion "demonstrably committed" to him by the Constitution and the law.

Had Chief Justice Marshall not entered his giveback caveat, this most basic of all questions would surely have been resolved by the general doctrine of judicial review expounded in *Marbury v. Madison*. Brennan, for the majority in *Baker*, had expressed some misgivings about making foreign affairs a special case in the Court's jurisdictional jurisprudence. It "is error to suppose that every case or controversy which touches foreign relations lies beyond judicial cognizance,"[32] he had written, adding that the political-question doctrine excludes courts from deciding "political questions" but not "political cases."[33] Unfortunately, he stopped short of explaining this new, presumably narrower basis for distinquishing between cases, although venturing that courts "cannot reject as 'no law suit' a bona fide controversy as to whether some action denominated 'political' exceeds constitutional authority."[34] By the time *Goldwater* came before the Court, however, the majority for that vision seems to have evaporated.

It seems unlikely that even with a majority on his side, Justice Brennan would have been able to formulate a coherent doctrine of judicial review based on the distinction between a "political case" and a "political question." Indeed, Brennan himself had warned against "semantic cataloging," echoing Professor Louis Jaffe's earlier comment on the same subject that "classification is not reasoning."[35] Unfortunately, "semantic cataloging" is still the prevalent means for deciding conceptually difficult cases without addressing the underlying structural issues. Courts, especially lower courts, announce that a case deals with "foreign relations" and that this makes the issue being litigated a "political question" requiring "judicial deference" to the political branches. None of the three terms are defined; they are used as if their content and relevance to the case were self-evident.

A 1940 decision of the D.C. Circuit illustrates this reliance on unreasoned categorization. "Among the questions which have been recognized as political rather than judicial in nature, none comes more clearly within the former classification than those which involve the propriety of acts done in the conduct of the foreign relations of our government."[36] Yet the facts of the case demonstrate the futility of such classification. At issue was the finality of a Mixed Claims Commission award that had virtually nothing to do with foreign relations.

More recently, in *Sneaker Circus, Inc. v. Carter*,[37] the Second Circuit panel stated the general principle thus: "To be decided on its merits, a case must . . . be justiciable per se. That is, it must be the kind of case which provides an appropriate occasion for judicial decision-making." What kind of case is that? The court's answer: "[It] must not involve a 'political question.' "[38] The reasoning is entirely circular. Moreover, nothing in this case tells us whether it is the courts or the political branches of government that are to decide what kind of case this is. If it is the courts, the doctrine of judicial abstention is surely redundant, merely reiterating what is already expressed in the text of the Constitution as interpreted by the landmark decisions on judicial review. On the other hand, if it is the political branches, it is the Constitution that becomes redundant, a repository of unenforceable limits on the exercise of political power.

In the practice of the lower federal courts even more than in the Supreme Court, there appears to be sympathy for the expansive view of the constitutional limitation on judicial review. This is usually manifest in extremely short conclusory opinions denying jurisdiction. For example, in *Durand v. Hollins*(1860),[39] an American plaintiff had sued the commander of a naval force that had destroyed his property in the bombardment of Greytown (San Juan del Norte) in Nicaragua. Defendant responded that he was carrying out the decision of the president, as commander in chief, to protect the lives and property of American citizens who were threatened by "an independent government, not recognized by the United States" that "had forcibly usurped the possession of the place."[40] The action was dismissed in a brief opinion stating that "as it respects the interposition of the executive abroad, for the protection of the lives or property of the citizen, the duty must, of necessity, rest in the discretion of the president. Acts of lawless violence, or of threatened violence to the citizen or his property, cannot be anticipated and provided for; and the protection, to be effectual or of any avail, may, not infrequently, require the most prompt and decided action."[41] Circuit Justice Nelson then cites *Marbury v. Madison* for the conclusory proposition that the "subjects are political."[42] A presidential "decision is final and conclusive."[43]

Even more summary was the 1958 decision of the Sixth Circuit rejecting as nonjusticiable a taxpayer suit claiming a right to withhold payment because Congress had appropriated revenues for military and foreign policies in violation of international law.[44] Instead of dismissing this argument for lack of standing or on the merits, the court felt constrained to hold that the complaint "involved political and governmental questions which are confided by the Constitution to the legislative and executive branches of the government, and over which the courts have no jurisdiction."[45] No effort is made in the five spare paragraphs of the decision to develop reasons for this view of the Constitution's distribution of powers, nor is a single judicial precedent cited. Equally brief and dismissive is the judgment of Judge June L. Green refusing jurisdiction on political-question grounds over a challenge to the constitutionality of the U.S. invasion of Grenada.[46] Thereafter, the D.C. Circuit simply dismissed the case as moot.[47]

Many courts seem particularly anxious to demonstrate adherence to a constitutionally mandated restraint on their power to decide cases where disposition on the merits would seem easy and would create no possible clash with the executive. In *Dickson v. Ford*,[48] for example, the Fifth Circuit ostentatiously declined even to reach the preliminary issue of a taxpayer's standing to challenge the constitutionality of military aid to Israel as violative of the First Amendment's establishment clause.[49] Instead, the court merely noted that "the conduct of foreign relations" is traditionally "committed by the Constitution to the executive and legislative—the 'political'—departments of the government."[50] Nowhere does the court try to explain why this is a "foreign-relations" rather than an establishment case. Similarly, a suit challenging the constitutionality of establishing diplomatic relations with the Vatican could easily have been denied for lack of standing or on the merits. Instead it was peremptorily dismissed as presenting a "nonjusticiable political question."[51] Suppose in establishing these diplomatic relations the president had made an executive order proclaiming Roman Catholicism the state religion? What does it take to awaken the judicial watchdogs of the Constitution in foreign-relations matters?

Another recent example is the 1984 *Tel-Oren*[52] case where the D.C. Circuit panel dismissed an action against Libya by a survivor of an armed attack on an Israeli civilian bus. While two of the judges focused on procedural or substantive aspects of the case, Judge Bork took the purist view that the claim required dismissal because adjudication "would raise substantial problems of judicial interference with nonjudicial functions, such as the conduct of foreign relations."[53]

Each of the above cases probably produced the right outcome, but by reaching their result by recourse to superficial categories rather than by reasoning, the judges failed in their duty to "say what the law is." If "easy" cases are so readily turned away, it is not surprising that the courts refuse to hear ones that present closer or more delicate questions, or that might lead to a conflict with political power. Thus the judges refused to decide whether a person in the United States, a native of Austria, could be detained in wartime as an enemy alien because of the absorption of Austria into the Third Reich in 1938 despite his departure from Austria in 1919.[54] The court felt the issue to have been judicially foreclosed by U.S. foreign policy, which had recognized the *Anschluss* with Germany. "Recognition of foreign nations, it is settled, is a political question," it ruled, "the determination of which by the legislative and executive departments of the government conclusively binds the court."[55] It is difficult to see why this should be so, why the court could not have weighed the operation of the detention order against defendant's asserted constitutional right to liberty, at least to the extent of examining the plausibility of the executive's assertion of a probable threat to national security. The court might have decided that issue either way; what is depressing is not so much the outcome as the refusal of U.S. judges even to consider something so basic to the principles of personal liberty for which the nation was fighting.

Finally, if ours is a nation of divided and limited powers, how is one to rationalize the decision of the Tenth Circuit that a presidential decision to enter into an agreement with another state by executive agreement without senatorial advise and consent rather than by treaty "presents a nonjusticiable political question"[56]—or the New York Circuit Court's decision in the 1861 case of *United States v. Baker*[57] dismissing without any inquiry into the facts a challenge to a presidential determination that an act of piracy had been transformed into one of "naval engagement" solely because of a state of (undeclared) war or belligerency?

If the courts will not weigh the property- or liberty-based claims of citizens or the claims of members of Congress to participate in governance, what use are the balances established by the drafters of the Constitution? Madison, writing as "Helvedius," wrote, "If we consult, for a moment, the nature and operation of the two powers to declare war and to make treaties, it will be impossible not to see, that

41

they can never fall within a proper definition of executive powers. The natural province of the executive magistrate is to execute law, as that of the legislature is to make laws. . . . A treaty is not an execution of laws: it does not presuppose the existence of laws. It is, on the contrary, to have itself the force of a *law*, and to be carried into *execution*, like all *other laws*, by the *executive magistrate*. To say then that the power of making treaties, which are confessedly laws, belongs naturally to the department which is to execute laws, is to say, that the executive department naturally includes a legislative power. In theory this is an absurdity—in practice, a tyranny."[58]

Why do judges feel excused from defending a constitutional line that Madison, in any event, thought as important in the field of foreign affairs as in any other aspect of the Republic's governance? Why do some courts feel that the Constitution's separation and balancing of power is preserved when they confine themselves to writing a memo-size dismissal of a citizen's serious claim of right by categorizing it, simply and without amplification, as "political" or concerned with "foreign affairs"? To the claimants in these cases, the issue looks neither political nor like a foreign-policy issue but like a question of personal freedom, compensation for injury, or respect for the Constitution. Those claims may yield to weightier constitutional priorities, but surely the claimant is entitled to be weighed on a scale that is not held by the claimant's political adversary.

The recent *Lowry*[59] case is a particularly egregious example of what happens to the system of checks and balances when courts apply the expansive version of the constitutional doctrine of judicial abdication. There the federal district and circuit courts refused to hear an action brought by 110 members of Congress during the Iran-Iraq war contending that the president had dispatched U.S. naval forces to the Persian Gulf where they were engaging in combat in disregard of the requirement of the War Powers Act. That legislation requires Congress to be notified when troops are introduced "into hostilities or into situations where imminent involvement in hostilities is clearly indicated by the circumstances."[60] Such notification, had it been given, would have triggered an automatic requirement for withdrawal of forces within sixty days unless during that time continued deployment was specifically approved by Congress.[61]

The district court concluded that it should exercise its "remedial discretion" not to hear "political disputes" in which there is no evident consensus in Congress whether the president has violated the law.[62] The court would feel obliged to hear the dispute only if there was a "true confrontation between the Executive and a unified Congress, as evidenced by its passage of legislation to enforce the Resolution."[63] In the absence of such "true confrontation," the issue was held not "ripe"[64] and was "dismissed as a prudential matter under the political question doctrine."[65] This result was affirmed in an even more terse decision by the D.C. Circuit Court.[66] In effect the judges were telling 110 members of Congress that if they wanted the courts to enforce a law, they should pass another law saying so. Even then, the court "as a prudential matter" might choose to duck. The only conclusion to be drawn from such dismissive disposition of a serious claim by a large number of interested parties is that the president is beyond the control of law when he acts in foreign affairs.

This is never said. Indeed, very little is said in some of the most egregious instances of judicial abdication. Terse opinions and terser denials of certiorari are the real repositories of the judicial purist's view that courts may not challenge the authority of coequal branches in their conduct of foreign relations. Justice William O. Douglas eloquently attacked this practice in dissenting from an order denying certiorari in *Commonwealth of Massachusetts v. Laird*[67] where that state sought an adjudication of the constitutionality of continued U.S. participation in the Vietnam War. There is no reason, he said, why the judges could not decide whether the Tonkin Gulf Resolution or other subsequent acts of Congress were the constitutional equivalent of a declaration of war. He thought this an ordinary question of constitutional construction and statutory interpretation, one not lacking in applicable legal standards but largely bereft of political policy content. The issue, he argued, was not whether the president ought to be fighting the war but whether he might do so constitutionally without specific congressional participation in the decision to use force.[68] In Douglas's view, while the courts admittedly may not decide questions of foreign policy, they may not shy from responsibility to decide whether those who make foreign policy are proceeding in accordance with the law and the Constitution. This view, in other words, rejects the notion that there is an inherent difference, easily and facially apparent, between political and other cases, between the conduct of foreign affairs and other kinds of government action. While the Constitution in this view commands the judiciary to show deference to the political branches' calculation of what is best for the nation, the Constitution quite as urgently commands the judiciary not to abdicate its responsibility as the sole umpire to weigh competing legal claims and entitlements. In discharging this inescapable judicial function, mere semantic cataloging neither offers relief from the responsibility to hear, consider, weigh, and decide nor excuses failure to enunciate a coherent set of principles for decision.

Many judges and most scholars probably accept Douglas's restrictive version of the constitutional basis for judicial deference in foreign-relations cases. They may reject altogether the theoretical underpinnings of the political-question doctrine. They may not believe that judges are constitutionally barred from a case with foreign-affairs implications. However, that does not necessarily mean they think that courts *should* decide such cases. A second, prudential line of jurisprudence has evolved that also cautions judges to stay away from the water's edge.

Prudential Reasons for Judicial Abdication

THE TENDENCY of judges to refuse to adjudicate cases involving foreign-affairs or national-security issues originated in a giveback tactic employed as part of an overall strategy of judicial expansion. Courts deployed an utterly inappropriate notion borrowed from British imperial jurisprudence, which the judiciary reinforced by use of straw dicta and double-entry bookkeeping.

That, however, is not the whole story. Were it so, it would be easy to refute the political-question doctrine and its penumbra insofar as it applies to foreign-affairs cases. It could be dismissed as a historic device of dubious origins, perhaps necessitated at an early stage of judicial ascendance, built on ill-considered dicta and kept alive with mirrors. It could easily be written off as a historic oddity incongruent with modern constitutionalism. However, the doctrine is not so easily disposable. The abdicationist doctrine, the notion that law stops at the water's edge, nowadays finds support in other, weightier *prudential* considerations. It is to these we now turn.

Although constitutional theory initially gave impetus to judicial abdication in foreign-affairs cases, today judges more frequently abstain because of prudential concerns. In some instances, both prudential and constitutional grounds are cited, but the judicial emphasis is increasingly on the former.

These prudential reasons for abstention fall into four somewhat overlapping categories. First, judges assert that cases involving foreign affairs present issues turning on factual evidence that the courts are unsuited to obtain or assess. Second, judges point out that foreign-affairs cases often present policy questions to which legal standards are inapplicable or unascertainable. Third, they caution that the cases present questions that must be resolved by foreign-affairs experts rather than judges because the outcome is likely to determine not only the well-being but even the survival of the nation in a dangerous world. Fourth, they evince concern that inconvenient decisions that judges might make on foreign affairs might be ignored by the political branches. In general, prudential considerations are cited by judges to escape a responsibility that many do not want, for which they feel ill prepared, and that might bring them bitter confrontation with the political branches. Each of these concerns is expressed through the ample, if chaotic, abdicationist jurisprudence.

THE FACTUAL EVIDENCE IS TOO DIFFICULT

It is true that cases turning on foreign facts present unusual evidenciary problems for judges. Not only are key facts sometimes esoteric and exotic, but often they shade into matters of opinion. Which state possesses a disputed piece of territory may be difficult to ascertain if it depends on interpretation of what the media call "fast-breaking developments." In response to that problem, the Supreme Court, despite occasional deviations,[1] has tended to accept as essentially unreviewable the determinations of the political branches pertaining to contested title to territory, sovereignty, and jurisdiction. This eagerness at least to appear guided by the executive is evident in Chief Justice Marshall's handling of the boundary issue presented by the 1829 *Foster v. Neilson* case.[2] The same concern can be seen in *Williams v. Suffolk Insurance Co.*, an 1839 Supreme Court opinion in which the Court asked rhetorically: "Can there be any doubt, that when the executive branch of the government, which is charged with our foreign relations, shall in its correspondence with a foreign nation assume a fact in regard to the sovereignty of any island or country, it is conclusive on the judicial department? And in this view it is not material to inquire, nor is it the province of the Court to determine, whether the executive be right or wrong. It is enough to know, that in the exercise of his constitutional functions, he has decided the question."[3]

The question in *Suffolk* was whether the Falkland Islands belonged to Argentina. If they tried to determine such questions for themselves, the judges said, "there would be an irreconcilable difference between the executive and judicial departments. By one of these departments, a foreign island or country might be considered as at peace with the United States; whilst the other would consider it in a state of war. No well regulated government has ever sanctioned a principle so unwise, and so destructive of national character."[4]

A similar self-restraining rule was applied in the 1890 case of *Jones v. United States*[5] where the Court was asked to accept the fact of U.S.

possession of the guano island of Navassa to validate the federal government's jurisdiction to prosecute a murder committed there. The power to declare U.S. jurisdiction was held to be "a strictly executive power, affecting foreign relations,"[6] and the Court added that its members, in ascertaining "any facts of which they are bound to take judicial notice" especially as "to international affairs," should merely "inquire of the Foreign Office or the Department of State."[7]

Similarly, who is the sovereign of a foreign nation is an oft-litigated issue that has been held a political question in a broad range of cases, the courts often not merely heeding the recognition policy of the executive branch but declaring that issue entirely nonjusticiable.[8] For example, where the United States recognizes a government in exile and a rival regime is actually in charge of the country, the lower courts often appear to feel foreclosed from making their own determination, choosing instead to follow the executive's lead without any independent inquiry.[9]

Abdication of this kind is often justified by reference to *Baker v. Carr*'s admonition to avoid "the potentiality of embarrassment from multifarious pronouncements by various departments on one question."[10] In *Oetjen v. Central Leather Co.*,[11] the Supreme Court held that it was not free to determine which government was the ruler of post-revolutionary Russia, for if it came to a conclusion different from that of the Department of State, that would "imperil the amicable relations between governments and vex the peace of nations."[12] Similarly, whether a foreign ship is a "public vessel" entitled to sovereign immunity as an instrumentality of its government, even though engaged in the carriage of goods for hire, has been held by the Supreme Court to depend solely on whether that "claim is recognized and allowed by the executive branch."[13]

Because of the complexity or paucity of factual evidence, judges have also tended to find it impossible to determine such questions as whether a war was going on in Vietnam or Cambodia. In 1978, Judge Wyzanski found that this "is a question which at this stage in history a court is incompetent to answer."[14] His judgment continued: A "court cannot procure the relevant evidence. . . . Even if the necessary facts were to be laid before it, a court would not substitute its judgment for that of the President, who has an unusually wide measure of discretion in this area, and who should not be judicially condemned except in a case of clear abuse amounting to bad faith."[15] In *Holtzman v. Schlesinger*,[16] a member of Congress had alleged that the

U.S. bombing of Cambodia had created a "basic change in the situation" negating whatever earlier congressional acquiescence there may have been for presidential warmaking. The Second Circuit simply remanded the case with instructions to dismiss because it called for the exercise of "military and diplomatic expertise not vested in the judiciary, which make[s] the issue political and thus beyond [the] court to determine."[17]

There are two related issues intertwined in these fact-related grounds for judicial abstention. One has to do with the judicial system's competence to decide complex issues of fact the *loci* of which are wholly or partially outside the United States. There is surely no inherent reason why a court in the District of Columbia cannot nowadays determine whether Cambodia is being bombed or a warrantless search has been conducted by U.S. agents in Mexico. The second issue relates to evidentiary probity and onuses of proof. If the president has determined that the lives of Americans abroad are in danger if military protection is not afforded them, that view has gravamen. A private citizen or member of Congress may have to overcome a heavy burden of proof to establish that the president's reason for action is fraudulent or without merit. Other presidential determinations, such as whether a treaty has lapsed due to war, may be entitled to some lesser degree of deference, still others to no presumptive weight. These, however, present issues of litigious procedure with which courts have extensive familiarity. Devising and applying suitable rules of evidence to foreign-affairs cases, as we shall see, should (and does) present no particular difficulty for our sophisticated federal judicial system.

No Applicable Legal Standards

Closely related to the perception that foreign-affairs "facts" are beyond courts' reach is the view that the field is one inherently lacking in what in *Baker v. Carr* is described as "judicially discoverable and manageable standards."[18] For example, in a recent dispute between two U.S. companies claiming title to the same oil by virtue of conflicting concessions awarded by the rulers of adjoining Persian Gulf states, the Fifth Circuit dismissed on the "ground that the question presented is political, being both constitutionally devolving on the executive and judicially unmanageable."[19] The judges had been advised by the State Department to remain neutral about the territorial dispute, and they dutifully complied.[20] They agreed that this dispute between U.S. commercial litigants was in reality a boundary dispute between two sovereign foreign nations that U.S. judges were unsuited to resolve not only because of its complexity but because, they added, in "their external relations, sovereigns are bound by no law; they are like our ancestors before the recognition or imposition of the social contract. A prerequisite of law is a recognized superior authority whether delegated from below or imposed from above—where there is no recognized authority, there is no law. Because no law exists binding these sovereigns and allocating rights and liabilities, no method to *judicially* resolve their disagreements."[21] That is surely news to the International Court of Justice, which recently has been involved in deciding six major boundary disputes submitted by states laboring under the "illusion" that there are ascertainable legal standards—that it's *not* a jungle out there.

Along the same line, the Supreme Court in *Banco Nacional de Cuba v. Sabbatino* (1964)[22] adopted another abdicationist concept, the "act-of-state doctrine," in part because the judges felt they could not ascertain the relevant legal standards applicable to title to goods confiscated in Cuba. "There are few if any issues in international law today," Justice Harlan wrote, "on which opinion seems to be so divided as the limitations on a state's power to expropriate the property of aliens."[23] Thus redress should be left to the political experts. "Following an expropriation of any significance, the Executive engages in diplomacy aimed to assure that United States citizens who are harmed are compensated fairly."[24] If courts were to decide, they would have to pick their way through "the fluidity of present world conditions" and would be drawn into "a patchwork approach toward the formulation" of law that might be "highly conjectural."[25]

This line of reasoning entirely ignores the established role of courts in clarifying murky areas of law by defining rules and imposing them on diverse fact patterns. The argument that courts must confine themselves to applying rules previously clarified by legislation or precedent pretends to a degree of judicial virginity that is simply not credible and thus seems almost indecent. Where there is no clear practice to support a rule of compensation for expropriated property, courts may be justified in refusing to invent such a rule, preferring a more modest normative requirement. It is surely insupportable, however, to argue that the judicial function does not operate in such circumstances. There are gray areas everywhere, but only in international matters is a claim of "no law" thought an acceptable judicial response to legal ambiguity. Nothing about foreign affairs inherently justifies their being exempt from the obligation of courts to answer as best they can the questions of law framed by litigants. If on close examination no clear legal standards emerge to guide the litigants in resolving their dispute, it is the duty of the courts to leave the parties' interaction to their own unencumbered search for a pragmatic modus vivendi by reaching the perfectly appropriate decision that the law imposes no requirements but leaves such relations to the pragmatic devices of the parties. Such a decision, however, represents a judicial assumption—and not an abjuring—of the duty to decide.

Too Much at Stake

Judges, as we have noted, are not immune to the popular perception that we live in a dangerous world in which the nation's well-being and security may depend on a willingness to engage in conduct that would not be tolerated domestically. This attitude may take the form of courts overlooking political conduct they would not permit in another context. This attitude might be understandable in extremis if the nation's very survival was at stake, and the courts certainly have shown leniency in such conditions.[26] However, leniency, in the form of abdicating the responsibility to review executive and legislative conduct for violations of due process, has not always been confined to extraordinary circumstances.

Some of the most dramatic judicial reticence is found in foreign-affairs cases that involve no such urgency. In the Supreme Court's 1937 *Belmont* decision,[27] for example, plaintiffs complained of the U.S. government's having taken their property without compensation in carrying out an agreement with the Soviet Union. Writing a summarily brief opinion dismissing the complaint as nonjusticiable, Justice Sutherland held that "the conduct of foreign relations was committed by the Constitution to the political departments of the government, and the propriety of what may be done in the exercise of this political power was not subject to judicial inquiry or decision."[28] The occasion for this abdication of judicial review was not a war or even a crisis but a perfectly ordinary decision made by the federal government in the course of normal diplomacy. No dire blow to the national interest would have resulted had the court decided on the merits of plaintiffs' claim or even if the federal authorities had lost the case, as a closer look at the circumstances makes clear.

A Russian corporation had deposited funds in Belmont's private New York bank. After the 1917 revolution, the new Soviet regime had expropriated the corporation and its assets. In November 1933 the Soviet claim to the account at Belmont's bank was transferred to the U.S. government by operation of an executive agreement (the "Litvinov Assignment") by which the two nations brought about a settlement of rival claims and a mutual exchange of recognition and diplomatic relations. The executors of Belmont's estate resisted turning over the deposit to the U.S. receiver on the ground that to do so would contravene the property provisions of the state and federal constitutions.

The Court, refusing to look at the issue of uncompensated expropriation, merely took judicial notice of the fact that the "recognition, establishment of diplomatic relations, the assignment, and agreements with respect thereto, were all parts of one transaction, resulting in an international compact between the two governments." That the conclusion of these "were within the competence of the President may not be doubted. Governmental power over internal affairs is distributed. . . . Governmental power over external affairs is not distributed, but is vested exclusively in the national government. And in respect of what was done here, the Executive had authority to speak as the sole organ of that government."[29] To support this extravagant proposition, Sutherland (inevitably) cited his opinion in *Curtiss-Wright*.[30] As for the argument that the Constitution bars the United States government from becoming the beneficiary of a Soviet expropriation of assets in the United States, Sutherland responded that "our Constitution, laws and policies have no extraterritorial operation, unless in respect of our own citizens."[31]

What would have happened if the Court had taken jurisdiction and decided that the Litvinov Assignment, since as it made the U.S. government the beneficiary of Soviet expropriation of private assets located in the United States, was a violation of constitutionally protected due process pertaining to property rights? Would the Soviet

51

Union have broken off its newly established diplomatic relations with Washington? Of course not. Moscow had only the slightest interest in the outcome of this case, which actually dealt with how U.S. and foreign creditors would be compensated out of assets in the United States for losses sustained by nationalization of property in the Soviet Union. It is also inconceivable that the Roosevelt administration would have altered by one iota its newly conciliatory policy toward Moscow had the Court refused to let the Litvinov Assignment transfer the Belmont account to a federal receiver.

Almost exactly the same issues presented themselves to the Supreme Court a few years later. The majority opinion written by Justice Douglas in the 1942 *Pink* case is less categorical, however, in endorsing judicial abstention.[32] But even Douglas was not wholly immune to the thaumaturgic invocation of "foreign policy" by the political branches of government. Once again the case involved neither the war power nor any matter threatening the national well-being but pitted the constitutionally protected right to private property against the presidential prerogative of recognizing foreign governments. At issue was whether U.S. title acquired through the Litvinov Assignment[33] could prevail in a conflict with Pink, the superintendent of insurance of the state of New York. In 1925 Pink had taken possession of the New York assets of the expropriated First Russian Insurance Company to protect its policyholders and creditors. He had liquidated those assets and paid off U.S. creditors and policyholders. The litigation between the U.S. and New York authorities turned on an amount in excess of $1 million remaining after this distribution. In 1931 the New York Court of Appeals had directed that these surplus assets be made available to satisfy other claims, including those of any foreign creditors having filed attachments prior to the commencement of liquidation proceedings.[34] Against this order the federal authorities countered with a claim based on the Litvinov Assignment seeking the surplus to satisfy claims of U.S. citizens arising out of unrelated Soviet expropriations.

The New York authorities, like Belmont in the earlier case, argued that if the Supreme Court validated the U.S. claim, it would be recognizing the extraterritorial effect in the United States of a confiscatory Soviet decree. Such recognition "would be unconstitutional and contrary to the public policy of the United States and of the State of New York."[35] The New York Court of Appeals upheld this argument in favor of Pink.[36]

In reversing the New York courts, Douglas, for the majority, was constrained by the sweeping propositions formulated by Justice Sutherland in *Belmont*. Thus Douglas wrote: "The conduct of foreign relations is committed by the Constitution to the political departments of the Federal Government; . . . the propriety of the exercise of that power is not open to judicial inquiry."[37] At the same time, in framing his judgment, he sought, with considerable subtlety, to shift the emphasis away from Sutherland's broad sanctification of unreviewable federal executive power to a narrower executive plenary discretion in recognizing governments and making arrangements incidental thereto.[38] He noted that the Litvinov Assignment was "part and parcel"[39] of the deal by which recognition had been negotiated by the president and was thus covered by article 2, section 2(3), of the Constitution. To this Douglas added that the agreement had also been approved by Congress, which had authorized the appointment of a commissioner to determine claims to be made by U.S. nationals against the Litvinov-assigned assets.[40]

A close reading of *Pink* also makes clear that the majority opinion, while deferring *pro forma* to the abdicationist language of *Belmont*, is careful not to treat the case as nonjusticiable. On the contrary, Douglas examined in great detail the counterpoised constitutional arguments advanced by New York and the federal authorities. In so doing, he explicitly did not conclude, like Sutherland in *Belmont*, that the foreign policy of the president invariably and generally trumps claims arising from the Constitution's protection of property rights. Rather, he held quite narrowly that a decision by the president, as part of the process of reconciling interests necessary to recognition of the Soviet regime, and with the specific approval of Congress, may secure priority for U.S. claimants who had been affected by Soviet expropriations over foreign claimants seeking to attach the same Russian assets in New York.[41] Such a foreign-policy-based shift in the priority of classes of claimants, favoring Americans over foreigners, "is not barred by the Fifth Amendment. . . . There is no Constitutional reason why this Government need act as the collection agent for nationals of other countries when it takes steps to protect itself or its own nationals. . . . There is no reason why it may not, through such devices as the Litvinov Assignment, make itself and its nationals whole from assets here before it permits such assets to go abroad in satisfaction of claims of aliens made elsewhere and not incurred in connection with business conducted in this country."[42] This tight rein of judicial review is slipped over the neck of the president with the reassuring whisper that "[o]bjections to the underlying policy as well as objections to recognition are to be addressed to the political department and not to the courts."[43]

That Douglas, even while deciding in favor of an "unreviewable" presidential policy, was actually cutting back on previously excessive judicial abdication did not escape the notice of Justice Frankfurter, another inveterate defender of the political-question doctrine who was later to feel driven to a stinging dissent in *Baker v. Carr*.[44] While voting with the majority, Frankfurter went out of his way to state that the presidential power over foreign relations is not dependent upon any narrow reading of the Constitution's recognition clause. "The President's power to negotiate such a settlement", he wrote, alluding to the assignment, "is the same whether it is an isolated transaction between this country and a friendly nation, or is part of a complicated negotiation to restore normal relations."[45] To counteract the subtle effect of Douglas's majority opinion, Frankfurter intoned the more orthodox formulation: "In our dealings with the outside world, the United States speaks with one voice and acts as one, unembarrassed by the complications as to domestic issues which are inherent in the distribution of political power between the national government and the individual states."[46]

The Supreme Court has also tended to be unusually forthcoming in applying the political-question doctrine to cases pertaining to aliens, even though this also cannot be thought among the most urgent of foreign-policy concerns. When the executive and legislative branches have acted in concert to affect the rights of an individual, this solicitude has extended to both, thereby also immunizing the acts of the legislature. In the 1952 case of *Harisiades v. Shaughnessy*,[47] for example, Justice Jackson wrote the opinion of the Court upholding the right of the government, acting under authority of the Alien Registration Act of 1940, to deport otherwise legally resident aliens because of membership in the Communist party, even if such membership was terminated more than a decade before passage of the act and regardless of evidence of the alien's subsequent repudiation of communism. The decision does not rest on the merits but on judicial abdication. No plea of unconstitutionality moved the judges to "say what the law is." According to the Court, "Any policy towards aliens is vitally and intricately interwoven with contemporaneous policies in regard to the conduct of foreign relations, the war power, and the maintenance of a republican form of government. Such matters are so exclusively entrusted to the political branches of government as to be largely immune from judicial inquiry or interference."[48]

The majority's reasoning turns upon a stated but essentially unexamined assumption that the national security and an effective foreign policy are advanced by giving the political branches unreviewable discretion over aliens' residency rights in the United States. A siege mentality is evident. At the height of the cold war, such an extraordinary power over persons within the jurisdiction of the United States may have seemed reasonable to many Americans. That it seems irrational when viewed from the contemporary perspective of less dangerous times should caution against leaving such important matters exclusively to the unchecked discretion of those branches of government most vulnerable to the gales of popular perception and passion.

In any event, that was the dissenting view of Justice Douglas. "This doctrine of powers inherent in sovereignty", he wrote, joined by Justice Black, "is one both indefinite and dangerous. Where are the limits to such powers to be found, and by whom are they to be pronounced? . . . History, before the adoption of this Constitution, was not destitute of examples of the exercise of such a power; and its framers were familiar with history, and wisely, as it seems to me, they gave to this government no general power to banish."[49] He thought it unconstitutional to deport a resident alien unless it could be shown that such a person constituted a clear and present danger, an onus not to be discharged by a mere allegation that he had once belonged to an organization advocating revolution. In particular, he thought it wrong for the Court to abdicate responsibility for defining and where necessary defending the rights of all persons within its jurisdiction. Should the definition of those rights be left to the legislature? "If so," he wrote, "then the mere assertion of an inherent power creates it, and despotism exists."[50] That despotism is not negated by popular approval of arbitrary political action is the very essence of the U.S. constitutional system and the rationale for judicial review.

The notion that foreign relations and national security are matters altogether too plenary and delicate to be entrusted to the judiciary appears to appeal particularly to some judges who formerly served in a political branch. Jackson, a former attorney general, only at the end of his career lost this proclivity for entrusting the political branches, and particularly the presidency, with broad, unreviewable discretion in foreign-relations and national-security matters. This orientation became particularly apparent in the justice's majority opinion, supported by Black, Reed, and Rutledge, in *Chicago & Southern Air Lines v. Waterman Steamship Corp.*[51] where the Court stretched to invoke the political-question doctrine in another matter only tenuously linked with a serious foreign-relations interest.

At issue was a decision by the Civil Aeronautics Board, approved by the president, granting a Caribbean air route to Chicago and Southern Air Lines while denying the competing application of Waterman Steamship Corporation. The federal district court had found the president's approval unreviewable, a conclusion rejected by the circuit court of appeals. Thus, the Supreme Court was faced initially not with the issue of which carrier was entitled to the route but which branch of government, the executive or the courts, should have the final word in reviewing the CAB's procedures. To complicate matters, the relevant statute specifically subjected to judicial review "any order, affirmative or negative, issued by the Board under this Act, except any order in respect of any foreign air carrier subject to the approval of the President."[52] Neither of the competing carriers in this case, however, were foreign, although the contested routes were international.

Jackson's decision noted that the case could have been resolved simply by construing the statute as exempting from judicial review this sort of order involving "foreign" routes approved by the president. That might have strained the language, but not necessarily the intent, of the law. However, this easy escape was not taken. Instead, Jackson chose to find important constitutional rights at stake—the prerogative powers of the presidency. "The President also possesses in his own right certain powers," he wrote, "conferred by the Constitution on him as Commander-in-Chief and as the Nation's organ in foreign affairs. For present purposes, the order draws vitality from either or both sources. Legislative and Executive powers are pooled obviously to the end that commercial strategic and diplomatic interests of the country may be coordinated and advanced without collision or deadlock between agencies.

These considerations seem controlling on the question whether the Board's actions . . . are subject to revision or overthrow by the courts."[53]

What led the Court to conclude that the president's approval rested on an inherent, unreviewable power rather than relying on the text of a statute expressly granting some but withholding other nonreviewable presidential discretion? Jackson was emphatic that the "President, both as Commander-in-Chief and as the Nation's organ for foreign affairs, has available intelligence services whose reports are not and ought not to be published to the world. It would be intolerable that courts, without the relevant information, should review and perhaps nullify actions of the Executive taken on information properly held secret. . . . They are decisions of a kind for which the Judiciary has neither aptitude, facilities nor responsibility and which has long been held to belong in the domain of political power not subject to judicial intrusion or inquiry."[54] For this sweeping abdication, Jackson cites, of course, Sutherland's opinion in *Curtiss-Wright*.[55]

Douglas's *Waterman* dissent does not directly address the claim of superior presidential wisdom but points out that "Presidential approval cannot make valid invalid orders of the Board."[56] He was plainly unimpressed by the majority's argument that the licensing of air carriers was an activity of such crucial importance to the Republic as to be beyond regulation by law or that the Court should decline to apply the law to the president for fear of trespassing on the domain of political power.

The cases in which one would expect the courts to reach for the political-question doctrine and avoid conflict are those that challenge the commander in chief's authority to engage in undeclared war. These cases do arise out of extraordinary circumstances that may justify greater judicial diffidence toward political authority than might be warranted by the absence of danger to national survival. In practice, however, most of the undeclared-war cases have not been rejected by the courts on prudential grounds. Instead, the courts tend to treat the cases as justiciable but dismiss them for procedural reasons, such as lack of standing.[57] Or, as in the *Prize Cases*, the courts bow to the political-question doctrine but then decide such cases on the merits, holding that presidential warmaking was implicitly authorized by congressional ratification.[58] Few of the Vietnam cases turn exclusively on the political-question doctrine. One exception is *Mitchell v. Laird*,[59] in which Judge Wyzanski, joined by Chief Judge Bazelon, rejected the basis for decision used in many other cases that although the Vietnam War did require some form of congressional assent, such assent could be inferred from military appropriations or extension of the draft.[60] Instead the court decided that President Nixon in 1969 had inherited ongoing military hostilities. "Even if his predecessors had exceeded their constitutional authority," Wyzanski wrote, "President Nixon's duty did not go beyond trying, in good faith and to the best of his ability, to bring the war to an end as promptly as was consistent with the safety of those fighting and with a profound concern for the durable interests of the nation—its defense, its honor, its morality. . . . In short, we are faced with what has traditionally been called a 'political question.' "[61]

Much about this opinion cuts across various schools of juridical thought on the several issues addressed. It proposes that what might be an unconstitutional activity when initiated by one president may become justified when continued by another who is doing his purported best to terminate the activity. Whether he is actually doing his best, however, is a political question beyond judicial scrutiny. Nevertheless, Judge Wyzanski added, this very "political question" may be subject to review if there has been "abuse amounting to bad faith."[62] Since a motion for rehearing en banc was denied,[63] the case stands as one of the rare applications (with an unorthodox exception seeming to allow for judicial review of executive bona fides) of the political-question doctrine in the midst of military hostilities, the one circumstance in which some form of judicial reticence might seem warranted.[64]

What can be summarized about these cases in which courts abdicate to save the nation from some dreaded catastrophe is that most must be seen to have conduced to, rather than prevented, damage to the national interest. That damage occurs when courts refuse to consider serious allegations of unlawful behavior brought against the political branches in circumstances where what is at risk is less the survival of the nation than the principle of legality.

JUDGES CANNOT COMPEL THE EXECUTIVE

Among the "prudential" grounds why courts should refuse to decide some kinds of cases, as outlined by Professor Alexander Bickel, is "the anxiety, not so much that the judicial judgment will be ignored, as that perhaps it should but will not be."[65] This is a backhanded advertence to that aspect of prudential judicial policy that seeks to avoid situations in which courts are seen as unable to enforce their writ against a noncompliant party. In *U.S. v. Lee*, Justice Miller defended the judiciary's refusal to decide disputes—foreign affairs were his example—when lacking "the power to adjust them."[66]

In a sense, this is the ultimate, or purest, prudential reason for judicial abdication—the desire to avoid an unwinnable confrontation with political power. It is manifest when courts seek to lower the stakes in a dispute, for example, by refusing to decide on the basis of the constitutional issues presented when less controversial grounds will do[67] or when judges apply the common presumption in favor of the constitutionality of statutes[68] and the regularity of an executive act.[69] Courts' sense of self-preservation counsels them to seek to dismiss cases on procedural grounds (standing, ripeness, failure to exhaust local remedies, or mootness) if that makes it unnecessary to reach the merits, thereby avoiding the possibility of a clash with political power.[70] Judges are also sensitive to the fact that the political agencies, by law, may limit or deprive them of their jurisdiction by committing the review of certain issues to other agencies.[71] While the Vietnam cases do not say so specifically, judges were undoubtedly influenced by the onerous consequences that might ensue if an unelected group of life-tenured officials were to order the elected president to end a conflict in which at the time half a million American lives were engaged. It is not difficult to empathize with Judge Wyzanski's view that in the middle of a war, constitutionally authorized or not, "a court would not substitute its judgment for that of the President."[72] Indeed, what is odd is the relative reluctance of the courts to use the abdicationist way out of cases in which recourse to it would appear comparatively comprehensible while deploying it in numerous situations where virtually nothing of great national importance appears to be at stake and executive compliance is not seriously in question.

History affords a few instances of genuine concern about enforceability. In *Cherokee Nation v. Georgia*,[73] Chief Justice Marshall applied the political-question doctrine to avoid deciding on the validity of certain state actions that seemed to violate Cherokee treaty rights but had the support of President Jackson. A year later, however, in *Worcester v. Georgia*,[74] after the Georgia courts had extended the state's usurpation by arresting and convicting two missionaries in Cherokee territory, the Supreme Court issued a writ of error and reversed the convictions on the ground that these had violated the Cherokee treaty. President Jackson contemptuously challenged the judges to enforce their own order: "Well, John Marshall has made his decision," he is reported to have exclaimed, "now let him enforce it."[75] Understandably, judges do not like to put themselves in that kind of confrontational posture.

That, however, was more than 150 years ago. While courts prudently continue to be wary of creating confrontations that may call into question in the political arena the very legitimacy of an unelected branch of government, the judiciary today is surely no longer as vulnerable as it had reason to feel two centuries ago when judicial review was an entirely novel aspiration. Various presidents[76] and several populist campaigns[77] that have sought in recent years to tamper with the independence of the Supreme Court have had little to show for the effort. The American public has accepted that a social compact that consciously elevates certain inalienable rights above the vagaries of democratic political decision must also cherish a nondemocratic body of decision makers deliberately insulated from popular political fashion and consciously protected from majoritarian will. As the ensuing cases will demonstrate, many courts and judges have chosen to risk countermajoritarian confrontation to live up to that difficult calling. They have realized that judicial legitimacy depends on a willingness to challenge, when it is not justified to accommodate, political authority.

When Judges Refuse to Abdicate

As WE HAVE SEEN, many judges still dismiss foreign-affairs cases as nonjusticiable. They do this because of conceptual adherence to a constitutional theory of limited judicial review in "political" cases or nowadays more frequently because of the practical difficulty in assessing factual evidence, the absence of relevant legal standards, or the delicacy of the issues. Whether for theoretical or prudential reasons, a widespread tendency to defer to the political decision makers and foreign-relations experts persists.

This tendency, however, is far from universal. Particularly in the Supreme Court, the political-question doctrine is now quite rarely used and may be falling into desuetude. This chapter will survey that significant countervailing trend, viewing it through nonabdicationist jurisprudence. That courts do decide "political" cases challenges the notion, explored in the previous chapter, that they cannot decide them. Such a survey will also demonstrate that these antithetical judicial tendencies remain largely unnoted and consequently unreconciled. This creates both a problem and an opportunity.

In particular, a problem arises from the way judges register their refusal to abdicate. When judges take jurisdiction in a case involving foreign affairs or national security, they never reject the political-question doctrine as such. Instead, they circumnavigate it, and they have developed several pragmatic ways to do this. The duty to abstain may be held specifically inapplicable in the circumstances of a particular case. This can be done by simply reclassifying the subject matter of the case; for example, deciding that it deals with treaty interpretation or a First Amendment claim rather than foreign affairs. Circumnavigation can also be managed by judicial double-entry bookkeeping. As we noted in chapter 2, courts frequently pay lip service to abstentionist dogma while taking jurisdiction to decide the case on its merits. Most simply, circumnavigation is accomplished by silently passing over the doctrinal or theoretical shoals, gliding past the prudential problems, while studiously avoiding all disquisition on jurisprudential issues.

Some of these strategies create problems for judges and researchers interested in measuring the true dimension of judicial restraint. Where abdication is rejected by double-entry bookkeeping or passed over in silence, no computer search will reveal that case as evidence of a deliberate judicial refusal to abstain. No jurisprudential trail is hacked through the jungle. Many cases dealing with foreign relations do not even mention the political-question doctrine and its penumbra, let alone explain its nonapplication. This may account in part for the doctrine's continuing vitality, particularly in lower federal courts.

This is not a matter of deviousness. When a federal judge one way or another refuses to abdicate, it is almost always in the context of construing a treaty, statute, or the Constitution, or resolving a clash between them. Since from one perspective these are perfectly ordinary judicial activities, courts may not feel constrained to explain why they are engaging in them. Less frequently, a judge may feel compelled by the issues to interpret customary international law, which is part of U.S. common law.[1] Again, this may be seen as perfectly ordinary, requiring no explication. In many of these kinds of cases, the court will simply describe what it is doing in such traditional jurisprudential terms; it will say that it is construing and reconciling the meaning and significance of legal instruments or weighing evidence of a legal order. By so characterizing its activity, the court rejects, sometimes overtly but usually only implicitly, the notion that it cannot perform such ordinary traditional juridical functions merely because a foreign-affairs interest may be at stake. In a sense, this is the mirror image of what courts do when they refuse to adjudicate: They use classification as a substitute for explication.

For example, as early as 1796, the Supreme Court demonstrated its competence to interpret and give domestic effect to a treaty between Britain and the United States that, the judges held, protected the rights of a British creditor against a Virginian debtor.[2] A Virginia statute had purported to abrogate the debt. The Court made its own interpretation of the law, the Constitution and the treaty, as well as customary international law. "By every nation, whatever its form of government," wrote Justice Wilson, "the confiscation of debts has long been held disreputable: and, we know, that not a single confiscation of that kind stained the code of any of the *European* powers, who were engaged in the war, which our revolution produced."[3] The point is not that this is what the Court decided but that it decided at all. Why Wilson thought himself entitled to decide is not discussed.

These comments should be juxtaposed with the frequently quoted dicta to the contrary in *Foster v. Neilson*[4] that the "judiciary is not that department of government, to which the assertion of its interests against foreign powers is confided; and its duty commonly is to decide upon individual rights, according to those principles which the political departments of the nation have established."[5] Had the Court applied that rule, it would simply have referred the plaintiff to the British Foreign Office. Obviously there are contradictory jurisprudential trends at work here. While, as we have seen, some judges are convinced that an independent review of the specialized facts in foreign-affairs cases is beyond judicial competence, others have acted upon a quite different premise.

The cases in which some in the judiciary have demonstrated their willingness and ability to decide cover a wide range of subjects, all of which undisputably to some extent affect U.S. foreign relations and national security. These include disputes between an executive assertion of its power to protect national security and conduct foreign relations on the one hand, and, on the other, countervailing constitutional or law-based claims to property or personal rights by individuals or institutions. Also included among the cases that courts have agreed to decide are disputes over the boundary between the powers of the executive branch and Congress. Whenever courts are drawn into deciding these sorts of disputes—and this is so regardless of which party wins—they demonstrate, though rarely expound, a conscious competence that reproves and rebuts the abdicationist judicial proclivity.

SECURITY AND FOREIGN POLICY INTERESTS V. PROPERTY RIGHTS

To the judiciary's credit, there is a long strand of federal decisions in which judges, often without comment thereon, have manifested a willingness to decide cases with foreign-affairs and national-security aspects and to do so quite undeterred by evident but scarcely unique fact-finding difficulties. When they do this, they are moved primarily by the importance of the rights at stake, elevating them above other countervailing considerations. Property rights, more than personal rights, seem to have been the particular subject of such judicial solicitude.

In its 1851 decision in *Mitchell v. Harmony*,[6] for example, the Supreme Court agreed to examine the actions of agents of the president as commander in chief in wartime, a prime topic for judicial reticence and application of the political-question doctrine. However, Chief Justice Taney not only took jurisdiction but awarded damages to Harmony, a U.S. civilian trader doing authorized business in U.S.-occupied areas of Mexico, for the seizure of his property by Lieutenant Colonel Mitchell, an officer in the U.S. armed forces in the war with Mexico. Mitchell's defense had been the traditional plea of necessity: that hostilities were under way, that he was obeying superior orders, that those orders were lawful in the circumstances because the property had been taken for military use, and even that he had reason to suspect Harmony of being engaged in illicit trade with the enemy.

Taney rejected all of these arguments as conclusory and approved the proceedings in the lower court where a jury had been instructed to determine whether there had been an actual danger of Harmony's goods falling into enemy hands, one that was "immediate and impending, and not remote and contingent." Also left to the jury was the decision whether the plea of military necessity was justified by "an immediate and pressing danger or urgent necessity existing at the time."[7] Taney, approving this charge, rejected the defense's argument that such decisions by military officers in the stress of combat cannot be reviewed by courts. "It is the emergency which gives the right" to seize property, he stated, "and the emergency must be shown to exist before the taking can be justified."[8] Mitchell's "distance from home, and the duties in which he is engaged, cannot enlarge his power over the property of a citizen, nor give to him, in that respect, any authority which he would not, under similar circumstances, possess at home."[9] Having concluded like the jury at trial that the reasons for and circumstance of the seizure of Harmony's property did not meet the "immediate and pressing danger" test, Taney concluded that it is "very clear that the law does not permit it."[10] The question, he said, was "whether the law permits [property] to be taken to insure the success of any enterprise against a public enemy,"[11] and the answer to that in our system, he insisted, is no.

Whether a particular deprivation of a constitutionally guaranteed right could be justified by recourse to the prerogative power of the commander in chief in defense of the national security is a question of circumstantial fact that is reviewable in judicial proceedings.

The 1952 *Steel Seizure Case*[12] is an even more surprising wartime instance of the Court's circumnavigating the political-question doctrine to protect property rights and other constitutionally based claims. Most remarkable in this respect is the celebrated opinion of Justice Jackson,[13] which came at the very end of his career. Jackson rejected as invalid the president's decision to nationalize a critical war industry hobbled by a strike. He was not deterred by the fact that the issue, arising in the midst of the Korean War, was fraught with the most serious foreign-relations and national-security significance. Indeed, none of the judges in the majority, not even Frankfurter, or any of the dissenting opinions thought the case presented a nonjusticiable political question.

In this most influential of Jackson's opinions, he outlined a theory of "fluctuating" presidential power in the constitutional "grey area" that varies according to whether he is acting with congressional authorization, in the face of congressional silence, or in violation of a legislated prohibition.[14] Sutherland's *Curtiss-Wright* opinion is dismissed in a mere footnote noting that "[m]uch of the Court's opinion is *dictum*."[15] Indeed, Jackson limits *Curtiss-Wright* strictly to its facts, citing it only to support the proposition that the president's power is "at its maximum" when his powers are reinforced by a significant delegation of authority from Congress.[16] Even then, the exercise of such power "must be scrutinized with caution, for what is at stake is the equilibrium established by our constitutional system."[17]

More important than the language of *Youngstown* is the Court's action and the circumstances in which it acted. The case clearly raised the most cogent foreign-policy and national-security issues, implicating the power of the president not only as the responsible authority for the conduct of American foreign relations in times of severe challenge but also as military commander in chief charged with protecting the national security during large-scale hostilities. By reversing the president, the Court turned its back on the political-question doctrine in the very circumstances where it had been thought most applicable. As in the *Mitchell* case a century earlier, the Court rejected the notion that the exigencies of military conflict insulate the president from judicial review of the limits of his constitutional powers. Emergencies may *reposition* those limits but do not transfer from court to White House the locus for defining them.

The Court in *Steel Seizure* also firmly rejected the argument that its adjudicatory functions must be suspended whenever credible claims are made by the executive branch that a case involves delicate political policy choices affecting the conduct of foreign relations. "I did not suppose, and I am not persuaded," Jackson said, "that history leaves it open to question, at least in the courts, that the executive branch, like the Federal Government as a whole, possesses only delegated powers. The purpose of the Constitution was not only to grant power, but to keep it from getting out of hand."[18] With that, Jackson, hitherto one of the foremost champions of judicial reticence, rejected Justice Sutherland's oft-quoted rationale in *Curtiss-Wright* and *Belmont* for endorsing the political-question doctrine, which holds that the powers of the presidency in the conduct of foreign relations are not merely delegated but are prerogatives inherent in his historical office and implicit in the nature of sovereignty itself.

This metaphysical notion of inherent powers Jackson treated almost with contempt, arguing that "no doctrine that the Court could promulgate would seem to me more sinister and alarming" than that the president's foreign-relations power can "vastly enlarge his mastery over the internal affairs of the country by his own commitment of the Nation's armed forces to some foreign venture."[19] The "Constitution did not contemplate that the title Commander in Chief *of the Army and Navy* will constitute him also Commander in Chief of the country, its industries and its inhabitants. He has no monopoly of 'war powers,' whatever they are."[20] And then this: "No penance would ever expiate the sin against free government of holding that a President can escape control of executive powers by law through assuming his military role."[21] Judicial review cannot be restricted by the invocation of alleged "inherent" presidential power, for "a judge cannot accept self-serving press statements of the attorney for one of the interested parties as authority in answering a constitutional question." Wryly, Jackson, the former attorney general, added that this must constrain a conscientious judge *even if the advocate was himself.*"[22]

Surveying the jurisprudence, Jackson found that judicial notions of inherent presidential powers have been invented by building on precedents that on closer examination turn out to be ones of judicial acquiescence in exercises by the president of authority expressly delegated by Congress and thus not "inherent" at all.[23] He held it egregiously inconsistent with the Constitution to recognize extraordinary emergency powers while leaving to those who seek their exercise the decision whether the extraordinary conditions justifying resort to them had arisen. Thus, while global experience "may be inconclusive as to the wisdom of lodging emergency powers somewhere in a modern government," it assuredly "suggests that emergencypowers are consistent with free government only when their control is lodged elsewhere than in the Executive who exercises them."[24]

It would be difficult to formulate a more concise or compelling argument to rebut the advocates of judicial abdication and the orthodox use of the political-question doctrine in cases involving foreign relations and national security. "With all its defects, delays and inconveniences," Jackson concluded, "men have discovered no technique for long preserving free government except that the Executive be under law, and that the law be made by parliamentary deliberations.

Such institutions may be destined to pass away. But it is the duty of the Court to be the last, not first, to give them up."[25] Douglas, his views so ably subsumed, offered only a brief confirmation of Jackson's thesis. Even Justice Frankfurter concurred: "To deny inquiry into the President's power in a case like this, because of the damage to the public interest to be feared from upsetting its exercise by him would in effect always preclude inquiry into challenged power."[26]

There have been more recent echoes of *Steel Seizure*. In *Ramirez de Arellano v. Weinberger*,[27] the D.C. Circuit Court agreed to adjudicate the alleged unconstitutional "taking" of land in Honduras as a result of the decision of U.S. officials to establish a military training facility on plaintiff's cattle ranch. In the rehearing by the appellate court, meeting en banc, the constitutional dimensions of the plaintiff's claim were duly noted by the majority.[28]

> The Executive's power to conduct foreign relations free from the unwarranted supervision of the Judiciary cannot give the Executive *carte blanche* to trample the most fundamental liberty and property rights of this country's citizenry. The Executive's foreign relations prerogatives are subject to constitutional limitation.[29]

The full court's reasoning rejected the political-question doctrine relied on by the district court, which had initially been affirmed by a panel of the appellate court.[30]

Even though *Ramirez* was eventually dismissed for mootness,[31] the court in its final disposition evidenced a willingness to continue monitoring the situation. It instructed the district court "to modify its judgment to effect dismissal without prejudice so as not to bar reinstatement of the suit in the event the challenged activity resumes."[32]

The Supreme Court also had occasion in the 1980 *Dames & Moore v. Regan* case[33] to reiterate the justiciability of disputes involving executive management of foreign-relations crises. After the taking of U.S. diplomatic hostages in Tehran, President Carter had frozen all Iranian assets in the United States.[34] Parties with claims against Iran were permitted by the presidential order to proceed to attachment but not to judgment.[35] Even that permission was later revoked by further executive order after the release of the hostages when it became necessary to divert those resources to establish the claims fund called for in the release agreement.[36] At the same time, the president also revoked the license by which attachment orders against some of these assets had already been issued.[37] Plaintiff, who had secured both an attachment and summary judgment, argued that his property rights were abridged by these successive executive orders, first by President Carter's revoking the license to bring attachment proceedings and second by President Reagan's barring all those claims lodged in U.S. courts that under the U.S.-Iran agreement had become eligible for resolution exclusively before the newly established claims tribunal.[38]

In many ways, these facts closely resemble those in the very differently decided *Belmont* and *Pink* decisions arising from the Litvinov Assignment.[39] Those cases were redolent of judicial deference. This makes it all the more significant that none of the Court's justices in *Dames & Moore* thought the case nonjusticiable by virtue of the political-question doctrine. Instead, the Court relied heavily on Jackson's analysis in the *Steel Seizure* case,[40] finding that the Carter orders were authorized by the International Emergency Economic Powers Act (IEEPA).[41] In the majority opinion, Rehnquist, who had been Jackson's law clerk when the *Steel Seizure* opinion was written, agreed that the president's authority could be sustained only by a judicial determination that he had acted within the mandate of a relevant act of Congress or the Constitution.[42] The first of these two tests was passed to the satisfaction of the Court after careful scrutiny of IEEPA, the relevant legislative framework for the exercise of emergency economic power.[43] The second test was also passed to the Court's satisfaction. Paraphrasing and quoting Jackson's *Steel Seizure* opinion, Rehnquist stated: "When the President acts pursuant to an express or implied authorization from Congress, he exercises not only his powers but also those delegated by Congress. In such a case the executive action 'would be supported by the strongest of presumptions and the widest latitude of judicial interpretation, and the burden of persuasion would rest heavily upon any who might attack it.' "[44] This part of the Court's analysis, while upholding the contested presidential actions, gives no comfort to advocates of unreviewable executive prerogatives in foreign relations and national security.

Property rights have also been at stake in cases presenting no national-security crisis or hostilities but where courts were nevertheless asked to abdicate their independent judgment for the sake of solidarity with the executive's foreign policy. These cases tend to present themselves as turning on questions of recognition of foreign governments, states, and title to territory. For example, in the *Oetjen*[45] and the *Guaranty Trust* cases,[46] the Supreme Court held that judges must accept as conclusive the State Department's determination of which of several contending parties is the government of a foreign country. By this reasoning, the Court in *Guaranty Trust* still felt itself compelled in 1938 to treat the Kerensky regime as having been the government of Russia as late as 1933,[47] even though it was clear to all that it had ceased to function since 1918.

Such abdication absolves the courts of responsibility for determining facts with important foreign-affairs implications, even though in so doing important consequences result for the party asserting a property claim. Some judges, however, have refused to be quite so submissive.[48] In *Salimoff & Co. v. Standard Oil Co. of New York*,[49] the highest court of the state of New York was faced with a suit between Standard Oil, an American company that had purchased petroleum from the Soviet government, and Salimoff, the former owner of expropriated lands from which the oil had been extracted. The case reached the New York Court of Appeals in 1933. Salimoff, pointing to U.S. nonrecognition of the Soviet Union, took the position that it was entitled to the proceeds of the sale because the lands had been seized by authorities that, unrecognized by the executive branch, were thus legally no better positioned than bandits and certainly incapable of passing good title. The Court, rejecting plaintiff's evidence of the regime's nonrecognition by the executive, said it would not "sit in judgment upon the validity of the acts of another [state] done within its own territory."[50] Was the unrecognized Soviet regime a "government," or must the court ignore that regime's evident ability to function? The judges decided that while the "government may be objectionable in a political sense," it "is not unrecognizable as a real governmental power which can give title to property within its limits."[51] Unanimously, they found that the Soviet regime, factually, *was* the effective "government in Russia"[52] for the limited purposes of passing valid title, no matter what the State Department said about the regime's diplomatic status.

The second instance is a 1961 case, also in New York, in the appellate division of the state supreme court. In that case, *Upright v. Mercury Business Machines Co.*,[53] Mercury had purchased typewriters from an East German (German Democratic Republic) government-owned manufacturer. That nation and government, although having functioned for more than a decade, had not yet been recognized by the United States. Nevertheless, Mercury had been allowed to import the machines. When the manufacturer sought payment, however, Mercury refused. The debt was assigned by the manufacturer to Upright, an American, who tried to collect it. Mercury argued that the courts should not help Upright because his claim was a facade for that of the unrecognized East German government.

This contention was emphatically rejected. "A foreign government," the court said, "although not recognized by the political arm of the United States Government, may nevertheless have *de facto* existence which is juridically cognizable" and which "may affect private rights and obligations arising either as a result of activitiy in, or with persons or corporations within, the territory controlled by such *de facto* government."[54] As far as suits of this sort are concerned, "only limited effect is given to the fact that the political arm has not recognized a foreign government."[55]

The court added: "It is a false notion, if it prevail anywhere, that an unrecognized government is always an evil thing and all that occurs within its governmental purview are always evil works."[56] Nonrecognition "does not mean that the denizens of such territories or the corporate creatures of such powers do not have the juridical capacity to trade, transfer title, or collect the price for the merchandise they sell to outsiders."[57] In a more recent case, a federal judge in the southern district of New York held that the unrecognized Republic of Palau was entitled to be treated as a "foreign state for purposes of jurisdiction." The court declined "to close its eyes to the *de facto* degree of sovereignty which the Palauans have exercised" in a period of political transition.[58] The judge found as an independently established fact that the "foundation laying period has ended and the transition to sovereign equality has begun."[59]

Quite a few federal judges have shown a willingness to decide such questions for themselves, so that one might conclude that as for recognition, two contradictory judicial trends coexist in the jurisprudence, one abdicationist, the other activist. The activist stance is sometimes adopted even in the face of vigorous resistance by the executive. For example, in the 1902 decision in *Tastar Chemical v. United States*,[60] the federal circuit court heard an importer's argument that a reciprocal trade agreement should be construed as including two French departments of Algeria as part of metropolitan France rather than as a colony. The executive branch strongly urged the court to take the contrary position and to rule that "this is not a judicial but a political question."[61] The judges demurred, finding as a matter of fact after considering evidence supplied by the French ambassador and the consul general at New York that "Algeria is as much a part of France as New York is part of the United States or as Long Island is a part of the state of New York."[62] Judge Coxe made it clear that in his opinion, "this is a question for the courts."[63]

Such assertions of judicial independence have occasionally been ventured even by the Supreme Court. In *Vermilya-Brown*,[64] that Court was asked to decide whether bases in Bermuda leased by the United States from Britain for ninety-nine years came within the jurisdiction of the Fair Labor Standards Act; that is, did they, in the words of the statute, constitute "any State of the United States or the District of Columbia or any Territory or possession of the United States"?[65] The State Department's legal adviser explicitly informed the Court that the act should be construed as inapplicable because the base agreements "were not intended to transfer sovereignty over the leased areas from Great Britain to the United States."[66] After asking "Is this a political question beyond the competence of courts to decide?"[67] the judges decided it was not, made an independent examination of the text of the statute and congressional intent in enacting it, and held the act applicable.[68] This drew an emphatic dissent from Justice Jackson in which he predicted that the decision would cripple U.S. relations with the United Kingdom and expressed dismay that his fellow justices should make a finding that "the Department of State feels constrained to inform us that it 'regards as unfortunate.' "[69] He reminded his colleagues that it "should be the scrupulous concern of every branch of our Government not to overreach any commitment or limitation to which any branch has agreed."[70]

Of course, U.S.-British relations easily survived this assertion of the judicial will to adjudicate. What then seemed to the State Department an issue of overweening foreign-policy significance can now be seen in all its historical triviality. While this does not reflect badly on the State Department's expert judgment of the day, it ought to make courts cautious about accepting as compelling such parochial views of a case's "political" importance. In the end, when it comes to assessing transcendent political significance, we are all guessing, although some are perhaps better positioned to do so than others, but we guess from different interest-based perspectives. State Department experts are likely to be sensitive, perhaps too much so, to the British Foreign Office but not to pecuniary rights of Bermuda-based employees. Those who conduct U.S. diplomacy are neither able nor intended to balance their short-term objectives and client-oriented concerns against countervailing interests expressed in the Constitution or legislation and asserted in litigation by citizens, corporations, or legislators. A balancing of interests, if it is to occur at all, must be done by judges. When judges demur, they are actually saying that the pursuit of foreign-relations goals—indeed their mere assertion by the executive—must necessarily trump other protected interests, that a question of balancing simply cannot arise. That is rarely a satisfactory formula for implementing the rule of law.

Fortunately, judicial balancing is apparent in many cases counterposing an executive assertion of a national-security interest and a citizen's constitutionally protected property interest. In *Algonquin SNG, Inc. v. Federal Energy Administration*,[71] the D.C. Circuit overturned oil-import license fees imposed by the Federal Energy Administration despite the FEA's determination that imports had reached such "quantities as to threaten to impair the national security."[72] The dissent by Judge Robb echoed the administration's argument that "the court should not interfere in this dispute between the President and Congress."[73] In his sharply worded decision, however, Judge Tamm said that an executive assertion that it is acting to protect the national security should not be treated by the court as "a talisman, the thaumaturgic invocation of which should, *ipso facto*, suspend the normal checks and balances on each branch of Government. Our laws were not established merely to be followed only when times are tranquil. If our system is to survive, we must respond to even the most difficult of problems in a manner consistent with the limitations placed upon the Congress, the President, and the Courts by our Constitution and our laws."[74] The imposition of these fees by executive fiat, the court decided, constituted a violation of the president's limited authority under the Trade Expansion Act of 1962 by seeking to raise revenue "in the manner of an Appropriations Committee of the House."[75] This was not authorized by the legislation, and if it were, that law would be unconstitutional.

As we saw in the preceding chapter, the foreign-policy interests deemed by some courts to preclude judicial determination of the merits often do not rise to the level of genuine national-security questions. Nevertheless, the executive often vociferously claims that these lesser matters too are exclusively committed to its foreign-policy discretion. Some courts have disagreed. In the confusing[76] 1972 decision by the Supreme Court in *First National City Bank v. Banco National de Cuba,*[77] a majority of the Court rejected the advice that in a suit involving title to foreign assets claimed by a hostile regime or its agencies, judicial deference should be given a letter from the government purporting to state the applicable principle of decision. The executive had argued that the Court had a duty to follow its advice in order to advance the interests of American foreign policy.[78] Only Justices Rehnquist, Burger, and White agreed, citing Sutherland's admonition in *Belmont* that judges should heed "the exclusive competence of the Executive Branch in the field of foreign affairs."[79] The other six judges, however, thought that such abdication, while purportedly based on respect for the Constitution's separation of powers, in fact transgressed that fundamental principle by virtually delegating the decision in specific adjudication to the executive branch.

In their opinions, concurring and dissenting, respectively, Justices Douglas and Brennan agreed that the executive branch cannot by simple stipulation determine whether a matter is a cognizable claim or a political question; that is a matter entrusted by the Constitution to the courts.[80] Justice Powell underscored this point with wry understatement: "I would be uncomfortable with a doctrine which would require the judiciary to receive the Executive's permission before invoking [the Court's] jurisdiction. Such a notion, in the name of the doctrine of separation of powers, seems to me to conflict with that very doctrine."[81]

In *Dames & Moore v. Regan*,[82] it was claimed that the president's settlement with Iran of the hostage crisis had been made at the expense of plaintiff's property and that the president's action had not been authorized by Congress.[83] The executive responded that to the extent the president's acts were not authorized by legislation, they were emanations of his sole prerogative powers in the conduct of foreign affairs. The Supreme Court rejected that claim. Justice Rehnquist, for the Court, passed in silence the issue whether this constituted a political question, proceeding directly to determine that when "the President acts in the absence of congressional authorization he may enter 'a zone of twilight in which he and Congress may have concurrent authority, or in which its distribution is uncertain.' In such a case," the judgment continued, "the analysis becomes more complicated, and the validity of the President's action, at least so far as separation-of-powers principles are concerned, hinges on a consideration of all the circumstances which might shed light on the views of the Legislative Branch toward such action, including 'congressional inertia, indifference or quiescence.' "[84]

In making this analysis, the Court, ignoring *Curtiss-Wright* and its theories of inherent and unreviewable presidential discretion in the conduct of foreign affairs, proceeded to examine meticulously the interlacing pattern of practice of presidents in making claims-settlement agreements on their own initiative and the long record of congressional acquiescence in that activity.[85] "Crucial to our decision today," the Court concluded, "is the conclusion that Congress has implicitly approved the practice of claim settlement by executive agreement."[86] In addition, prior judicial decisions such as *Pink* were cited for the narrow proposition that the president "does have some measure of power" (impliedly of his own) to enter into executive agreements, at least of the kind here in contention, that are intended to normalize relations between the United States and a foreign state.[87]

The Court further made the evidenciary point—a controversial one, as our ensuing discussion of the *Chadha* case will show—that "a systematic, unbroken, executive practice, long pursued to the knowledge of Congress and never before questioned . . . may be treated as a gloss on 'Executive Power' vested in the President by s 1. of Art. II."[88]

One may agree or not with that principle of constitutional interpretation, but there can be no gainsaying the Court's firm grasp of jurisdiction over an issue of intense political controversy, one distinctly affecting the foreign policy if not the security of the United States. None of the judges deemed it worth discussing the political-question doctrine, much less abdicating their power to determine the constitutionality and legality of what must surely be accounted a very politically sensitive presidential foreign-relations initiative.

In 1989, the Supreme Court was again faced with a case involving Iranian claims. This time the plaintiff was Sperry Corporation, which had succeeded in negotiating a settlement with Iran while its claim was pending before the Iran–United States Claims Tribunal to which it had gone after its court-ordered attachments were voided by the executive decrees upheld in *Dames & Moore*.[89] Sperry's complaint concerned the U.S. Treasury's demand for a percentage of the settlement as a "user's fee" to reimburse the U.S. government for expenses incurred in connection with the tribunal's arbitration. Sperry argued that this "fee" was an unconstitutional tax because it had not been levied by legislation originating in the House of Representatives. The Court, again passing the political-question doctrine in silence, proceeded to adjudicate the issues raised by Sperry.[90] Although the government won this case, that success took the form of a judicial decision on the merits, not judicial abdication. The same may be said of the decision in which the Supreme Court, again without deference to abdicationist doctrines, decided that a gold-based monetary limit for air carriers' legal liability, established under a treaty to which the United States is a party (the Warsaw Convention),[91] had not been superseded in U.S. law by a subsequent (1978) congressionally enacted demonetarization of gold.[92] It concluded that the gold-to-dollars conversion factor established under the convention, although unrealistic in market terms, did not violate the intent of the congressional demonetarization law or the convention.[93]

The executive won the case. In reaching that conclusion, however, the judges not only ignored the political-question doctrine but did not feel obligated to heed the Civil Aviation Board if they found it, after rigorous examination of textual and contextual evidence, "to be [acting] contrary to law established by domestic legislation or by the Convention itself."[94] The Court had no doubt about its powers. "In determining whether the Executive Branch's domestic implementation of the Convention is consistent with the Convention's terms," the judges said, "our task is to construe a 'contract' among nations."[95] This they did by recourse to text and such evidence as could be adduced of the parties' intent and their conduct in implementing the agreement during the fifty years of its operation.[96] No mention was made of the danger of this yielding to "multifarious pronouncements" or of the need to defer to the political agencies in interpreting treaties. Indeed, as might be expected, the dissent by Justice Stevens is even more emphatic on this point, stating that "even if some deference were to be accorded to the CAB's views, the CAB's position would have to be rejected since it conflicts with the plain meaning of the Convention."[97] What the convention means is for the courts to say. "On this matter, the CAB's views are not entitled to any special deference."[98]

SECURITY AND FOREIGN-POLICY INTERESTS v. CIVIL RIGHTS

Even in Britain where judicial deference is still the established doctrine Lord Devlin, in a 1962 concurring opinion in *Chandler v. Director of Public Prosecutions*,[99] emphasized the reason for treating with caution all self-serving governmental evidence of the importance of state interest when it seeks to abridge the rights of individuals. He called for careful judicial scrutiny of the government's contention that defendant had engaged in a "purpose prejudicial to the safety or interests of the state" within the meaning of the Official Secrets Act of 1911.[100] While conceding that the government undoubtedly was best suited to define the requisites for safety and the interests of the nation, he warned: "Men can exaggerate the extent of their interests and so can the Crown. The servants of the Crown, like other men animated by the highest motives, are capable of formulating a policy ad hoc so as to prevent the citizen from doing something that the

Crown does not want him to do. It is the duty of the courts to be as alert now as they have always been to prevent abuse of the prerogative."[101]

In the United States, this call to alertness is heeded by some courts even in cases involving delicate foreign-relations and national-security concerns. Limiting the degree of deference given to the "foreign affairs prerogative" of the executive and legislative branches, the D.C. Circuit, in Freedom of Information Act litigation, felt entitled "to consider and weigh data pertaining to the foreign affairs and national defense of [the] nation,"[102] holding that "whatever weight the opinion of the [political] Department, as a presumed expert in the foreign relations field, is able to garner, deference cannot extend to blatant disregard of countervailing evidence."[103]

Other judges too have not felt constrained to recede from deciding difficult factual issues presented by cases involving actual hostilities. In the previously discussed Vietnam War case, *Commonwealth of Massachusetts v. Laird*,[104] Judge Coffin, for a panel of the First Circuit, wrote that judges must discharge their duty to decide whether "both Congress and the executive have acted unconstitutionally in sustaining the hostilities without a Congressional declaration of war."[105] And having held this issue justiciable, he also accepted that "a court must be prepared to adjudicate whether actions are justified as emergency ones needing no declarations, or have gone beyond this bound. In the latter event the court must adjudicate whether Congress has expressly or impliedly ratified them."[106] Far from shunning these tasks as too political, the court thought that "on a question so dominant in the minds of so many, we deem it important to rule as a matter of constitutional interpretation if at all possible."[107]

Judge Coffin observed that "[s]cholars have probed 'the political question' and found it just as much an impenetrable thicket as have the courts."[108] He felt justified in refusing to hide behind it. Similarly, in *Berk v. Laird*,[109] the Second Circuit held that Berk's claim that orders to fight must be authorized by joint executive-legislative action was fully justiciable. Admittedly, these cases did not alter the result, which was judicial approval of executive action.

The Vietnam cases are in the category of the most difficult of the personal-rights cases, those in which judges are asked to make rulings affecting ongoing hostilities or to review conduct pertaining to hostilities recently concluded. The pressure on a court not to interfere with the discretion of the constitutionally ordained commander in chief are formidable. Yet as we have noted, they were resisted early in its history by the Supreme Court in *Mitchell v. Harmony*.[110]

The temptation to abdicate was also resisted by the Supreme Court at the end of World War II in *Yamashita*.[111] At issue was the extent to which the judiciary is authorized by the Constitution and law to review the jurisdiction, procedures, and decision of a military commission that had tried the wartime commander of Japanese forces in the Philippines. The U.S. Congress, exercising its prerogative under article 1, section 8(10), of the Constitution to "define and punish . . . Offences against the Law of Nations" had enacted Articles of War authorizing military commissions appointed by overseas military command to try and to punish offenses against the law of war, whether committed by U.S. or foreign combatants.[112]

The Supreme Court, asked to review the death sentence imposed on General Yamashita by one such tribunal, "recognized throughout that the military tribunals which Congress has sanctioned by the Articles of War are not courts whose rulings and judgments are made subject to review by this Court. . . . Correction of their errors of decision is not for the courts but for the military authorities which are alone authorized to review their decisions."[113] Nevertheless, the justices added, "courts may inquire whether the detention complained of is within the authority of those detaining the petitioner."[114] This authority is specifically vouchsafed by the Articles of War themselves, which permitted the courts "to grant writs of habeas corpus for the purpose of an inquiry into the cause of restraint of liberty,"[115] but even in the absence of such statutory mandate, the right of habeas corpus would undoubtedly be protected by the Constitution itself.

It is inherently the courts' duty when the jurisdiction and procedures of a military commission are challenged to "inquire whether the detention complained of is within the authority of those detaining the petitioner."[116] The judgment of the military commission is dispositive only if it is found to "have lawful authority to hear, decide and condemn."[117] As to each of these three elements of due process, the Supreme Court made an independent determination.[118] Only after careful examination of the commission's statutory authority and its authority under the laws of war to determine whether each charge postulated an offense recognized by those laws did the Supreme

Court conclude that "the order convening the commission was a lawful order, that the commission was lawfully constituted, that petitioner was charged with violation of the law of war, and that the commission had authority to proceed with the trial, and in doing so did not violate any military, statutory or constitutional command."[119]

Yamashita supports the proposition that at a minimum, courts can never abdicate the duty to determine whether in any particular set of litigious circumstances the political branches have exercised their broad discretion within the parameters established by law and the due-process requirements of the Constitution.

The temptation to avoid deciding a case is probably strongest when it compels a judge, if he takes jurisdiction, to evaluate potential damage to the national interest in a situation of alleged deep military secrecy and diplomatic delicacy. In such disputes, it is usually the executive that urges courts to refuse to decide. Yet there have been notable instances where the courts have been pulled into just such a confrontation at the instigation of the executive, usually in instances where the president seeks to enjoin private conduct. The *Pentagon Papers* case[120] is the most dramatic of the litigations in which judges, asked to take the government's word, nevertheless have assumed responsibility for weighing complex national-security evidence. There, the Supreme Court denied the government's request for an injunction against publication of classified information by the *New York Times*. In so doing, it first had to balance evidence of dangers to the national security against the costs of infringing interests protected by the First Amendment. This forced the judges to inspect a vast and complex array of specialized and sensitive foreign-relations evidence.[121]

In seeking to enjoin publication of a classified study of Vietnam policy at a time when hostilities were still under way, the government precipitated the Supreme Court into a direct conflict between presidential assertion of sole discretion in national-security matters and a countervailing claim by citizens to rights protected by the First Amendment. But instead of deferring to the executive's claim that it be given a free hand to determine the steps necessary to bring a military conflict to a successful conclusion, the Supreme Court endorsed the opposite notion: that in any instance involving prior restraint on freedom of expression, there is "a heavy presumption against its constitutional validity," that the government "carries a heavy burden of showing justification for the imposition of such a restraint"—a burden the government was found not to have met.[122]

The *Pentagon Papers* case involved making a factual determination about the extent of damage to the national interest that might result from publication of secret information. An instance in which a court did grant an injunction against publication is the *Progressive* case.[123] There, the court was convinced by the weight of the government's evidence. Only then was a magazine prohibited from publishing an article describing how to build nuclear weapons. Such cases present the court with a choice between evaluating sensitive and complex foreign-affairs materials or taking the government at its word. At least some judges, choosing to do the former, have demonstrated that the judiciary, as well as the relevant procedural law, has become remarkably adept at managing the special problems posed by judicial review of evidence of this sort. The methods developed for protecting secrets while they are reviewed by judges, discussed in chapter 9, provide ample grounds for believing that courts can handle quite effectively cases involving such sensitive information.

This is a healthy antidote to the tendency of foreign-relations and national-security managers to withdraw from adjudication a broad range of cases in which their actions are challenged as illegal or unconstitutional. The if-you-only-knew-what-we-know defense of the foreign-policy establishment has never been fully endorsed by the judiciary and is becoming even less credible as judicial procedures and judges develop more sophisticated means to scrutinize and evaluate the relevant evidence without endangering national security or secrecy.[124]

As we have noted, difficulty in discerning applicable legal standards as much as evidentiary problems in ascertaining the facts has persuaded many courts to refuse to adjudicate foreign-affairs cases. Refusals to say what the law is may also be motivated by a judge's conviction that national-security considerations require abdication so that the nation may speak to others with a single voice. Federal cases provide dramatic exceptions, however, in which the judiciary has insisted on playing its normal role in interpreting the law and balancing competing legally justified interests.

In *Zweibon v. Mitchell*,[125] the plaintiffs, members of the Jewish Defense League, which had been demonstrating against Soviet policy, sued for damages based on allegedly unlawful electronic eavesdropping ordered by the attorney general. The latter urged the court to accept that he had acted "in the exercise of his authority relating to the nation's foreign affairs and [in ways] deemed essential to protect this nation and its citizens against hostile acts of a foreign power and to obtain foreign intelligence information deemed essential to the security of the United States."[126] The district court, dismissing, concluded that when there is a "clear threat to this country's foreign relations, it is the executive and not the judiciary, which should determine whether or not an electronic surveillance requires prior judicial authorization."[127] Rejecting this proposition and the precedents cited in support, the circuit court held that "despite broad dicta in some of these cases, none stands for the proposition that the Executive Branch is immune from constitutional strictures in the conduct of the nation's foreign affairs." The judges thought that the jurisprudence "clearly subjected the Executive Branch to the normal system of constitutional checks and balances, and . . . has clearly indicated the limited ability of the President to justify actions taken in the United States on the basis of conditions abroad or relations with foreign powers."[128] The circuit court showed remarkable courage in treating the pronouncements to the contrary in *Curtiss-Wright* and *Waterman Steamship* as unpersuasive dicta.[129] Where citizens' rights of privacy are concerned, the judges ruled, "the decision whether [these] may constitutionally be invaded is not a 'political' question . . . ; rather, it is a question of providing a bulwark against Executive excess, a task which the Fourth Amendment deliberately allocated to the neutral officials of the judiciary."[130] The courts must be particularly alert "when national security is used as a talisman to invoke extraordinary powers,"[131] and they must resist use of the "war power" by the political branches "as a talismanic incantation."[132]

An equally remarkable (and perhaps unexpected) example of judicial activism is found in Judge Bork's opinion in *Finzer v. Barry*.[133] Here, the plaintiff, one with whose endeavors Judge Bork probably felt considerable sympathy, headed the Young Conservative Alliance of America. He and his followers sought to picket the Soviet and Nicaraguan embassies in Washington, D.C., but were restrained by a District of Columbia law (nominally defended by Mayor Barry but actually by the U.S. attorney, *amicus curiae*) that restricts picketers to locations more than five hundred feet from the targeted embassy except when otherwise specially permitted by the chief of police.[134] Arguing that this abridges rights guaranteed by the Constitution's First and Fourteenth amendments, plaintiffs sought an injunction against the law's enforcement and a declaration of its unconstitutionality.[135] The State Department entered the controversy to argue that the D.C. law merely implements an international treaty obligation to protect diplomats and their embassies from harassment.[136]

Judge Bork's opinion recapitulates the classical political-question doctrine as requiring deference to the political branches in "foreign-affairs" matters.[137] However, he quickly added: "Deference to the judgment of Congress and the President in these matters is, of course, by no means absolute."[138] His judgment then makes a scholarly, careful appraisal of Congress's legislative authority under article 1, section 8, of the Constitution "[t]o define and punish . . . offenses against the law of nations" and balances the means chosen against the costs to the constitutionally protected right of free speech.

Although he concluded that the restrictions on the latter were reasonable, Bork added: "Strictly speaking, it may be doubted whether there is any need for any particular deference to the judgment of the political branches in order to uphold this statute."[139] If such deference is required by the doctrine, moreover, it is of a very different kind from that evident in writings of some of the more abdicationist judges. Bork emphasized that his court did not decide to uphold the statute " 'simply because the government has sent its lawyers into court to defend it.' The presence of a first amendment claim requires that the court examine the balance struck by the political branches. The deference we owe is not to the government's *legal* judgment that the statute is constitutional, but to their factual discussion of the nature and depth of the foreign relations interests that are involved. . . . Once we accept that these interests exist, it becomes the responsibility of the court to determine whether they justify the statute before us."[140] Thus defined, the political-question doctrine is no barrier to full adjudication of the means employed by Congress and the government. Only after making a thorough examination of the international legal obligation and practical considerations of diplomacy as well as the effects of the District's regulatory scheme did the court conclude that it "is impossible for us to see how the compelling interest at stake could be served with a regulation that had any significantly smaller impact on speech."[141] To demonstrate the active role of the judiciary in umpiring such conflicts between competing constitutionally protected interests, however, Bork added: "If, on the other hand, Congress tried to protect foreign representatives from all affronts, it would have to rule off limits all utterances anywhere tending to bring foreign governments into disrepute. That, of course, is unthinkable. The first amendment would have been destroyed over wide areas in the name of international law."[142]

Similarly, in a 1986 decision reminiscent of the previously discussed Jonathan Robbins case, the government sought the extradition of an alleged Irish terrorist.[143] The Ninth Circuit ruled that the government's assertions of national-security and foreign-policy interests could not preclude the court from determining whether the plaintiff's constitutionally protected right to "liberty" would be infringed by his return to Britain. Thereby the court assumed jurisdiction over the issue whether he had committed a nonextraditable "political offense," rejecting the contention that "such a determination involves political questions that only the executive branch of the government can resolve."[144] It added, "We believe that even if unique, sensitive information that is available to the State Department bears on this factual issue, there are adequate mechanisms—such as *in camera* disclosure—for ensuring that the material can be produced for judicial consideration."[145]

The Second Circuit recently reasserted its duty to say what the law is in a case brought by Planned Parenthood against the Agency for International Development.[146] Plaintiff challenged the legality and constitutionality of contractual provisions in the government's family-planning grants to institutions operating abroad. These forbade recipients from performing or promoting abortions anywhere, even with funds from other sources. The court held that this suit was not barred by the political-question doctrine.[147] Responding to the agency's claim that the case presented "nonjusticiable political questions," the judges wrote: "While courts are not competent to formulate national policy or to review controversies which 'revolve around policy choices and value determinations constitutionally committed' to Congress or the executive branch, it is a court's duty to determine whether the political branches, in exercising their powers, have 'chosen a constitutionally permissible means of implementing that power.' . . . Assuming that the [agency] declares a foreign or national policy that the United States 'will no longer contribute to . . . organizations which perform or actively promote abortion,' it does not follow that requiring appellants to agree to allegedly unconstitutional limitations on their free speech is also foreign or national policy. Nor can AID transform the [contractual] Standard Clause into foreign policy simply by affixing the label 'foreign policy.' . . . Appellant's constitutional challenge to the Standard Clause merely requires the court to apply well-established principles of First Amendment jurisprudence, an area traditionally vested in the federal courts."[148]

In addition to these cases in which courts have explicitly refused to apply the political-question doctrine, there are numerous instances in which judges have decided important foreign-relations and national-security issues with no mention of the doctrine.

Thus, whether a treaty is self-executing and creates a private cause of action has usually been decided by courts without reference to the doctrine or deference to the political branches.[149] So too the question whether a senatorial reservation to a treaty has the force of law.[150] Courts have also interpreted the legality of some statutes' application by the federal executive, even when the application had major foreign-policy effects. A court has decided that the Nuclear Regulatory Commission was not precluded by the National Environmental Policy Act of 1969 from licensing the export of a nuclear reactor to the Philippines without evaluating health, safety, and environmental impacts in the recipient nation.[151] This conclusion was reached by judicial interpretation of environmental legislation and its extraterritorial impact against the background of other, sometimes potentially contradictory legislation dealing with atomic-energy exports as well as by careful judicial scrutiny of the legislative and executive policies intended to promote nuclear nonproliferation.[152] By taking jurisdiction, but without considering the abdicationist precedents, the court incidentally but necessarily immersed itself in complex weighing of countervailing aspects of U.S. foreign policy: our global environmental concerns and the commitment to supply dependable nuclear energy to states agreeing to abide by the treaty on nonproliferation.

In recent years, courts have also decided on the merits such questions as whether the imposition of sanctions on Libya by presidential order, resulting in the termination of plaintiff's contract with that government, constitutes a "taking" of property in violation of the Fifth Amendment.[153] They have ignored the government's invocation of the political-question doctrine[154] and decided on the basis of careful weighing that the treaty-based claim by Haitian "boat people" to a right of "nonrefoulement" does not take priority over a legislatively based program to interdict undocumented aliens on the high seas.[155]

Abdication may be rejected explicitly or in judicial silence. It may occur in a case the government loses or wins on the merits. What these cases have in common is only the judges' refusal to suspend normal judicial review in disputes where the government asserts a "thaumaturgic" power to use unfettered discretion in the national interest. As we have seen, in its 1952 *Harisiades* opinion,[156] the Supreme Court had seemed to declare just such an enclave of nonreviewability in matters pertaining to the deportation of aliens suspected of leftist sympathies. Nonjusticiability, however, has not become the invariable rule. For example, in 1979, the D.C. Circuit,[157] while upholding on the merits the attorney general's regulations subjecting to deportation nonimmigrant Iranian postsecondary students who had failed to make the required annual report to the Immigration and Naturalization Service (INS), nevertheless asserted jurisdiction to review whether the INS had used its statutory discretion to make a "discriminatory classification" against this unpopular group. Moreover, the judges insisted that the attorney general's action must be "supported by a rational basis" and cannot be "wholly irrational."[158]

In *Jean v. Nelson*,[159] the Eleventh Circuit, sitting en banc, also undertook to determine whether INS officials had abused the discretion granted them under the act. Arguments before the court challenged the detention without parole in Florida of Haitian illegal aliens pending final adjudication on the merits of their petitions for asylum. Although the court acknowledged that immigration issues "reflect policy imperatives and fundamental principles of national sovereignty that [could] not be easily dismissed,"[160] it ordered the case remanded to the lower court[161] with the admonition that it determine whether there was "a facially legitimate and bona fide reason" for the decision to deny parole.[162] Similarly, the D.C. Circuit has decided that the courts have jurisdiction to review the denial of a visa to an alien based on a belief by the executive that his admission would be contrary to national-security interests. The judges determined that the admission of a person invited to address an American audience did involve an infringement of protected rights and ordered the lower court to make a fuller examination of the factual evidence upon which the denial was based.[163]

In *Kleindienst v. Mandel*,[164] the Supreme Court considered a similar case, denial of an entry permit by the attorney general to a foreigner invited to speak to a gathering of U.S. nationals. While the majority upheld the denial—opposed vociferously by Justices Douglas, Marshall, and Brennan—they did review the attorney general's action to determine whether it was within the discretion given him by the relevant legislation. None of the Court's judges thought that such a review was barred by the political-question doctrine once they had satisfied themselves that "First Amendment rights are implicated."[165]

One provision of the visa law made ineligible persons "who advocate the economic, international and governmental doctrines of world communism" while granting the attorney general discretion, upon "recommendation by the Secretary of State," to waive the bar in specific instances.[166] The majority held that the executive's statutory discretion in applying this test was very broad and that such a delegation by Congress was constitutional in the circumstances. But it was the Court that decided, on review of the evidence, that the excluded alien fitted the ineligible category established by the law (he tended to describe himself as a "revolutionary Marxist")[167] and that the First Amendment costs of his exclusion had been mitigated when he addressed the meeting by telephone. Not only did the Court review the factual basis of the attorney general's conclusion that the excluded alien fell into the excludable category established by law,[168] but the majority explicitly joined the dissent in rejecting the request of the attorney general for "a broad decision that Congress has delegated the waiver decision to the Executive in its sole and unfettered discretion, and any reason or no reason may be given."[169]

Further examples of some federal courts' reluctance to give way to invocations of the political-question doctrine where personal rights have been affected are to be found even in that former redoubt of unfettered political discretion,[170] the right to travel. In its decision in *Kent v. Dulles* in 1958,[171] the Supreme Court seized the initiative for judicial review. The *Kent* case clearly dealt with a national-security issue: the right of Americans suspected of leftist sympathies to travel abroad. Kent, a U.S. citizen denied the passport necessary for travel, had sued the secretary of state, who asserted that his denial was based on a belief that the plaintiff, presently or previously, had communist beliefs and associations. Under applicable legislation,[172] the secretary had authority to issue passports "under such rules as the President shall designate."[173]

Douglas wrote the 5–4 majority opinion. Faced with the attorney general's claim that the grant of a passport is "a discretionary act,"[174] Douglas replied that the issue was not whether the secretary had discretion but "the manner in which the Secretary's discretion was exercised."[175] That issue, he held, must be subject to judicial review when a citizen asserts that his Fifth Amendment right to travel had been violated in an arbitrary manner.[176] The liberty to travel, the Court held, like freedom of speech, may be abridged only upon a showing—to the *Court's* satisfaction—of "the gravest imminent danger to the public safety" and only if it can be demonstrated that "the Congress and the Chief Executive moved in coordinated action." In the instant case, the majority found "[n]o such showing of extremity, no such showing of joint action by the Chief Executive and the Congress to curtail a constitutional right."[177]

This decision constitutes a sharply worded repudiation of the notion, explicit in the broad version of the political-question doctrine, that when a party asserts a legal or constitutional right that is in conflict with the right of the political branches to conduct foreign relations or protect the national security, judges should refuse to weigh the competing interests. The effect of Douglas's opinion was to compel the secretary to demonstrate to the judges, marshaling persuasive evidence, that serious damage to a U.S. foreign and security interest is likely to follow the granting of a passport and that this risk outweighs the damage to the citizen that would result from frustrating his right to travel abroad. In such a weighing process, the views of government experts should be given due consideration, but it is the judges who decide.

Not only does Douglas's opinion implicitly reject the application of the political-question doctrine[178] while manifesting the justiciability of an issue the executive had declared to be of major foreign-relations and national-security importance; it also in effect overrules by silence the small kernel of stare decisis in *Curtiss-Wright*, insisting that if a constitutional liberty is to be regulated, the executive's authority must have been validated by legislation and that, even in foreign-affairs matters, such legislation must also embody specific judicially reviewable standards "adequate to pass scrutiny by the accepted tests"[179] as set out in such delegation cases as *Panama Refining*.[180]

The majority in *Kent* expressed no reserve about its competence to review decisions based on secret sources and involving evaluation of sensitive security information. Similarly, in a 1990 case, Supreme Court judges expressed no qualms about ruling on the legality of U.S. secret agents' warrantless searches and seizures of an alien's property in Mexico. Chief Justice Rehnquist, for the majority, examined the relevant constitutional text, history, and jurisprudence to conclude that the Fourth Amendment's prohibitions on unauthorized search are inapplicable abroad. He also examined the political and strategic implications of the issues raised, noting that the United States "frequently employs armed forces outside this country. . . . Application of the Fourth Amendment to these circumstances could significantly disrupt the ability of the political branches to respond to foreign situations involving our national interest."[181] Thus, if "there are to be restrictions on searches and seizures which occur incident to such American action, they must be imposed by the political branches through diplomatic understanding, treaty, or legislation."[182]

While at first glance this looks like a reversion to the political-question doctrine, the opinions demonstrate the opposite. In deciding that the Fourth Amendment's reach does not extend beyond the water's edge, the Court implicitly held that its jurisdiction is not so limited. In deciding the issue not on jurisdictional grounds but on the merits, the judges took into account all of the sources normally associated with thorough judicial review. That the majority may have come to the wrong conclusion on the merits is arguable; that it came to its conclusion on the merits rather than by abdication is not. The political-question doctrine was simply passed over in silence.

Further erosion of the doctrine, this time by near silence, was also evident in the Supreme Court's recent *Chadha* decision.[183] Here, the argument for judicial deference to the political agencies was raised not by the president but by Congress. The case is remembered primarily for its holding unconstitutional a large number of statutory provisions popularly known as the "legislative veto."[184] By this device, Congress had sought to give itself the power to repudiate, instance by instance, executive actions implementing legislatively delegated administrative discretion. In *Chadha* the discretion concerned aliens, a subject within Congress's legislative jurisdiction, specifically under article 1, section 8(4), of the Constitution and more generally under the necessary-and-proper clause (article 1, section 8(18)).

The political-question doctrine appears only incidentally in the Court's review. In defending its exercise of the legislative veto, Congress had argued that any exercise of this plenary power over aliens is within its sole legislative discretion and thus unassailable by judicial review.[185] Counsel for Congress urged the Court to apply the political-question test of *Baker v. Carr*. If the Court decided this case, it was argued, the judges would be trespassing on a matter on which, as Brennan had expressed it, there was "a textually demonstrable constitutional commitment of the issue to a coordinate political department."[186] That would constitute "an assault on the legislative authority."[187] Rejecting this line of advocacy, the Court replied that "if this turns the question into a political question virtually every challenge to the constitutionality of a statute would be a political question. . . . No policy underlying the political question doctrine suggests that Congress or the Executive, *or both acting in concert and in compliance with article 1*, can decide the constitutionality of a statute; that is a decision for the courts."[188] (Emphasis added.) Writing for the majority (and the dissent does not challenge this part of the judgment), Chief Justice Burger added:

> It is correct that this controversy may, in a sense, be termed "political." But the presence of constitutional issues with significant political overtones does not automatically invoke the political question doctrine. Resolution of litigation challenging the constitutional authority of one of the three branches cannot be evaded by courts because the issues have political implications in the sense urged by Congress. *Marbury v. Madison* . . . was also a "political" case.[189]

As for the importance the Court will attach to the acquiescence of one branch in the gloss placed on the Constitution by the long-standing assertions of the other, Chief Justice Burger implicitly seemed to disagree with Rehnquist's *Dames and Moore*[190] formulation of the weight judges should attribute to historical precedents established by the action or inaction of the political branches as evidence of the Constitution's meaning. In *Chadha*, the Court thought that the willingness of presidents to sign a large number of laws containing the disputed legislative-veto provision was of no evidentiary weight in determining its constitutionality: The "assent of the Executive to a bill which contains a provision contrary to the Constitution does not shield it from judicial review."[191] The majority opinion, however, did reiterate the evidentiary "presumption that the challenged statute is valid,"[192] a presumption that in this case was successfully rebutted by reference to both the text and architecture of the Constitution as well as extensive examination of the drafters' intent.[193]

Whether one agrees or disagrees with the outcome invalidating the legislative veto,[194] it is impossible to read the decision without realizing that it constitutes another powerful dismissal of the political-question doctrine in an area (regulation of aliens) once thought inherently unsuited to judicial review. Moreover, the case demonstrates the willingness of the Supreme Court to take responsibility for defining the contested boundaries between executive and congressional authority, even to the extent of reviewing, and if necessary rejecting crucial border compromises worked out by the political branches themselves.

CONGRESSIONAL V. EXECUTIVE POWERS

Chadha exemplifies an activist judicial role in umpiring disputes between Congress and the executive that requires definitive interpretation of the political branches' respective constitutional authority. This judicial willingness to say what the law is did not falter in *Chadha* merely because the issue was political or pertained to a regulatory category, aliens, where judges traditionally have allowed the political branches wide latitude. In marked contrast with its failure to do so in *Goldwater*,[195] the Supreme Court took jurisdiction over a troublesome, drawn-out boundary dispute between Congress and the presidency and in a clear opinion definitively laid the debilitating uncertainty to rest. This may be a far greater act of judicial deference to national security than any abdication.

That was also the gravamen of Judge Harold Leventhal's remarkable opinion, written for a unanimous D.C. Circuit panel in the 1977 *AT&T* case.[196] This litigation, like *Chadha*, appeared to be between an individual and the executive but was in reality a dispute between a committee of the Congress and the president. The case was another of those in which the executive branch sought to invoke the political-question doctrine not as an absolute defense to protect one of its asserted prerogatives but as an offensive weapon to obtain an injunction. The executive sought an order to prohibit the American Telephone and Telegraph Company from complying with a subpoena of its records issued by a subcommittee of the House of Representatives investigating the attorney general's issuance of warrantless "national-security" wiretaps.

The court categorically rejected this application of the doctrine. "Where the dispute consists of a clash of authority between two branches . . . judicial abstention does not lead to [an] orderly resolution of the dispute," Leventhal wrote. "No one branch is identified as having final authority in the area of concern. If negotiation fails—as in a case where one party, because of chance circumstance, has no need to compromise—a stalemate will result, with the possibility of detrimental effect on the smooth functioning of government."[197] "In our view," the court continued, "neither the traditional political question doctrine nor any close adaptation thereof is appropriate where neither of the conflicting political branches has a clear and unequivocal constitutional title, and it is or may be possible to establish an effective judicial settlement."[198]

The first of these conditions, the judges thought, is met in a broad range of foreign-policy disputes. "The executive would have it," Leventhal wrote, "that the Constitution confers on the executive absolute discretion in the area of national security. This does not stand up. While the Constitution assigns to the President a number of powers relating to national security, including the function of commander in chief and the power to make treaties and appoint Ambassadors, it confers upon Congress other powers equally inseparable from the national security, such as the powers to declare war, raise and support armed forces and, in the case of the Senate, consent to treaties and the appointment of Ambassadors."

"More significant, perhaps," Leventhal continued, "is the fact that the Constitution is largely silent on the question of allocation of powers associated with foreign affairs and national security. These powers have been viewed as falling within a 'zone of twilight' in which the President and Congress share authority or in which its distribution is uncertain. The present dispute illustrates this uncertainty. The concern of the executive that public disclosure of warrantless wiretapping data may endanger national security is, of course, entirely legitimate. But the degree to which the executive may exercise its discretion in implementing that concern is unclear when it conflicts with an equally legitimate assertion of authority by Congress to conduct investigations relevant to its legislative functions."[199]

In its order, the court emphasized that "[w]e have not accepted the contention that the executive determination that national security may be involved is conclusive and not subject to any further inquiry, nor have we accepted the rival claim that Congressional right of access to documents for legislative purposes is at any time absolute."[200]

Significantly, the courts in this litigation at first required the political branches to attempt to arrive at a compromise of the access problem.[201] That led to a clarification and narrowing of the dispute, and the court was then able to invent a solution that involved in camera monitoring by the judges.[202] They took up the task of ensuring by inspection of classified documents against "inaccuracy" in executive editing of wiretap orders presented to the subcommittee, "for example, executive abuse of the 'foreign intelligence' rubric."[203] The judges were clearly daunted neither by the fact-finding problem nor the need to preserve secrecy. Having established its competence, the court conditionally granted the injunction sought by the executive, subject to revocation if the judicially prescribed process proved unworkable or failed to secure the necessary interbranch cooperation.

Executive-congressional disputes frequently center on the constitutional parameters of the president's power to enter into international agreements without senatorial consent or specific legislative authorization. In 1978, sixty members of Congress challenged the constitutionality of the president's decision to surrender title to the Panama Canal Zone by self-executing treaty rather than by legislation disposing of federal property in accordance with article 4, section 3(2), of the Constitution.[204] The D.C. Circuit upheld the president on the merits but rejected his argument that adjudication was barred by the political-question doctrine. In the words of Judge MacKinnon,[205] "The construction of treaties is the peculiar province of the judiciary." Thus "the question is purely judicial; it is committed by Art. III, s 2 to the courts established pursuant to Art. III, s 1 in which the 'judicial power [is] vested.' It is the type of controversy that the United States courts decide every day, and there is no lack of judicial and manageable standards for resolving it."[206]

Similarly, the D.C. Circuit in 1987 held that it was not prevented by the political-question doctrine from resolving on the merits the question whether an international agreement had been superseded by a subsequent, allegedly inconsistent statute,[207] and the Second Circuit rejected the notion that it was barred from considering whether an "orderly marketing" agreement with Korea had been concluded by the president in a manner consonant with the authorizing legislation.[208] In the latter case the court went so far as to apply a "presumption of reviewability." It held that while the terms of an international agreement were a nonreviewable exercises of executive discretion, the way the agreement was made is not similarly exempt. "It is by now a commonplace," the judges said, "that an agency's violation of its own procedures may constitute a denial of due process, adjudicable in the courts."[209]

More recently we have the further instance of the political-question doctrine's nonapplication by the Supreme Court in the *Japan Whaling* case.[210] At issue was whether the secretary of commerce had violated a mandatory requirement of law, the 1978 Packwood Amendment,[211] that required him to impose import sanctions on states he certified to be operating in violation of the International Convention for the Regulation of Whaling.[212] By 1981, Japan was in violation of the zero quota set in accordance with the treaty by the International Whaling Commission. Faced with import sanctions, Japan then entered into a bilateral agreement with the United States in which it undertook to cease whaling by 1988. In return, the secretary of commerce agreed not to certify Japan, thereby preventing the application of the sanctions envisaged by the Packwood Amendment.[213] The suit was brought by conservationist groups to compel compliance with the law.

Faced with the government's argument, derived from *Baker v. Carr*, that any decision of the Court would present the danger of "embarrassment from multifarious pronouncements,"[214] Justice White, for the Court, briefly paid lip service to the political-question doctrine but then reiterated that "the courts have the authority to construe treaties and executive agreements, and it goes without saying that interpreting congressional legislation is a recurring and accepted task for the federal courts."[215] He continued:

> It is also evident that the challenge to the Secretary's decision not to certify Japan for harvesting whales in excess of IWC quotas presents a purely legal question of statutory interpretation. The Court must first determine the nature and scope of the duty imposed upon the

Secretary by the Amendments, a decision which calls for applying no more than the traditional rules of statutory construction, and then applying this analysis to the particular set of facts presented below. We are cognizant of the interplay between these Amendments and the conduct of this Nation's foreign relations, and we recognize the premier role which both Congress and the Executive play in this field. But under the Constitution, one of the Judiciary's characteristic roles is to interpret statutes, and we cannot shirk this responsibility merely because our decision may have significant political overtones.[216]

Having thus found the issue wholly justiciable, a five-justice majority, after canvassing the relevant evidence and arguments, concluded that the law neither explicitly required nor intended the invariable imposition of sanctions in circumstances where the same purpose could best be advanced by means such as the present U.S.-Japanese executive agreement.[217] The four justices who thought otherwise did so on a contrary reading of the statute, its history, and intent.[218] None, however, doubted their right and duty to umpire this issue, whatever its significance for the conduct of U.S. foreign relations.

The courts' disposition of the previously discussed *Lowry* case[219] indicates less judicial willingness to adjudicate disputes where members of Congress seek to recapture their share of the war power. Nevertheless, even here there are counterindications. *Lowry* may be interpreted to mean not that a dispute over authority to engage the United States in hostilities is nonjusticiable but that it may be adjudicated by the courts—but only when Congress's adversary position has become manifest through a patent confrontation with the president. Even when that condition has not been met, some federal courts have indicated discomfort with any blanket rule of abdication in such "war-powers" cases. Thus, abdication was rejected specifically by the D.C. Circuit in connection with U.S. involvement in the Nicaraguan Contra insurgency. A claim by members of Congress and Nicaraguan citizens in connection with those hostilities had been denied by the district court on political-question grounds.[220] On appeal, the circuit court held: "Without necessarily disapproving the District Court's conclusion . . . we choose not to resort to that [political-question] doctrine. . . . [W]e find other bases for dismissing the suit."[221]

In sum, if as in *Steel Seizure*, *Dames and Moore*, and *Chadha* a clash between political power and a countervailing legal interest is clearly seen by the Supreme Court to call for adjudication rather than deference, even when there are foreign-affairs implications, then the heart of the political-question doctrine has been pierced. The purist version of the doctrine asserts that the Constitution requires such clashes to be resolved by the political process, not by the courts, particularly when, to quote *Baker v. Carr*, there might otherwise be a danger of multifarious pronouncements. Burger, in *Chadha*, demolishes this argument by pointing out that "since the constitutionality [of the exercise of political power] is for this Court to resolve, there is no possibility of 'multifarious pronouncements' on this question."[222] This is a point long noted by scholars[223] but never before specifically embraced by the Supreme Court. The danger to national security and the coherence of national policy, the judges seem increasingly to realize, is aggravated when courts abdicate; the threat of multifarious pronouncements is diminished when courts discharge their normal umpiring function.

There is another aspect of *Chadha* that bears on the judges' duty to umpire. In *Chadha*, the Supreme Court declared unconstitutional the "legislative veto," a device by which Congress sought to give itself the right to judge whether the executive branch was exercising a legislatively delegated discretion in ways consonant with its mandate. Although depriving the legislators of that safeguard, the Court assured Congress that the legislative veto was unnecessary to ensure that the executive branch would stay within the limits of authority set by laws delegating discretionary power to executive officers. In such instances, said the majority, the legality of presidential exercises of discretion can *always*[224] be tested by recourse to adjudication. No exception was made for foreign affairs, or national security. This failure to make an exception cannot have been inadvertent in a case dealing specifically with aliens. In effect, in nullifying a congressional control over executive *exces de pouvoir*, the Supreme Court promised to substitute its own umpiring vigilance, a promise wholly incompatible with the premise of nonjusticiability underlying the traditional version of the political-question doctrine, which proceeds from the notion that the political process, as in Britain, should generally police itself.

The willingness of some courts to treat foreign-affairs cases like any others is still, on balance, the exception to the abdicationist tendency.

Significantly, however, as will be further developed in chapter 6, this tendency has had some important support from an unlikely source—the executive and Congress. In at least two important areas of litigation, judicial reticence has been overcome in part by a legislative mandate, supported by the executive, requiring the courts to say what the law is. These are in the *act of state* and *sovereign-immunity* classes of litigation. In these the political branches have made clear their preference for judicial disposition of types of foreign-affairs cases they expressly wished to see depoliticized.

Mandated Adjudication: Act of State
and Sovereign Immunity

JUDGES, when they refuse to take jurisdiction over foreign-affairs cases, purport to be deferring to the political branches' superior wisdom in such matters and to the need for secrecy, speed, unison, and flexibility in defense of the national interest. In most of the cases we have examined, this judicial reticence sails under the flag of the political-question doctrine. When they apply that doctrine, the courts purport to be following the intent of the Constitution. In particular, the more deferential judges perceive their reticence as strengthening the capacity of the political branches to carry out assigned responsibilities in dealing with foreign states and governments.

This makes it significant that Congress and the president in recent years have taken the initiative in actually *requiring* courts to decide two categories of disputes in which judges have habitually acted with deliberate reticence. Applying two abdicationist legal theories—the act of state doctrine and the doctrine of sovereign immunity—judges had refused to decide large categories of foreign-affairs claims precisely because they believed the politicians and diplomats better positioned to resolve disputes testing the legitimacy of foreign governments' laws and activities. While the courts claimed to be deferring to foreign laws and governments, in practice they were deferring to the U.S. political branches, which were thought better suited to dealing with the effects of laws and actions of foreign states.

Notably, Congress and the president, regarding both juridical doctrines, have enacted laws in recent years mandating that courts decide rather than abdicate. This refusal by the political branches to tolerate judicial deference is highly suggestive. Evidently, the president and Congress do not take for granted that judicial reticence in foreign-affairs and national-security matters invariably advances the national interest. More important, the recent history of legislation to compel the courts to decide some foreign-affairs cases and the courts' agreement to do so, albeit sometimes given grudgingly, strongly sug-

gest that judicial abdication in foreign-affairs cases is not constitutionally required after all.

The act of state and sovereign-immunity rules precluding adjudication rested on essentially the same separation-of-powers arguments
that underpin the political-question doctrine. Nevertheless, Congress
has spoken decisively in the recent past to restrict both these additional doctrinal bases for judicial abstention. Instead of welcoming
the judges' reticence, the political branches have actually sought to
propel the judiciary to say what the law is. The courts, while not necessarily overjoyed to be thrust forward, have not seen in the Constitution any significant barrier to their being vested with these new
responsibilities in an area from which they had abdicated.

ACT OF STATE

The act of state doctrine is traceable in the jurisprudence of the Supreme Court at least to the 1806 decision in *Hudson v. Guestier*.[1] It is,
strictly speaking, "a special kind of rule of decision, not a rule of abstention."[2] Technically, the doctrine did not make an issue nonjusticiable but did bring to bear a judicially fashioned choice-of-law rule
that has the effect of taking the decision out of the hands of U.S.
courts.[3] Thus, the result, and more important the rationale, is much
the same as with other principles of judicial abdication. This has led
some Supreme Court judges, notably Chief Justice Taney[4] and more
recently Justice Powell,[5] to treat the act of state and political-question
doctrines as more or less interchangeable.

The essence of the act of state doctrine is a refusal to rule on the
legitimacy of a foreign government's actions or laws insofar as these
have taken effect entirely within the foreign jurisdiction. To do otherwise, judges have reasoned, is to risk the courts' embroiling the
United States in disputes with foreign governments, perhaps against
the wishes of the political branches.

The doctrine's choice-of-law rule is best illustrated by the decision
of the Supreme Court in *Banco Nacional de Cuba v. Sabbatino*.[6] That case
was brought by an agency of the Cuban government to recover the
U.S. proceeds from the sale of a shipment of Cuban sugar for delivery
outside Cuba. Cuba argued that U.S. courts should not sit in judgment on the legality of its laws or decrees since these had operated to

transfer title to the disputed property while still in Cuba. If Americans have a quarrel with this Cuban law, such a grievance should be pursued through the channels of diplomacy, not the courts. The defendant asserted that the sugar had belonged to a company largely owned by Americans that had been confiscated in Cuba. Defendant further averred that this taking was unjust, discriminatory, and in violation of international law. The lower federal court agreed, leading the judge to conclude that he need not defer to the act of state doctrine but could decide the case on its merits because the doctrine should not be interpreted to require courts to immunize those acts of foreign states that are in violation of international law.[7] The circuit court affirmed.[8] In the Supreme Court, however, the act of state doctrine was reinstated, thereby effectively resolving the dispute in Cuba's favor. The Supreme Court expressly refused to decide whether the Cuban expropriations were violations of international law.

Athough the Supreme Court agreed that the act of state doctrine is not required by notions of sovereignty and international law, or even by the Constitution, it added that the doctrine does "have 'constitutional' underpinnings. It arises out of the basic relationships between branches of government in a system of separation of powers. It concerns the competency of dissimilar institutions to make and implement particular kinds of decisions in the area of international relations. The doctrine as formulated in past decisions expresses the strong sense of the Judicial Branch that its engagement in the task of passing on the validity of foreign acts of state may hinder rather than further this country's pursuit of goals both for itself and for the community of nations as a whole in the international sphere."[9] This is particularly so when the international law pleaded is less than absolutely clear or is not based on a treaty to which the United States and the foreign state are parties.[10] These reasons for abdication are virtually identical with those that inform the political-question doctrine.

In effect, the Supreme Court applied prudential reasons for refusing to "say what international law is" in a case where the determination of the applicable rules might otherwise have been dispositive. Instead, the majority appeared to defer to the political organs of Cuba. In reality, however, it was to the U.S. government that the judges were deferring, having concluded that the dispute with Cuba over the confiscated property of American citizens would be better resolved in a diplomatic forum.

Similar grounds for deference to the political branches were controlling in a later decision of the Third Circuit. That court, holding the act of state doctrine applicable, emphasized "concerns for preserving the 'basic relationships between branches of government in a system of separation of powers,' and not hindering the executive's conduct of foreign policy by judicial review or oversight of foreign acts."[11]

This sounds exactly like the theoretical and prudential reasons for abdication usually urged by the executive in foreign-affairs cases. The political branches, however, were not entirely delighted by these displays of judicial modesty. Shortly after the Court's *Sabbatino* decision, Congress took the unusual step of legislating that decision's partial repeal. The "Hickenlooper Amendment" to the Foreign Assistance Act of 1964[12] provides: "Notwithstanding any other provision of law," unless the president determines otherwise, "no court in the United States shall decline on the ground of the federal act of state doctrine to make a determination on the merits giving effect to the principles of international law in a case in which a claim of title or other rights to property is asserted . . . based upon (or traced through) a confiscation or other taking . . . by an act of that state in violation of the principles of international law."[13] Congress thereby sought to give U.S. investors in foreign lands additional protection by requiring judges to ensure that their jurisdictions did not become a "thieves' market" for the product of foreign expropriations.[14]

Although the executive initially opposed this law, it later became its enthusiastic supporter.[15] The courts, on the other hand, while grudgingly applying the law,[16] have been reluctant to give it more than the narrowest construction.[17] Old habits die hard. Only very recently, with considerable prodding from the executive, has there been some glimmering indication of a greater willingness to take jurisdiction by construing narrowly not the Hickenlooper law but its target, the act of state doctrine.[18]

What makes this interesting is that here we see a counterindicated phenomenon: the political branches acting as the engines pulling the judiciary into cases involving an important category of foreign-relations cases. We see the astonishing sight of legislators and secretaries of state urging, even compelling, the judges in cases fraught with foreign-relations significance to say what the law is. Thus compelled, the courts have agreed with Senator Hickenlooper that the law mandating adjudication is "a constitutional exercise of Congress' powers."[19]

In changing the law, Congress was responding to the rapidly expanding private foreign-investment sector of the U.S. economy, which had greeted with anger the *Sabbatino* decision. Business interests wanted the courts to begin enforcing internationally recognized standards against deviant foreign expropriations whenever the subject of an illegal seizure or the funds paid for seized assets found their way into the American market. They had concluded, rightly, that ordinary judicial process would provide a better way to protect their interests than diplomatic maneuvers. The executive had at first preferred to keep matters in its own hands. Overridden by Congress and pressured by the foreign-investment community, however, the State Department gradually changed its mind, concluding that judicial activism in the application of international law to foreign expropriations would strengthen rather than weaken its hand in dealing with foreign regimes tempted to steal U.S. citizens' assets. It is now common ground that the interests of both the business community and foreign policymakers are best served by letting the courts perform their normal function.

FOREIGN SOVEREIGN IMMUNITY

Sovereign immunity is a doctrine that is found in some form in the jurisprudence of almost all nations. It serves to protect from legal process the governmental activities and entities of one state within the jurisdiction of another. In the United States, the doctrine first received the imprimatur of the Supreme Court in an 1812 decision written by Chief Justice Marshall.[20] The Court noted that judicial recognition of immunity was supported by the law and practice of nations, but it went on to enunciate another basis for judicial abdication. The judges were of the opinion that in such cases the decision should rest not with them but with the executive branch. The latter should make a "suggestion" whether a foreign sovereign should be immune to a legal proceeding brought against it, and such a suggestion should be deemed binding by the courts. As the courts began to apply this approach, the judges increasingly, indeed exclusively, looked to the

State Department rather than the facts and the law of nations to make the determinative case-by-case finding whether a foreign state entity was entitled to immunity.[21] The effect of this, in essence, was to transfer the adjudicatory process to the executive.

Sovereign immunity's justification is rooted in international legal theory, especially in deference to the "perfect equality and absolute independence of sovereigns" that international law is thought to establish.[22] However, while international law may indeed mandate the immunity of at least some instrumentalities of foreign governments, it has nothing to say about how a court determines whether a particular defendant is entitled to have a claim of immunity validated. Britain's queen is surely immune to a prosecution for parking her car in a New York bus zone, as is Her Majesty's ambassador. But what about the ambassador's private secretary or first cousin? What of the president of Aeroflot, the Soviet government's commercial airline? Or the deposed King Michael of Romania?

American judges tended to solve such close-call issues by refusing to decide, preferring that they be resolved case by case by the executive. Since the answer to the close-call question "Is *this* defendant immune?" is usually dispositive of any dispute in which it is asked, the effect of judicial reticence was to transfer the essence of many legal disputes between businesses or persons and foreign governments, their representatives and entities, to the State Department. Once again, the U.S. courts' willingness to defer to the State Department in deciding whether a foreign government could defeat a suit against it or one of its emanations by an assertion of immunity has its rationale in peculiarly American constitutional and prudential considerations: Courts must not become enmeshed in situations that might give rise to a serious cause of conflict between the United States and a foreign government or that might hinder the conduct of international relations. The courts were also solicitous of the need for the nation to speak with a single voice in such matters.

Until the twentieth century, the immunity doctrine "seemed to have no exceptions."[23] Toward the middle of the twentieth century, however, states increasingly began to engage in commercial enterprise, the sort of activity that gives rise to disputes otherwise indistinguishable from the normal grist of the judicial mills. If a government enterprise is suit-proof, it would appear to be in an anomalous position vis-à-vis the market in which it competes. On the one hand, it would have the apparent advantage of being suit-proof. If it did not opt to carry out its contractual obligations, for example, it could not be forced by litigation to do so or to pay damages. On the other hand, private entrepreneurs would probably be reluctant to do business with an immune party, thereby placing the immune enterprise at a competitive disadvantage. Consequently, governments began to re-think the utility of the doctrine and decided to restrict its application.

Most nations came to believe that these "private" or commercial activities by public authorities should no longer be protected from or-dinary commercial litigation by the sovereign-immunity doctrine. Thus it was that governments themselves began to take the initiative to restrict sovereign immunity.[24] In the United States, this movement was first manifested in the Tate Letter.[25] Named after the acting legal adviser of the State Department, it expounded the view that in future sovereign immunity should be recognized only in cases involving a foreign state's public acts, not in those based on commercial ones.

The Tate Letter purported to change the rules as to who or what was entitled to sovereign immunity. It outlined a set of exceptions to generalized immunity of states and their instrumentalities that were to be applied case by case. However, it did not change the judicially created rule that it was the State Department that would determine who was entitled to immunity. Courts continued to act entirely in ac-cordance with the "suggestions" of the executive. So it was that the department was forced to establish a quasi-judicial administrative process to determine, for each action, whether a foreign govern-ment's request for immunity should be accepted or rejected and to communicate its decision to the court.

Prior to the Tate Letter, the department's role in making this deter-mination had not been particularly onerous. Since all activities of for-eign governments were entitled to immunity, the department merely certified to the applicable judge that X was or was not the representa-tive or emanation of a foreign government. The only issue in most of these pre-Tate cases had been whether a foreign regime claiming im-munity had been accorded recognition by the United States. After Tate, however, the department found itself in the "awkward position of a political institution trying to apply a legal standard to litigation already before the courts"—a complex standard, at that—in circum-stances where "it does not have the machinery to take evidence, to hear witnesses or to afford appellate review."[26] As the Senate Judiciary Committee observed, from "the standpoint of the private litigant, considerable uncertainty results. A private party who deals with a foreign government entity cannot be certain that his legal dispute with a foreign state will not be decided on the basis of nonlegal considerations through the foreign government's intercession with the Department of State."[27] In a number of cases, "considerations of foreign policy had determined a grant of immunity where the criteria of the Tate Letter did not call for it."[28] Nevertheless, the courts seemed eager to continue to abstain from reviewing the department's processes or determinations.[29]

In addition to leaving private litigants at the mercy of the executive's diplomatic priorities, this practice also sent a very damaging message abroad. It projected a judicial system lacking in independence, sensitive to orders from the political branches rather than the rule of law. From the mid-1960s, the practicing bar and the Departments of State and Justice began to seek a better way of handling such cases. While they shared the concern of litigants about the inequity of a practice that made the legal process so evidently subordinate to political considerations, the executive had another reason for seeking to end the practice of judicial deference. The State Department had begun to recoil from a practice that thrust it into the middle of numerous ordinary lawsuits, making a dispute about contractual obligations into issues in which the friendly relations between the U.S. and foreign governments were at stake. It bridled at the pressure being exerted by foreign diplomats demanding that the department agree to "suggest" the immunity of a defendant in one adjudication after another. Yet this conundrum was inescapable as long as the courts continued to put the real burden of deciding the litigous outcome on the executive branch. As long as there were no immutable rules and the decisions were being made by the State Department, each denial of immunity, no matter how well founded, could be perceived by the foreign government as a deliberately unfriendly act calling for a political response.

By the early 1970s, the State Department began to ask: Will no one rid us of these troublesome disputes? It decided to shed a responsibility that had made the department vulnerable to intense pressure from other governments and in which its unfettered discretion, the vaunted policy flexibility, had become a source of embarrassment in the conduct of foreign relations. Increasingly, the political branches came to realize that in much otherwise ordinary litigation involving foreign governments, minor disputes tended to become foreign-relations causes célèbres because the courts refused to adjudicate; that if judges could be made to take jurisdiction, the foreign-relations implications of a case would tend to diminish. This awakening resulted in congressional enactment of the Foreign Sovereign Immunities Act of 1976,[30] which codified the restrictive theory of immunity and established its criteria but transferred to the courts exclusive jurisdiction for applying them. The Supreme Court has upheld and implemented the new system,[31] thereby accepting the political branches' view that these sorts of cases, whatever their vestigial foreign-relations aspects, would better be treated like any other suit.

The judges accepted Congress's view that legislation may direct the courts to say what the law is. They held the law valid on the ground that the Constitution empowers the legislature to prescribe the jurisdiction of the federal courts (article 1, section 8, clause 9; article 3, section 1), to define offenses against the law of nations (article 1, section 8, clause 10), to regulate commerce with foreign nations (article 1, section 8, clause 3), and "to make all Laws which shall be necessary and proper for carrying into Execution . . . all . . . Powers vested . . . in the Government of the United States," including the judicial power of the United States over controversies between "a State, or the Citizens thereof and foreign States."[32] Once the act was upheld, it came to be applied as a matter of course, succeeding in largely depoliticizing the issue of foreign sovereign immunity. Routine sovereign-immunity cases now make up a considerable portion of the federal courts' dockets.

This suggests that it is also time to rethink other ritual deference by the courts to the political branches. The political-question doctrine, like the act of state and sovereign-immunity doctrines, is a judge-made rule of abstention. All three doctrines operated until recently to shift the onus for saying what the law is from the courts to the politicians and diplomats. This was done in the name of avoiding embarrassment in the conduct of foreign relations. However, that the political branches themselves took the initiative to repeal some of this judicial abdication strongly suggests that these political agencies do not necessarily believe themselves helped by a general rule of judicial abdication in ordinary legal disputes that happen to have "foreign" aspects. Such abstinence, far from clearing the path for those charged with formulating and implementing foreign and security policy, may merely complicate their tasks by needlessly politicizing matters better determined not as an incident of foreign policy but the administration of justice. More important, each instance of judicial abdication erodes the belief of Americans, and of foreigners, in our vaunted system of government under law.

If that is so for cases involving acts of state and questions of sovereign immunity, it may also be true of other kinds of cases to which the political-question doctrine has been applied by courts altogether too anxious to defer to the political branches. If adjudication is not a constitutional trespass in some kinds of cases previously thought to have been committed exclusively to the president and Congress, perhaps the Constitution does not require judicial abstinence in those other matters either. If there are prudential reasons favoring the courts' taking jurisdiction in some foreign-affairs cases, perhaps the blanket invocation of prudential reasons for denying jurisdiction in others also needs to be reexamined. Such a reexamination by the political branches and the judiciary can benefit from the experience of a constitutional system very like our own in which the courts have deliberately chosen not to follow the path of abdication but have taken a measured direction of their own that could serve as a model worth emulating.

Abolishing Judicial Abdication:
The German Model

GERMAN JUDGES ON WHETHER TO DECIDE

I F OUR JUDGES were to embark on a new approach to cases dealing with sensitive foreign-relations and national-security issues, they could be guided by the experience of their German brethren. While our legal culture is based on the common-law tradition of Great Britain, the British model is misleading for the reason, examined in chapters 2 and 3, that the object of the colonies' revolutionary enterprise had been to sever their tie to the mother country's system of executive prerogatives and parliamentary supremacy. These notions continue to hold sway at Westminster, making it profoundly different from our traditions of constitutionalism, limited and divided powers, and judicial umpiring. It is in the constitutional development of the German Federal Republic, designed after World War II to emulate our system of checks and balances, that useful analogies may be sought.

The German Constitutional Court, the final interpreter of the Federal Republic's constitution, operates in a system of separated powers, protected rights, and federalism readily comparable to our own. Like our Constitution, the German Basic Law neither requires nor precludes judicial reticence in foreign relations. The judges are thus left free to steer their own course. Unlike American courts, however, they have chosen a path of activism, rejecting invitations to imitate the abdicationist U.S. practice. Moreover, they have developed a coherent theory applicable to the adjudication of foreign-affairs cases that is reasonable, works adequately, and provides a thread of jurisprudence that is pursued with far greater consistency than in the American practice. This judge-made German jurisprudence has staked out a middle course between judicial abdication and rampant judicial interference in the making and execution of foreign and security policy, one that satisfies systemic imperatives of the rule of law and political flexibility. In arriving at their solution, the German

107

judges have evolved a consistent doctrine and a practice that could be helpful in seeking to develop principled rules to replace the incoherence of our theory and practice.

The German theory begins at the opposite doctrinal pole from ours, then moves in practical increments toward a pragmatic middle position. In theory, the German courts are logically consistent: Everything is adjudicable. "The difference between law and politics, particularly in constitutional matters," a leading German judicial commentator has observed, "does not seem to impress the German judicial system."[1] In particular, "constitutional law, with its broad general clauses and its vague conceptions of values, offers a particularly wide scope for interpretation. Any wish to keep political considerations out of this interpretation would be doomed to failure at the outset."[2]

An American student of the German system, Professor D. Kommers, has concluded: "There is no 'political-question' doctrine as such in German constitutional law."[3] At the level of general theory, German courts have defined a bold position: "*All* questions arising under the Basic Law are amenable to judicial resolution if properly initiated under one of the eighteen different procedures authorized for the resolution of constitutional issues. These issues include the highly politicized field of foreign affairs."[4] Even though, as Justice Kondrad Hesse has observed, "separation of powers constitutes the basic organizing principle of the [German] Constitution,"[5] this has not been translated by the German judiciary to require abstention from questions raising political questions. Specifically, German judges have been careful to avoid creating any theoretical basis for exempting from the scope of their authority to review legislation and executive initiatives the broad category of legal disputes arising out of the conduct of foreign relations or efforts to protect the national security. In German jurisprudence, such cases are as amenable to adjudication as any other.

This can be illustrated by a few leading examples from German constitutional litigation. In 1954, the Constitutional Court decided the *Status of the Saar* case, an action brought by one-third of the members of the Bundestag (lower house) under procedures set out in article 92(1), paragraph 2, of the Basic Law. Unlike the situation in the United States, where as we saw in the *Lowry* case the matter remains obscure, the German Basic Law explicitly gives such a group of legislators standing to sue.[6]

The legislators' complaint focused on a recently signed treaty between the German Federal Republic and France concerning the status of the Saar, or more precisely on the law purporting to implement that agreement in Germany. Plaintiffs argued that this treaty and law would derogate from several of the Basic Law's guarantees to German citizens by instituting a special status for the Saar that would differentiate between its inhabitants and those of other German *Länder* (states of the federation). They pointed out that the purport of the agreement was to "Europeanize" the Saar[7] and in particular that the German federal government had struck an unconstitutional deal with France by which Paris, in return for renouncing annexation, received Bonn's acquiescence in a regime imposing mandatory political constraints on that particular state.

These restrictions, the plaintiffs argued, violated numerous articles of the Federal Republic's Basic Law.[8] For example, one provision of the treaty reserved certain external-affairs functions to an unelected Saarland Commissioner, who was to be appointed by the Western European Union, an intergovernmental regional organization. In the complainants' view, the Basic Law did not permit such derogations from sovereignty, nor did it allow invidious derogations from citizens' entrenched rights, including a constitutional right to equality.[9] In particular, the treaty was alleged to violate article 146, which provides for popular participation in the eventual transformation of the Basic Law into a constitution for a unified Germany. By vesting external affairs powers in a commissioner, it was urged, the Saarlanders could be deprived of the right to participate in the legal rites of eventual reunification.

The federal government initially saw no reason even to answer these allegations, preferring to urge the court to dismiss them as "essentially political . . . and . . . thus nonjusticiable."[10] The court flatly rejected this maneuver. Although the judges ultimately did conclude that the treaty was constitutional, they were careful to emphasize that exercises of the treaty-making power are never immune per se to judicial review. On the contrary, treaties, like legislation, are circumscribed by constitutional limitations enforceable in litigation. The fundamental principles imposed by articles 19(2) and 79(3) of the Basic Law, had they been found violated by an international agreement, would have compelled the court to invalidate the treaty's domestic effect.[11]

In the event, after the court upheld the treaty, it was not ratified by the requisite plebescite. Somewhat later, the Saar was able to join the Federal Republic on terms of complete equality with the other *Länder*.[12] Nevertheless, the *Status of the Saar* case set the jurisprudential direction of the German Federal Constitutional Court, one to which it consistently adhered thereafter. Essentially, the court regards itself as charged by the Basic Law with responsibility for saying what the law is in any case properly brought before it by parties with standing. The court's jurisdiction and the justiciability of disputes does not vary according to the subject matter. Thus, a foreign-relations and national-security case is as inherently reviewable as any other. The court, not the political authority entering into the agreement, has the constitutional responsibility to interpret whether it accords procedurally and substantively with the normative guidelines set by the Basic Law.

The constitutionality of a law implementing a treaty was again considered by the court in the *Inter-German Basic Treaty Case*.[13] In this instance, the challenge was to Chancellor Willi Brandt's *Ostpolitik*, which had led to an agreement between the two Germanies normalizing aspects of their relations. The constitutionality of the law was questioned by the state of Bavaria, ruled by a branch of the conservative opposition to the federal government led by Brandt's Social Democrats. The federal authorities once again sought to induce the Constitutional Court to adopt the political-question doctrine. As before, the judges refused. "There is no question that the constitutional order cannot be altered by a treaty," they said, carefully reserving for themselves the duty to determine whether a conflict between constitution and a treaty had arisen. The limits imposed by the constitution on the exercise of political power are equally applicable to the conduct of international relations, they added, because that is the very essence of the *Rechtsstaat*, a "state under law."[14] In a *Rechtsstaat*, the final responsibility for the protection of this constitutional order must rest squarely with the court.[15] Nothing done by government is beyond judicial review. That is what the rule of law means in Germany.

Addressing the merits of the complaint, the judges reiterated that the entrenched rights of Germans and the constitutionally established goals of governance, such as the reunification of Germany, cannot be renounced or restricted by any action of the political organs. Although the court found that the treaty did not transgress these basic norms, its decision made clear the central role the judiciary intended to play in ensuring that international agreements, or any exercise of political authority, fully comported with the national values and purposes entrenched in the Basic Law.

In 1975, a number of German nationals mounted a somewhat similar constitutional challenge to certain agreements concluded by the Federal Republic normalizing relations with Poland and the Soviet Union.[16] They alleged that those agreements failed to carry out the requirements of the Basic Law "to protect German nationals and their interests as against other nations."[17] Again the court had no conceptual problem with taking jurisdiction. It did not dismiss out of hand the plaintiffs' complaint that the agreements failed to regain their lost property rights in those parts of prewar Germany incorporated into Poland in 1945. The judges also considered the complaint that the treaty failed to achieve hoped-for family reunifications. Once again the court upheld the government, but only after testing the agreements against the normative standards established by the constitution and its framework of civil rights.

Although the expansive rhetoric that accompanies the taking of jurisdiction by the Constitutional Court in these cases is in marked contrast with that found in some U.S. courts, the actual outcome in both systems would probably have been the same. In a flat confrontation between the terms of a treaty and a claim based on the Constitution, American judges nowadays are unlikely to refuse to rule. The German treaty cases, however, establish a far more expansive basis for judicial review, one that has equal application to nontreaty cases. For example, the Constitutional Court has taken jurisdiction over disputes involving the exercise of tactical discretion in the conduct of foreign affairs. In the *Rudolph Hess* case of 1980,[18] the court was petitioned by the son of that well-known prisoner then still serving a life sentence for war crimes in Berlin's Spandau jail under the authority of the occupying Allied powers. Rudolph Hess had been committed by a judgment of the Nuremberg Tribunal in 1946. The petitioner sought the court's help in compelling the German federal government to make a more active diplomatic effort to free him, the only remaining such prisoner, in accordance with the alleged "constitutional tradition"[19] that the state owes its citizens a duty of protection against other states.

The Constitutional Court agreed that this general duty is judicially enforceable by individuals, that the judges could review the officials' policy to determine "whether they went beyond the limits of their allotted discretion, or whether in their action they were guided by an erroneous belief about the legal constraints on their discretion."[20] The court also asserted its right to determine whether genuine steps had been taken to seek Hess's release and whether the authorities were committed to further efforts on his behalf.[21] Moreover, the court added, in choosing the means to carry out their constitutional mandate, the authorities must be seen not to have acted arbitrarily (*mit Willkur*),[22] and the judges assumed responsibility for reviewing the government's actions to ensure that this due-process-like standard had been met in practice. The case offers a striking contrast, for example, to the summary refusal of the Fourth Circuit to consider whether the president was making sufficient effort to locate American soldiers missing in action in Indochina, as ordained by the Hostage Act.[23]

An especially expansive rejection by the German judiciary of the abdicationist doctrines favored by some American judges is found in a peculiar flurry of suits brought during 1983, collectively called the *Tabatabai* litigation. Here, the Düsseldorf Regional Court and Appellate State Court were called upon to decide the weight to be given to an intervention by the Foreign Ministry declaring that it recognized the diplomatic immunity of Dr. Tabatabai, an Iranian professing to be a special envoy on a negotiating mission to the Federal Republic. Upon entering Germany, Tabatabai had been apprehended by customs officials while in possession of 1.7 kilograms of "smoke opium."[24]

In America, even after passage of the Foreign Sovereign Immunities Act (see chapter 6), the courts almost certainly would treat such government intervention as dispositive of the diplomat's status. The German lower court, however, rejected the Foreign Office's intercession in Tabatabai's favor, proceeding instead with a criminal indictment. Although it was twice reversed by the appellate courts, the trial court sentenced Tabatabai to three years' imprisonment, an outcome he evaded by leaving the country after being declared persona non grata by the authorities.

In the final stage of this litigation, the criminal panel of the Federal Court of Justice took the position that it was "not bound by the legal view of the Foreign Office [that] . . . established the immunity of the accused. Regardless of the competence of the Foreign Office to shape the relations of the Federal Republic of Germany with foreign countries," the judges said, "the courts have to examine, within their own competence, whether immunity has been established in a specific case: here, whether the accused is exempted from German jurisdiction according to the general rules of international law (Section 20, Judicative Act)."[25] Having thus given itself the final word, however, the court agreed with the government's view of the matter and, reversing the verdict of the lower court, ordered the conviction quashed.[26]

It will be evident from this selection of German cases that many of the courts' bold assertions of broad jurisdiction are found in litigation the government has won. It would be wrong, however, to conclude from this that the taking of jurisdiction is illusory. That the courts will not permit otherwise valid foreign-relations objectives to be pursued by means that violate explicit (or even implicit) constitutional norms has been further demonstrated by several recent decisions of the Constitutional Court where the government has lost on the merits. These have held, for example, that treaties may not retroactively impose duties or illegalize previously legal activities since such provisions would violate the *Rechtsstaatsprinzip* of the Basic Law.[27] Most recently, the Constitutional Court held unconstitutional the German electoral law by which the voters of the merged German Democratic Republic would have participated in the first postunification election of the German Federal Republic, a move with the most serious potential foreign-policy implications.[28] As a result, the law had to be revised before the reunification election could be held.

A particularly dramatic example of German judicial review reversing a government policy despite foreign affairs and national security implications is found in the controversial *Citizenship* case.[29] This was a naturalization claim brought by Tiso, a person born in East Germany of an Italian father and East-German-born (but at the time of the son's birth expatriated) mother. Plaintiff had acquired a certification of citizenship from the authorities of the German Democratic Republic. In 1969 he escaped to the West with a passport obtained from the Italian consulate general in East Berlin after satisfying those authorities of his Italian nationality. Once in West Germany, however, Tiso claimed recognition by the Federal Republic of his status as a naturalized German citizen. The Bonn government rejected this claim on the ground that his East German naturalization had not made him a German in the sense of being a citizen of the nation designated

"Germany" by the German federal constitution.[30] Petitioner asserted that this decision violated at least twelve articles of the Basic Law.

The court ruled the complaint not only justiciable but justified.[31] In an extraordinarily long and thorough opinion, the court reversed the federal government's contention in a matter of considerable importance to foreign relations and national security. In effect, the judges decided that persons naturalized by the East German regime were constitutionally entitled to recognition of their status as German citizens in the Federal Republic. In the circumstances of a divided Germany, one democratic, the other Communist, this decision raised the specter of an ever more unpopular East German regime compensating for the flight of its nationals by recruiting large numbers of Eastern European, Asian, and African immigrants to staff its depleted infrastructure, then granting those persons citizenship. To some, including the ministries concerned with such matters, this seemed to pose the danger of an uncontrollable flood of ethnic non-Germans becoming entitled to automatic citizenship in the Federal Republic.[32]

The court reached its conclusion by making its own findings based on the Basic Law and relevant international law. Those findings significantly contradicted the views of the federal government.[33] The basic laws of both East and West Germany, the judges held, confirm the concept of the juristic unity of the German nation.[34] Moreover, in such actions as its payment of reparations to German victims of nazism and to Israel, as well as in treaty negotiations, the German federal government's actions and rhetoric were held to have been based on the indivisibility of German nationhood, despite its de facto partition.[35]

German indivisibility, the court continued, has also been the consistent legal policy espoused by the three western occupying powers, who continued to have residual responsibility for the status of Germany.[36] This, the judges said, rather than the position taken by Bonn authorities in connection with Tiso's application, was the proper definition of the status of Germany, one that could be altered only in accordance with the Basic Law through an act of popular self-determination.[37] The court added further ballast to its conclusion by pointing out that the Basic Law's self-determination provision is supported by the UN Charter, the international Human Rights Covenants,[38] and various agreements between the Federal Republic and Eastern European nations.[39] Even the International Court of Justice's assertion of the right of self-determination in the *Western Sahara*[40] advisory opinion was interpreted by the German judges as supporting their rejection of the authorities' narrow interpretation of Tiso's rights under the naturalization law.

Only once, in passing, does the Court mention the right of the government, in the name of "public order," to exercise broad political discretion over immigration and citizenship. The executive had argued that international law prohibits the automatic extension of citizenship by West Germany to someone like Tiso with whom the Federal Republic had no real nexus. Moreover, the authorities had urged that the court should avoid "multifarious pronouncements" by heeding the ministerial interpretation of applicable international law. Rejecting this, the judges interpreted their obligation differently. They agreed that the court should follow the government's lead in interpreting international law, but not if that interpretation is "obviously contrary to international law."[41] They were able to conclude that the federal government's interpretation of international law was correct by purporting to apply not the version of that law set out in the government's brief but rather the different positions previously taken consistently by the authorities. Again, citing the many instances in which the federal government had expressed its adherence to a "one-Germany" legal theory, the court declared its readiness to conform to that pattern of interpretation rather than to the ministerial views expressed for the purpose of prevailing in a specific suit involving the rights of one claimant.

That the highest constitutional court of the German Federal Republic felt itself free to override a policy decision of the government in a matter of such political importance, unmistakably asserting its power as the ultimate guardian of constitutional legality, is the result of its having long rejected the political-question doctrine as a matter of formal conceptual jurisprudence even while deciding the substance of various cases in the government's favor. While usually giving the political authorities ample political discretion to conduct foreign relations, the German judges have been careful to reserve full power to determine on the basis of all relevant evidence whether a particular exercise of discretion is within the ambit of unfettered choice of means allocated to the political sector by the constitution. They have done so, however, in a way that has not led to constant friction and confrontation with the political organs.

Another example of judicial independence is the 1989 decision of the German Federal Constitutional Court in the *Asylum Case*,[42] which proceeded from the government's refusal to grant asylum to several Sri Lankan Tamils. The lower court had upheld the federal authorities' judgment that applicants were not such "victims of political persecution" as were entitled to political refuge in Germany by operation of article 16(2)(2) of the Basic Law. In overturning this decision, the Constitutional Court refused to apply a standard of proof weighted in favor of the ministerial determination. Instead, it considered in great detail evidence of current and historical conditions in Sri Lanka as well as evidence of the political activities of the applicants. On this evidence, the court concluded that petitioners were constitutionally entitled to asylum.

There is good reason why the German courts should have decided to weigh the evidence in such a case themselves rather than deferring to the ministerial evaluation. Since it is the government that is seeking to exclude, deport, or extradite, its evidence should be as rebuttable as that of any other self-interested party.

The German judges seem to have understood, as some American counterparts have not,[43] that rules pertaining to evidentiary weight and onus of proof need to take into account the degree of disinterested expertise, or self-interest, of political authorities' assertions about disputed questions of fact that are crucial to the outcome of a case. They also understand that a distinction should be made between evidence presented by the foreign ministry and by other ministries (Justice, or the attorney general) that can lay less claim to foreign-relations expertise. Finally, as in the *Citizenship Case*,[44] they have understood the distinction between evidence of a consistent pattern of governmental conduct and legal rhetoric as opposed to a mere opportunistic ministerial statement supporting a particular litigious interest.[45]

German Judges on How to Decide

In effect, the German courts have redefined the issue. It is not *whether* but *how* judges should decide: what evidentiary credence courts should give to the government's assessment of the facts; how much room they should leave the policymakers to choose among options;

on what terms constitutionally protected yet conflicting public and private interests are to be reconciled.

The focus, in other words, has shifted in German courts from the issue of jurisdiction to the task of creating rules governing the weight and probity of government evidence in foreign-affairs litigation. Even while asserting its unlimited right of review, the German judiciary has developed evidenciary presumptions that favor the political organs. In the *Inter-German Basic Treaty Case*, for example, the Constitutional Court, while firmly asserting its jurisdiction, applied a presumption of constitutionality. In interpreting the agreement, it ruled that "in the event several interpretations are possible the Court should choose the one which is congruent with the strictures of the Constitution."[46]

In assessing disputed facts, the German judiciary has also developed a presumption that favors the government's "story," its account of why it chose to pursue one among several available courses of action or why it used one rather than another means. The judges, having satisfied themselves that the government's foreign-policy objectives are lawful, will disallow the means chosen only upon a showing of bad faith or arbitrariness (*Willkur*). This is illustrated by the *Schleyer Kidnapping Case*[47] where the Constitutional Court said that the tactical question of whether to negotiate with terrorists for the release of a hostage, plaintiff having urged that this was required by the constitutional guarantee of respect for "life" (article 2(2) of the Basic Law), was within the discretion of the politically responsible organs of government unless the discretion was demonstrably being exercised in bad faith.

While the German courts are willing to enter the political thicket at the behest of parties challenging the constitutionality of a foreign-policy objective or the means employed to attain it, in effect they give the government the benefit of any reasonable doubt. To put it another way: The complainant must discharge the onus of proving the essential ingredients of unconstitutionality or illegality in the challenged actions of the government. This is a difficult onus to discharge in an area—foreign affairs and national security—where conjecture reigns but does not constitute proof and some or even most of the facts are uniquely within the purview of the foreign office.

This is demonstrated in the *Pershing 2 and Cruise Missile I Case*, decided in 1983 by the Constitutional Court.[48] Several persons had complained that the Federal Republic's agreement allowing Allied forces to deploy a new generation of weapons with nuclear warheads on its territory significantly increased the chances of a Soviet nuclear strike against Germany. They contended that this violated the government's duty, prescribed by article 2(2) of the Basic Law, to protect its nationals' "life." The court responded that the injury forming the basis of the complaint must be shown to be both actually foreseeable and also caused by or attributable to the federal government's decision to deploy these weapons.[49] Neither foreseeability nor causality could be demonstrated to the court's satisfaction.

Nevertheless, the court treated the petitioners' allegations with great seriousness before concluding that it would be impossible for the judges to ascertain, "because there are no relevant criteria,"[50] the probable effect on the Soviet Union of the German government's decision to permit the weapons' deployment. Assessments of this sort, the judges concluded, are within the jurisdiction of the appropriate organs of the federal government. It is their responsibility under the Basic Law to make the determinations necessary to secure the defense of the Federal Republic.[51] What steps are required to achieve this is "within the ambit of political decision and responsibility,"[52] and the Basic Law does not permit the judges to substitute their assessment of the political risks for that of the appropriate political organs.[53]

While this test superficially resembles the one stated by Justice Brennan in *Baker v. Carr*,[54] which allows U.S. courts to abstain from adjudicating cases in which there is a lack of judicially ascertainable standards for deciding the issues, the similarity is misleading. The German judges' position is not that there is a category of cases beyond their power to decide but that where the applicable standards for making a judgment are highly subjective, they will decide, but may also give greater leeway than otherwise to the policymakers. In Germany it is not difficult to be heard in a case purporting to hold the government to a vaguely defined legal standard, but it is quite hard to win. The judges will reverse the political decision only where the petitioner can demonstrate that the government was acting in bad faith: if, for example, it can be shown that an action purportedly taken to pursue a lawful objective (to strength NATO defenses) was actually motivated by an unlawful one (to enrich the minister of defense or one of his constituents).

While the German court thus recognized the enforceable constitutional obligation of the state not to endanger the lives or well-being of its citizens, it pointed out that the dangers of deploying the missiles, if such there were, would proximately arise not from the deployment itself but from the reaction of foreign states. The Basic Law could not be interpreted to have accorded a foreign government the power to determine by threats and demands the constitutionality of actions that in themselves posed no danger to the lives or health of German citizens.[55]

The same position was taken in 1987 when the court decided the *Chemical Weapons Case*[56] where article 2(2) of the Basic Law was invoked by plaintiffs in an effort to prevent the storage of nerve gas and other poisonous substances on German soil for military use. Again, the court first determined whether the Basic Law gave the government discretion to enter into such an agreement and second, whether its political judgment had been exercised without mendacious arbitrariness or willful disregard of the facts. Once the judges were satisfied on these two counts, they deferred to the political judgment of the responsible political organs of government. In other words, the judges employed a test that requires that the court to satisfy itself that the government's policy (1) is a means to attain a constitutionally sanctioned objective and (2) is at least rationally defensible as a means to attain that objective. In this way, the German court has asserted—and circumscribed—its power of review. Consistently, the German judges have demonstrated seriousness in their treatment of even fanciful allegations made by petitioners in foreign-relations cases, certainly when compared to the dismissiveness with which many American judges treat similar suits. At the same time, the German courts have not made it easy for critics of government policy to use the judiciary to achieve what the political process has denied them.

The judicial presumption in favor of the government's story is augmented by what is tantamount to a presumption in favor of the government's account of the content of international law. In the aforementioned *Hess* case, for example, petitioner argued that the federal government was misconstruing the limit that article 107 of the UN Charter, dealing with the special status of the former Axis powers, placed on Germany's legal options in seeking Hess's release from prison. To this the court responded that a truly conclusive or defini-

119

tive interpretation of the relevant international law could be given only by the International Court of Justice[57] and that in the absence of such clarification, a national court must recognize that "it is of great importance to the interests of the German Federal Republic that it speak in international forums with a single voice."[58] For this reason the court must "exercise the greatest measure of restraint" before finding the government's interpretations of its rights and duties under international law in error. The court could contradict the policymakers on such a matter only "if the Government's interpretation of an international law were shown to be willfully wrong so as to affect directly the rights of a citizen." It must be demonstrated, in other words, that the government's interpretation "is not comprehensible."[59]

The judges defined the test to be applied—*arbitrariness* (*Willkur*)—and concluded that the onus of proving it rested with the plaintiff, who had failed to discharge it to their satisfaction. "It is not the place of courts to replace the views of the competent organs of foreign policy with their own," the court reiterated. When it is asked to assess the effectiveness of various foreign-policy options, the court must accept the government's view unless it has been shown that the policy chosen cannot be justified "by any sensible view of the matter."[60]

This should be set against the previously noted refusal of the Constitutional Court in the *Citizenship Case* to accept the argument of the federal authorities that their denial of plaintiff's claim to German citizenship was mandated by international customary law. There, however, the court was able to point to wide discrepancies between the government's contentions and quite different accounts of the law given by the government on other occasions.

Besides developing evidentiary presumptions favoring the government, the German courts in taking jurisdiction over foreign affairs cases have interpreted the Basic Law to give the political organs *Spielraum*: wide, but judicially reviewable and not unlimited, policy discretion. In the *Saar* case, for example, the Constitutional Court held that in interpreting the validity of that treaty and the legislation enacting it, the judges "above all . . . should not lose sight of . . . the political realities which are the starting point from which the treaty emerges, as well as the political realities which the agreement seeks to establish or to alter."[61] The Basic Law, said the court, must be read in the political context in which it was operating, such as the military occupation of the Federal Republic by the three western Allied powers. "While all exercises of state power in the German Federal Republic must be limited by the terms of the Basic Law," the judges added, "it is nevertheless necessary to imagine whether, in these circumstances, only agreements are to be held constitutional which give full effect to the Basic Law, or whether it is not more satisfactory that the steps contemplated by the agreement have been taken with the intent, and have the tendency, to advance [the nation] towards a full realization of the prescribed constitutional conditions at least to such an extent as these are politically achievable. The Federal Constitutional Court considers itself obliged to answer this question by adopting the latter position."[62]

In effect, the judges applied a half-a-loaf theory that justified their conclusion that the political settlement envisaged by the Saar agreement was "well within the ambit" of political discretion[63] because it tended to launch the step-by-step dismantling of the Saar's status as a French-occupied territory, one that legally severed it from the rest of the German Federal Republic but also envisioned the gradual restoration of the Saar's constitutional legitimacy within the German state. "Within such boundaries [of their discretion] the treaty-making organs of the Federal Government are only politically accountable for their content and agreed measures."[64]

Specifically, a judicial finding of unconstitutionality is excluded if the effect of the agreement, as interpreted by the judges on a full review of the record, is to create conditions more nearly in accord with the constitution than would otherwise exist.[65] "The bad," the court intoned, "must not be allowed to defeat the better merely because the best is . . . unattainable. This the Basic Law cannot intend."[66] The question whether the agreement will advance or retard the prospects of the Saar rejoining the greater part of the Federal Republic that already enjoys all the rights established by the Basic Law in the period before the conclusion of a final peace treaty "is a question of political judgment" beyond the Constitutional Court's competence.[67] Beyond the judges' competence, however, not *inherently* but only because it is an issue on which reasonable persons might differ. Precisely in such a close call will the judges defer to the judgment of the political branches. Even so, this is no carte blanche. "A finding of unconstitutionality," the judges cautioned, "could be made if it were evident that the effect of the agreement were to retard those prospects. That is not here the case."[68] In effect, the judges asserted their inalienable right to make the call, but where it is close, they agree to give the benefit of the doubt to the government.

The *Saar* case demonstrates that in discharging its responsibility for judicial review, the court will (1) take into account the circumstances and where appropriate interpret the meaning of the constitutional requisites in the light of existential reality and the range of options available to the political authorities, and moreover, (2) where the constitutionality of an agreement depends upon an informed judgment of its likely future operational effect, the judiciary will substitute its prognosis for that of the political organs only in extraordinary cases.

A similar reading of the constitution to give the government broad discretion in the shaping of foreign policy was enunciated by the Constitutional Court in the *Inter-German Treaty Case*. There the judges specified that the Basic Law must be read to give the authorities the leeway to decide which policies are most likely to serve the national interest in matters concerning foreign relations and agreements with foreign states.[69] However, the principle of "judicial self-restraint" (rendered in English by the German court) does not imply the foreshortening or weakening of judicial competence to decide. It does require the judges to "refuse to play politics" by "trenching upon the area created and circumscribed by the Basic Law as appropriate for the unrestricted operation of the political institutions."[70] What those areas are is for judges to say. The constitution, as interpreted by the court, defines the obligatory ends of national policy, but the political branches of government have wide yet not unlimited discretion in the means to be employed. In particular, the court remains the final arbiter of whether the means can reasonably be seen to be directed toward attaining the mandatory or permissible ends.

Thus the court in the *Inter-German Treaty Case* managed to uphold the constitutionality of the treaty while asserting its right fully to review the constitutionality of its terms and objectives.

The *Hess* case makes this duality particularly clear: The court's broad power of review coexists with the political organs' broad discretion in questions of policy. In holding justiciable the suit brought by Hess's son, the lower court had also declared that the Federal Republic has "a wide discretion" as to "whether and how they will provide this external protection" to which Hess was entitled under the constitution.[71] That discretion, said the court, was necessary because the duty of protection imposed on the government by the Basic Law, while real and judically enforceable, is owed by the political authorities not only to the imprisoned Hess but also to the nation as a whole. Where relations with other states are concerned, it is thus for the government to balance its duty toward the individual German against the interests of the entire community. "The Government's political judgment applicable to this balancing," the judge concluded, "is not reviewable by a court."[72] On the other hand, he said, the courts will review whether the authorities have violated a requirement of law, exceeded their allotted discretion, or misunderstood "the legal constraints on their discretion."[73]

When the case reached the Constitutional Court, it endorsed this summary of the standard of review. Although the case was plainly justiciable, the Constitutional Court's judges held that the government's "breadth of discretion in foreign affairs is justified in that foreign relations and events are not solely within the [political] control of the German Federal authorities, but are frequently beyond its control. In order to pursue the political objectives of the Federal Republic within the limits of what is permissible by international and constitutional law, the Constitution accords the organs of foreign policy a very wide discretion in assessing the practicality and feasibility of various policy options."[74]

It suffices if the federal authorities have demonstrated to the court's satisfaction that various steps have been taken to secure the liberty of the subject of the petition and that it is intended to take further measures.[75] The mere fact that initiatives taken so far have failed does not demonstrate that other steps would have been more successful.[76] For example, the complainant failed in his contention that the authorities should have used more arguments based on errors of law in Hess's conviction and should have raised the matter publicly in the forum of the United Nations[77] because he cannot demonstrate that such tactics would have been more successful than those chosen, in their discretion, by the authorities.[78] The onus of proof, in other words, is with those challenging the government.

Again, in the case testing the validity of the German treaties with Poland and the Soviet Union, the constitutional Court emphasized that the Constitution must be read to give the foreign-relations establishment a range of options. "In examining such agreements," the judges said, "one must consider *ab initio* that the Federal Government, in foreign policy matters, as in all matters requiring the exercise of political judgment, in general has a broad area of political discretion."[79] In practice, this means that the court will not declare unconstitutional a treaty (i.e., the legislation enacting it) merely because it fails to achieve what some may regard as optimum results in advancing constitutionally prescribed rights, goals, or values. The judges are not in a position to conclude that given the politics of the other party to the agreement, a better result could have been obtained in the circumstances.[80] "If the Constitutional Court were to rule otherwise," its members concluded, "it would be entering a sphere in which those bearing responsibility for foreign policy must retain the freedom of movement that is necessitated by the fact that what is involved is primarily the pursuit of political objectives and values."[81]

This summary of key cases makes clear that the German judiciary has reserved for itself the right to decide but that the judges tend to listen sympathetically to the policymakers. In practice, there has been little serious conflict between the political and judicial organs. It is also evident from the jurisprudence that foreign-policy cases are not litigated on an entirely level playing field. The German judiciary applies a rather narrow standard of review in foreign-relations questions that explicitly gives the political organs sufficient latitude to make policy choices without judicial second-guessing.

This achieves results that have not seriously discomfited the political branches while reassuring litigants with claims against the government that they will have their day in court. Measured by outcomes, the German judiciary, taking jurisdiction in virtually every instance, has upheld the contested foreign-policy and security initiatives of the political branches in roughly the same proportion (which is to say equally often) as the U.S. federal courts have by practicing abdication. The judicial results in the two systems are about as similar as the judges' conceptual formulations are different. In its theoretical pronouncements, neither judiciary is entirely candid about what it is doing. The German judges sound more assertive, just as their American counterparts, sometimes by practicing double-entry bookkeeping, have tended to sound more reticent, than they really are.

Nevertheless, the German Constitutional Court has at least managed to develop a seamless theory and by and large has given it a consistent application. That theory is consonant with the rule of law. No litigant in the German courts will be refused a hearing because the issue is too political, the interests too important, the facts too difficult, or the law too inscrutable.

Closer to home, the experience of Canada became a relevant standard of comparison once its federal system (in place since 1867) was augmented in 1982 by a constitutionally entrenched Charter of Rights and Freedoms. It is thus instructive that the Supreme Court of Canada used its very first opportunity (a case based on the guarantee in section 1 of the charter of the right to "life, liberty and security of person," which, plaintiff alleged, would be violated by a Canadian-U.S. agreement to permit U.S. cruise-missile testing in Canada) to reject out of hand the government's contention that the supreme court's jurisdiction in foreign-affairs cases should be circumscribed by adopting the political-question doctrine.[82] "I have no doubt," wrote Justice Dickson, "that disputes of a political or foreign policy nature may property be cognizable by the courts."[83] The Canadian Supreme Court's approach to the missile-testing case corresponds closely to the approach developed by the German Constitutional Court.

Courts do not merely decide cases. They speak, by word and example, as teachers. One should not underestimate the salutary effects of this approach on the legal culture of a society, manifesting that in government none are omnipotent and that the last word belongs to the least dangerous branch.

A Rule of Evidence in Place of the
Political-Question Doctrine

How much of a wrench would it be were U.S. courts to adapt and adopt a doctrinal approach similar to the one used by German judges? As we have seen, American judges have failed to impose uniformity, thereby leaving open the possibility of reform even while demonstrating the need for it. Further, there is evidence that the German approach is not really so alien to our jurisprudence.

In 1837, Chief Judge Cranch of the D.C. Circuit Court wrote an opinion that presaged the German jurisprudence. It categorically refutes the doctrinal basis for judicial abdication underpinning the political-question doctrine. At issue was whether the postmaster general of the United States could be ordered to pay a debt owed to one Stokes. Attorneys for the executive branch had argued that an order of mandamus to an officer acting under presidential authority would constitute a judicial attempt "to control the executive power, to assume the functions of the president, and to make [judges] the executive in the last resort." In granting the order nevertheless, Cranch replied that this "argument rests, almost entirely, upon the force of the word 'control'; which . . . implies an interference with some right or power of the person to be controlled. To command a person to do what, by law, he is bound to do, and what he has no right to refuse to do, is not to control him in the exercise of any of his functions, but to compel him to execute them. Before it can be shown that such a mandamus . . . would control the executive in any of its functions, it must appear that the executive has a discretion to do or not to do the thing commanded."[1]

This summarizes the tendency of at least some U.S. courts to reject the theory that the separation of powers requires judicial deference to the executive branch's views concerning the scope of its constitutional powers. Except in foreign affairs, such skepticism has long been the predominant jurisprudential mode. In the broad American constitutional tradition, like the German, it is not ordinarily left to the political actors to decide whether they have acted *intra vires*. Cranch's brilliant analysis of the proper role and function of judicial review in the new Republic led him to conclude that the "officers of the United States . . . stand on ground different from that occupied by the English executive officers, whose offices are created, and whose duties are assigned, by the king. . . . There is no analogy, therefore, between the executive officers of the king of England, and the executive officers of the United States . . . and the fact, if it be a fact, that there are no English cases of mandamus against the officers of the crown, affords no reason why a mandamus should not issue against an executive officer of the United States."[2] The Supreme Court affirmed this decision on appeal.[3]

The case posed a purely domestic issue. President Jackson had insisted on not paying Stokes, whereupon Congress passed a special act requiring the government to do so. While the nub of the case turned on an interpretation of ministerial duty, the argument by counsel for Postmaster General Kendall went much further, opening up the entire subject of the relation of the president to his subordinates in their performance of statutory duties. Kendall, seeking to immunize himself, chose to rely heavily "upon statements by Hamilton, Marshall, James Wilson, and Story having to do with the President's power in the field of foreign relations."[4] On appeal, the Supreme Court, essentially echoing Cranch, adopted the view that by legislating, Congress automatically empowered the courts to superintend the president's constitutional duty to "take care that the laws be faithfully executed." By that act, said the Court, Congress brings into operation the process of judicial review to ensure that the execution is faithful to the intent of the law.[5] When the president is constrained by a law, he is under a duty. It is for the courts, in a case or controversy, to declare what that duty encompasses.

This rejection of *Kendall's* argument for executive autonomy cannot readily be interpreted to admit an exception in matters of foreign relations or national security. There too, political discretion is circumscribed by the Constitution and statutes. If the United States is a nation in which political power is limited by legislation and the Constitution, then neither the executive nor Congress may exercise any (including foreign-relations) powers in a manner precluded by law—law it is for the courts to illuminate in the event of conflict or ambiguity.

This in no way precludes the notion, which informed the holding in *Curtiss-Wright* and has not since been seriously challenged, that the Constitution, legislation, or the common sense that forms the interpretative penumbra of both may give the president and his subordinate officers broad leeway within the established boundaries of law to make and execute the external policy of the United States. It does, however, make inescapable the conclusion consistently upheld by the German, but only intermittently by the American, judiciary that there can be no cases that are nonjusticiable per se merely because they affect the nation's interaction with the world.

The German courts are as sensitive as ours to the plea that the vicissitudes of conducting foreign relations makes it necessary that legal norms be construed, when the text allows, to give the policymakers maximum flexibility and latitude. There are very few results achieved in American courts by judicial abdication that could not have been reached had they taken jurisdiction. If, as seems likely, the public wants the management of foreign relations to be vested primarily in the hands of the president and his international-affairs experts, that preference, expressed in law, can be accommodated by the judicial process without the unseemly and injudicious, if not downright anti-constitutional, spectacle of judges shunning their ineluctable responsibility to say what the law means.

This requires balancing between the imperatives of constitutionalism and flexibility, a process well within the competence of the judiciary. A wise president and a sensitive Congress are also perfectly capable of making that determination, but these qualities of the political branches cannot simply be assumed; they must be demonstrable to the least dangerous branch. That, surely, is the right way to perceive the role allocation intended by the separation of powers. Professor Louis Henkin has aptly stated this need for balance: "Ordinarily, the appropriate judicial reply to a challenge to an act of Congress or to an executive action is that the political branch acted within its constitutional authority. But there is no warrant for the court to be mesmerized by incantations of 'national interest' or 'national security.' There is reason for due deference to the executive, but not for undue deference—for due judicial humility, but not undue humility."[6]

Evidentiary Weight

It has been common ground among judges since the beginning of the nineteenth century that the courts should refrain from ruling on the political sagacity or prudence of a policy or action being pursued by the executive or a policy that has been legislated by Congress so long as each is operating within the ambit of discretion allotted it by law and the Constitution. It is surely impossible to find a court that would disagree with that proposition or would blatantly review political choices among several legally and constitutionally sanctioned policy options. But that is not the sort of judicial reticence to which the historical political-question doctrine has summoned some judges. They have added a far more controversial corollary to the proposition: Courts are not to determine whether a political discretion in any particular instance has been exercised in accordance with the norms and within the ambit of the powers allotted to the executive or legislative branch by law and the Constitution. It was this corollary that Justice Douglas sought to refute in criticizing the Supreme Court's refusal to grant certiorari in a case challenging the legality of the Vietnam War. The "issue in this case," he said, "is not whether we ought to fight a war in Indochina, but whether the Executive can authorize it without congressional authorization. This is not a case where we would have to determine the wisdom of any policy."[7] Or as Chief Justice Burger put it in *Chadha*, the Court may not question the wisdom of congressional policy enacted into a law about aliens, but it has an inescapable duty to decide "whether Congress has chosen a constitutionally permissible means of implementing that power."[8]

If the courts were able to formulate a clearly enunciated theory for distinguishing between a judicial duty to examine the legality and constitutionality of any governmental policy affecting protected rights and interests and a duty to abstain from reviewing the policymakers' choice of ends and means from a permissible range of options, then the basis for a new and less contentious (although perhaps also unnecessary)[9] political-question doctrine would have been put in place. In practice, however, such a theoretical dichotomy might not in itself suffice to resolve the underlying problem, for as we have seen, American judges feel a genuine reluctance to be the final arbiters of questions the answers to which may have consequences for the security and viability of the nation. They feel uncomfortable with the data generated by such cases, which they have difficulty understanding and some of which may be too sensitive to be tested by the adversarial process of open courts. They may also feel that in foreign policy, consistency is essential and that the costs of fragmentation of authority are too high a price to pay even for legal accountability.

In other words, even if it were possible to envisage a new theoretical formulation for judicial review of cases bearing on the conduct of foreign affairs, it would still be necessary for judges to confront the prudential problems posed by foreign-relations cases. The first of these special prudential problems is the evidentiary one. Specifically, any theoretical reformulation would have to say something about the weight judges should give to the story—the fact-based and expert-interpreted contextual circumstances—told to the court by the president's or the Congress's foreign-relations and national-security establishment. That story—for example, the "spin" put upon the circumstances in which an act of executive discretion was exercised—is bound to have a significant effect in many instances where judges would seek to determine whether the policy options chosen are legally and constitutionally permissible.

This is because the boundaries of the constitutionally permissible are not marked by stone fences. Rather, they tend to be elastic, expanding and contracting in accordance with the context of circumstances in which power is exercised. Therefore, once the courts undertake to review the legality and constitutionality of an exercise of power in the conduct of foreign relations, they are immediately drawn into an assessment of those rather special circumstances that constitute the field of international relations, a field in which arcane expertise (on weapons strategy or economic impact, for example) and subjective perceptions (on the dangers to the United States of a particular "enemy" or action of a foreign government) mingle to confound the competence of the ordinary judicially cloistered judge.

This is a problem that can best be understood from the court's perspective in evidentiary terms. Should the secretary of defense and his challenger, a military recruit, stand on an equal footing in testifying to the circumstances in which the soldier has been ordered into combat? Whom should the court believe when hearing evidence intended to demonstrate whether the president acted in response to an actual or anticipated "attack upon the United States"[10] or its citizens abroad? Who is to be believed about whether forces being dispatched overseas are going "into hostilities or into situations where imminent involvement in hostilities is clearly indicated by the circumstances?"[11] Yet if judges are to review the legality and constitutionality of the president's action, such questions are likely to emerge at the heart of the litigation and cannot be avoided by the court. The scope of the president's lawful discretion is profoundly affected by the answers. To put the matter another way, how ready should judges be to entertain, and be persuaded by, evidence that particular means chosen by a political branch were less than compelled by the circumstances or that other, less legally or constitutionally objectionable means might have accomplished the same or "equivalent" ends? These sorts of questions are fielded by the German courts but make American judges quite uncomfortable.

A kind of answer was provided by the Supreme Court in the 1932 case of *Sterling v. Constantin*.[12] It is useful only by analogy since that case involved judicial review of the discretionary executive power of governors rather than the president. However, the Supreme Court thought that this test of the emergency powers of a governor was covered by the jurisprudence applicable to a comparable exercise of extraordinary presidential powers. Plaintiff, a Texas oil producer, brought an action to restrain the governor of Texas from violating his property rights protected from state action under the Fourteenth Amendment. The defendant, as governor of Texas, had proclaimed martial law over several oil-producing counties of the state, declaring that wasteful production by some operators in defiance of state conservation law and the violent feelings thereby engendered in the public constituted insurrection and riot beyond civil control, justifying the use of state military force against producers to compel their adherence to production restrictions.

The Supreme Court began by declaring the issue justiciable on the ground that when "there is a substantial showing that the exertion of state power has overridden private rights secured by [the federal] Constitution, the subject is necessarily one for judicial inquiry."[13] Second, the Court held that in exercising this power of review, it could inquire into the fact matrix behind the governor's decision to empower himself by a declaration of martial law. This entailed an inquiry into not only the law but also the facts because "when questions of law and fact are so intermingled as to make it necessary, in order to pass upon the federal question, the court may, and should, analyze the facts."[14] Third, however, in conducting this review of law and facts, the Court should recognize that in "the performance of its essential function, in promoting the security and well-being of its people, the State must, of necessity, enjoy a broad discretion."[15]

Applying those principles, the Court set about the task of balancing. It accepted that the governor exercises no greater responsibility than that constitutionally his as "Chief Executive and Commander in Chief of its military forces to suppress insurrection and to preserve the peace."[16] He is therefore "appropriately vested with the discretion to determine whether an exigency requiring military aid for that purpose has arisen."[17] Citing as analogous its prior decision on the use of military force by the president, the Court agreed that this power "is to be exercised upon sudden emergencies, upon great occasions of state, and under circumstances which may be vital to the existence of the Union." In making his decision to take other actions affecting civilians, the governor, like the president, has "a permitted range of honest judgment as to the measures to be taken in meeting force with force, in suppressing violence and restoring order, for without such liberty to make immediate decisions, the power itself would be useless."[18]

However, this discretion is neither absolute nor unreviewable. It must be exercised "in good faith" and in "the honest belief" that the measures are needed to prevent insurrection.[19] Thus, it "does not follow from the fact that the Executive has this range of discretion, deemed to be a necessary incident of his power to suppress disorder, that every sort of action the Governor may take, no matter how unjustified by the exigency or subversive of private right . . . is conclusively supported by mere executive fiat."[20] In other words, the Court will give much weight to the governor's determination of action required by the circumstances, but his opinion is not conclusive for the Court, which at a minimum will review to ensure that he was acting in good faith and in an honest belief that the circumstances constituted a real emergency for which extraordinary measures were the appropriate response. This test is comparable to the *Willkur* principle applied by German courts, discussed in chapter 7.

A more recent example of the possibility and importance of devising an evidenciary standard suitable to foreign-affairs and national-security review is found in the 1977 Supreme Court decision in *Fiallo v. Bell*.[21] Fiallo was the father of an illegitimate male minor claiming for his child the right to preferential immigration status. The relevant statute accords this to the "parent" or "child" of a U.S. citizen. However, Congress had further specified that the preferential status should extend to illegitimate children of U.S. mothers but not to those of U.S. fathers.[22] It was this provision that was being challenged as unconstitutional. A three-judge federal district court, upholding plaintiff's ineligibility, ruled that while Congress's political discretion regarding admission of aliens is "exceptionally broad," it is nevertheless judicially reviewable.

This required the court to enunciate a standard of judicial review, and it devised one that was essentially evidentiary. The judges held that the distinction made by Congress between claims through the father and those through the mother could be held unconstitutional *only* if it was "wholly devoid of any conceivable rational purpose" or "fundamentally aimed at achieving a goal unrelated to the regulation of immigration."[23] This placed an evidentiary onus on the plaintiff, similar to one applied by German courts, that he was unable to discharge. In other words, the court ruled that the onus of proving that the law had trespassed over the threshold of inequality to establish the unconstitutionality of a legislated standard—in which good faith, intent, the cost of alternatives, would all come into play—is on the plaintiff.

The Supreme Court's majority opinion by Justice Powell essentially upholds the evidentiary rule devised by the lower court, even relating it to the political-question doctrine. With some disregard for syllogistic logic, it states that "[t]he reasons that preclude judicial review of political questions also dictate a narrow standard of review of decisions made by the Congress or the President in the area of immigration and naturalization."[24] The problem with this syllogism is that if a rule "precludes" judicial review, it cannot "also dictate" an evidentiary rule establishing the standard for review. What the Court seems to mean is that the political-question doctrine should not preclude judicial review but that review should occur under a tailored rule of evidence that accords enhanced credence to the "story" asserted by the political branch (its version of the contextual facts) as the policymakers defend their choice of means. Powell cites with approval the decision of Frankfurter in *Harisiades v. Shaughnessy* that the grounds for exclusion of persons or categories of aliens is "wholly outside the power of this Court to control"[25] without seeming to recognize that it was a new and quite different rule of judicial control he was enunciating, one fundamentally at odds with the Court's abject abdication in *Harisiades*.[26] While he accepts the government's categorization of immigration matters "as involving foreign policy,"[27] his decision nevertheless reviews the basis of this peculiar statutory distinction between mothers and fathers and explicitly denies that its legislative justifications are beyond judicial review.[28] The Court opts for a theory of "limited judicial review."[29] This actually amounts less to endorsement than repudiation of the *Harisiades* line of jurisprudence, which purports to "preclude"[30] review.

The *Fiallo* court achieves this volte-face without accepting a full judicial review in which "policy questions entrusted exclusively to the political branches" are determined *de novo* by judges. The reason for this restraint is cast in terms of the constitutional separation of powers, much as in judicial justifications for the political-question doctrine. Judges, the court dutifully reiterates, "have no judicial authority to substitute [their] political judgment for that of the Congress."[31] The consequence of the *Fiallo* decision, however, is to replace an exclusionary rule with an evidentiary one.

This is approximately the position taken by the German Constitutional Court,[32] and it should become the standard "interpretation" of the political-question doctrine in contemporary American practice if the doctrine is to be congruent with the rule of law—that as with other matters, courts will review the legality and constitutionality of foreign-policy and national-security acts of the Congress and the executive but not their efficaciousness or wisdom as governmental policy. In gray-area cases such as *Fiallo*, it may be difficult to distinguish wisdom from constitutionality, particularly when assessing a law that seeks on rationally defended policy grounds to discriminate between similar but not identical categories of persons. What clearly emerges from both the majority opinion and the compelling dissent of Justices Marshall and Brennan, however, is that the Court understood that the judges must be seen to have the last word. While the dissent may be right to characterize the *Fiallo* majority's standard for review as "toothless,"[33] it was wrong, given the two-hundred-year history of this jurisdictional debate, for the dissent to call it "abdication."[34]

Rather, it was one small step for judicial review of foreign-affairs disputes otherwise properly before the courts.

We may be on the verge of a new era in which avoidance or abdication is no longer the Supreme Court's response when government thaumaturgically invokes the "national-security" or "foreign-policy" talisman. Except in *Goldwater*, the Court has lately avoided invoking the political-question doctrine, yet it achieved this truce largely by turning away petitions for review of foreign-affairs cases. Meanwhile, in the lower courts, as we have seen, "the political question doctrine has had a busy life."[35] However, when the Supreme Court occasionally does grant certiorari in such matters now, it seems increasingly willing to review the allegation of *exces de pouvoir*, and as we have seen in chapter 5, even if the case has evident national-security and foreign-policy elements, judges currently appear somewhat more willing to review the legality and constitutionality of the act. This subtle shift, if it is one, deserves clearer doctrinal enunciation by the Court. Thus, the debate ought soon to move on: from whether review is permissible (justiciability) to what the proper standard of review should be—a matter of onus and evidentiary weight.

That too raises questions quite as controversial, but different and manageable, as those presented by adherence to the doctrine of abstention. In *Fiallo*, for example, Marshall and Brennan, concluded in dissent that despite its protestations, Congress's discrimination between male and female parents was void because based on "reasons unrelated to foreign policy concerns or threats to national security" and that whatever the ends sought, any gender-based classification must "serve important governmental objectives and . . . be substantially related to achievement of those objectives" and must not be "illogical and unjust."[36] "Logical and just" is a tougher standard for judicial review of an exercise of political discretion than the "devoid of conceivable rational purpose" test adopted by the majority. But majority and dissent agreed that their difference was precisely that: disagreement over the applicable *standard* of judicial review where a coordinate political branch of government seeks to defend the constitutionality of its choice among policy options. Moreover, the justices evinced understandable disagreement over whether the distinction between genders served a genuine national-security purpose. They did not disagree, however, about where the final word on that issue properly resides—in the Court.

135

Constitutionality, majority and dissent agreed, is for courts to determine. Increasingly, such a view of the judiciary's role seems to be shared by almost all the justices in the cases they have recently accepted. When it grants certiorari, the Court now seems invariably disinclined to treat as beyond challenge the story told by a political branch about the circumstances in which it made its policy choice. But since most cases with foreign-policy or national-security implications do not reach the highest tribunal, the Court has a hortatory obligation it must soon discharge. In the lower courts, the nonjusticiability of foreign-relations cases is still prevalent doctrine, rooted in older Supreme Court cases, prodigious obiter dicta, and prevailing jurisprudential myth. Sooner or later this chaotic condition will have to be set right, if necessary with the help of Congress, by a comprehensive new theoretical pronouncement from the highest tribunal.

The Special Cases: In Camera Proceedings
and Declaratory Judgments

W E MAY HAVE something to learn from Germany, but we are also differently positioned. American foreign relations are infused with the special circumstances that go with being a superpower. Our foreign policy defends the frontiers of our national interest, but it is also the arrowhead of security for many other democratic nations that rely on us for their defense. Some of these democracies—Japan is the leading example—have been partially disarmed as a consequence of settlements ending great wars. Others live under military restrictions imposed by international agreement (Germany) or a voluntary (Switzerland) or imposed (Austria) policy of neutrality or are simply too small or weak to rely on their own capacity for self-defense.

Admittedly, the special role of the United States as the leader of an expanding coalition of democracies is no longer one of absolute paramountcy, as it was in the decades following the Second World War, and the threats facing what was called the western alliance have diminished since the mid-1980s with the disintegration of the rival Communist camp. Nevertheless, U.S. foreign policy is still of special, indeed unique, significance in stabilizing the global system. This means that U.S. courts must be aware of our foreign policy's special global role and its implication for the role of judges in reviewing the constitutionality and legality of policy choices made by foreign-policy managers.

Here the U.S. federal judiciary cannot expect guidance from its German brethren because Germany, even since reunification, has eschewed for historical reasons any assumption of a foreign-policy responsibility comparable to that of the United States. Thus, the German Federal Republic's judiciary, in taking jurisdiction over foreign-affairs cases, took quite a different and less complex responsibility than would American courts if they were similarly to extend the scope of judicial review.

In particular, two aspects of the U.S. leadership role have not loomed nearly as large in the context of postwar divided Germany: the government's legitimate need to protect a substantial hoard of secret data, sources, and methods, and its obligation as a superpower to use force quickly and decisively in confrontations with other states in some circumstances. The German courts cannot offer much guidance on how courts can protect crucial secrets of state to which a litigant seeks access in preparing a case, and they are unable to be of any help in resolving the problem of how to deal with a legal challenge to a contemplated or ongoing use of military force. Yet no American advocating greater judicial activism may properly evade these two salient, delicate problems—*evidence* and *remedies*. Here, foreign models cannot help. While the problems presented by sensitive evidence and the broadsword effects of injunctions are not uniquely associated with foreign-relations cases, it is in that area that they seem to loom as particularly formidable bars to the very idea of resolving conflicts by ordinary judicial recourse.

However, American courts are not without guidance. This can be found not abroad but at home within the perimeters of the national legal culture. Far from foreign-affairs litigation, the system already has developed workable procedures for balancing important national and private interests in a litigious setting. These are applicable by analogy and demonstrate that the judiciary can manage such special problems as protecting security secrets and preventing decisions that would guillotine national strategic initiatives in medias res. In these other adjudicatory contexts, courts have already developed and tested the procedural options that mitigate against the direst consequences of judicial intervention. Two of these will be considered here: the ex parte *in camera* procedures for dealing with sensitive evidence and the *declaratory judgment* as an alternative remedy to ameliorate the guillotine effect of injunctions and mandamus.

The Need to Preserve Secrecy

The risk that litigation will cause embarrassing disclosures of secret information arises in both criminal and civil cases. In criminal proceedings, however, the government usually has the option of sparing its secrets by abandoning a prosecution if it cannot persuade the judge to limit discovery or close the trial.[1] Civil proceedings, how-ever, sometimes present problems of disclosure from which there is no such ready, if costly, escape. Faced with a conflict between the assertion of a private right against an alleged government wrong, courts have had to weigh the social costs of allowing a plaintiff access to sensitive information necessary to his or her cause. When such information impinges on national security or the conduct of foreign relations, the defendant agency will typically seek safety behind the political-question doctrine. As we have seen, judges frequently per-mit recourse to that shield, in part because they share the govern-ment's concern that important secrets will be disclosed in the process of litigation.

This concern has been exaggerated. The risks of harmful disclo-sures are not insuperable. In enacting the Freedom of Information Act (FOIA), Congress has demonstrated the possibility of striking a constructive balance between the individual rights of litigants and the collective security of the nation.[2] The procedures tested in FOIA liti-gation point the way to a balancing approach that could be applied to any civil suits with foreign-affairs or national-security implications.

The Freedom of Information Analogue

Although the FOIA cases for the most part do not involve foreign affairs, they all pertain to the management of sensitive information and thus afford guidance for balancing the same competing inter-ests when they surface in some foreign-policy and national-security litigation.

Congress enacted the FOIA based on two amply justifiable as-sumptions: first, that there are secrets in the possession of policy managers that must be protected from public disclosure if the collec-tive self-interest of the citizenry is to be sustained; second, that policy managers sometimes exaggerate and use the need for secrecy in part to enhance and protect their political power and to escape judicial review. Acting on these two assumptions, Congress in 1967 devised a compromise designed to enhance public access to information with-held through overclassification while allaying genuine security con-cerns. Unique in its scope, the act reversed the prevalent presump-tion in favor of secrecy, substituting one in favor of openness. Rather than list categories of information to be released, it established categories of privilege that are exceptions to citizens' right to know. Governmental information that does not fit one of the exemptions must be made available on request, whatever the applicant's reason for seeking disclosure.

Two of the nine exempt categories are foreign-affairs-related. Exemption (b)(1) protects from disclosure matters "specifically required by Executive Order to be kept secret in the interest of national defense or foreign-policy," and (b)(3) covers information "specifically exempted from disclosure by statute."[3] These two categories have given rise to a repertory of practice well able to guide legislators to enacting more general rules governing all sensitive foreign-affairs and national-security information in civil litigation. In other words, if courts were to assume jurisdiction over foreign-affairs cases in the ordinary way without invoking the political-question doctrine or similar abdicationist strategies, they would be helped if they had specific legislative authority and guidance for balancing the rival imperatives of secrecy and disclosure to advance legally protected private rights with the least cost to public security. The experience of the FOIA presents a ready-made, if flawed, example of judges seeking to strike that balance.

Exemption (b)(1) of the FOIA refers to the president's power to classify national-security information.[4] There are only three levels of secrecy in the American system: *confidential*, relating to information that "could reasonably be expected to cause damage to the national-security"; *secret*, relating to information that "could reasonably be expected to cause serious damage to the national-security"; and *top secret*, relating to information that "could reasonably be expected to cause exceptionally grave damage to the national-security." Under the statute, any—but only—properly classified information may be withheld from public dissemination. That leaves open the key issue whether an item has been classified properly.

Oddly, the law was at first silent on this salient issue of which organ is empowered to determine whether a secret has been classified "properly." The confrontation that forced a legislative reconsideration of this gaping lacuna did not arise under this section but in litigation implicating the even broader exemption from disclosure contained in section (b)(3), which allows agencies to withhold information that must be kept secret in accordance with the requirement of any other statute. Exemption (b)(3) was soon being invoked frequently by reference to the National Security Act, which creates a presumption of secrecy about information that involves national-security. The CIA, FBI, and the National Security Agency used the provision freely as a shield, provoking litigants into raising the "lacuna" issue: In a dispute about access, who should make the ultimate determination of what is "properly" protected from disclosure?

This issue was confronted squarely in *EPA v. Mink*.[5] Until the Supreme Court decided *Mink*, the lower courts were unsure whether they could hear and determine the validity of a challenge to an agency's classification or categorization. Not only was the act silent, but it made no provision for judicial inspection of sensitive information the government was seeking to withhold and envisaged no in camera procedures to permit judicial review without public disclosure. In practice, it soon became apparent that this void essentially nullified the statute. In *Mink*, the Supreme Court forced the problem to a crisis by holding that Congress had not intended courts to review the agencies' classification decisions.[6] However, the judges invited Congress to clarify its position. In 1974, Congress complied. It amended the Freedom of Information Act to authorize judicial review in camera of the appropriateness of governmental classification of a requested document.[7]

This has not entirely laid to rest the difficult problem created by the clash of competing public and private interests and values. However, the law did deal with the tension between individual and collective rights by placing the onus for achieving balance squarely on the judiciary. It has not always welcomed that trust. Subsequent decisions have accepted that the exercise of the discretionary power to review assertions of privilege based on the legislated categories of information exempt from disclosure now rests with the district courts, but the judges have also demonstrated their unease by interpreting their new mandate quite narrowly. For example, it has been held that the courts need not review even in camera documents agencies seek to withhold unless there is independent evidence of the agency's bad faith.[8] This is not an easy standard for petitioners to meet since the prima facie showing must be made without recourse to the withheld evidence.

Even so, there has been enough in camera practice to demonstrate that judges are able to examine withheld information without endangering its confidentiality. In FOIA litigation, agencies now routinely submit information regarding classified materials to a judge, who

makes the preliminary determination of their sensitivity and importance in chambers. In *Halkin v. Helms*,[9] for example, the district court
examined in camera an affidavit from the National Security Agency,[10]
a procedure upheld on appeal with the remark that *"[i]n camera* resolution of the state secrets question was inevitable."[11] The affidavits
must provide extensive summaries in place of the raw materials being
sought by litigants. Typically, the summary itself is classified top secret[12] and gives "a detailed explanation of intelligence sources, methods, or NSA *modus operandi.*"[13]

Similarly, the CIA,[14] the Department of Defense,[15] and the FBI[16] all
now regularly submit affidavits to district-court judges summarizing
highly classified information and explaining their reluctance to disclose the requested materials to litigants. No government agency now
seeks to block these preliminary excursions of the judiciary into the
probity of an agency's reason for nondisclosure.

The willingness of these agencies to disclose and discuss sensitive
information in chambers is indicative for foreign-policy litigation. If
the government can disclose secret information in camera in a FOIA
suit, there is no reason the same procedure could not be applied in
other litigation. There have been no complaints of leaks or premature
disclosure in connection with these FOIA judicial procedures.

More often than the full texts of secret information, summaries are
what judges now routinely review. For the most part, courts have
been satisfied with chamber examinations of affidavits from the agencies seeking to prevent disclosure. The judges rarely require production of the requested documentation in its entirety. Nevertheless, the
affidavits are usually useful in providing detailed information regarding the classified documents themselves. Moreover, since judges
have the power to order production of the raw material, the agencies
are less likely to cheat in preparing the summaries.

Although "only in the exceptional case would the district court be
justified in relying solely on *in camera* affidavits,"[17] these help judges
by supplementing other information presented by claimants. They
usually provide a more detailed explanation of why certain information is being withheld, and they often give a sanitized account of the
information. Affidavits submitted in camera frequently also establish
an index to the documents.[18] These are usually disclosed to counsel,
providing a rudimentary but useful road map through the documentation jungle.[19]

Nevertheless, it is apparent that federal judges continue to interpret their statutory mandate quite narrowly. Only rarely in the many FOIA cases involving national-security information have they demanded to see the raw information. The prevailing practice is for judges to be satisfied with summaries and to treat the agencies in a studiously nonconfrontational manner when evaluating them. In the sixteen years since the *Mink* amendment first gave courts the power to review classifications, only one has ordered the declassification of a CIA document.[20] Judges have treated their role under FOIA very gingerly, creating what amounts to a strong presumption in the classifiers' favor. In *Ellsberg v. Mitchell,* for example, the D.C. Circuit stated that "the more plausible and substantial the government's allegations of danger to national-security . . . the more deferential should be the judge's inquiry into the foundations and scope of the claim."[21] In another suit, the D.C. District Court gave summary judgment for the National Security Agency without allowing the litigant to examine the withheld documents in camera despite his having been a former member of that agency.[22] In many instances, the judges do not even review affidavits in camera, satisfied by the agency's public justification if there is no evidence of bad faith.[23] When judges do require an affidavit, they tend to accord them extraordinary "deference."[24]

While FOIA practice demonstrates the reticence of judges in availing themselves of their post-*Mink* powers of review, that reticence may account in part for the excellent record of agencies in complying with court orders for in camera production of summaries or even raw materials for which privilege is being claimed.[25] A recent example is *Patterson v. Federal Bureau of Investigation* where the FBI responded to an order for in camera access to two withheld documents by "submitting *all* of the unredacted documents at issue as well as the declaration of . . . the FBI Assistant Director in charge of the Intelligence Division."[26]

The courts have the power to review in camera any document for which the government claims an exemption under the FOIA.[27] Although this power has not been broadly exercised, it is clear from the history and language of FOIA that Congress respects the ability of the federal judiciary to determine independently the propriety of classification and to decide what information may be released to the public.[28] At times, this authority has been used to reprimand the classifiers, as in *Jaffe v. Central Intelligence Agency* where, skeptical of the CIA's claims, the court quoted directly from classified documents to demonstrate "dubious classification practices."[29] Again in *Stern v. Richardson*,[30] the court ordered disclosure of several FBI documents after concluding that the documents did not fit any of the exemptions claimed by the FBI.

The FOIA cases are not the only instances of civil litigation where secrets may be at issue.[31] They are, however, the most numerous category and serve as a useful analogy. Some of the cases do deal with foreign affairs but of course only to the limited extent of seeking information. They are not suits to compel a change of policy, at least not directly. Thus, they are not typical of the bulk of cases for which judges have fashioned their general policy of nonjusticiability. The FOIA was not designed to remedy the larger problem of judicial abdication and deference to the political branches, nor did it seek to repeal or amend the political-question doctrine as it applies to foreign-affairs cases. It does not seek a general change in the policy of judicial reticence comparable to that brought about by the Hickenlooper Amendment and the Foreign Sovereign Immunity Act (see chapter 6). The FOIA practice does, however, clearly show how Congress might legislate to empower judges, giving them a coherent mandate to decide cases with foreign-affairs implications, aided by in camera and where necessary ex parte procedures to protect crucial secrets and sources. The FOIA cases also demonstrate that the courts, if mandated, are likely to be more than sensitive to the security needs of the political organs and that a de facto presumption will tend to operate against discovery and other disclosure of information that might seriously endanger the national interest. While the FOIA example demonstrates that judicial review offers no easy road to private litigants in actions against government agencies, it also demonstrates the way to allay the fears most commonly adduced to keep an entire area of government activity beyond the reach of judicial review.

In Camera Proceedings Initiated by the Government

As noted above, the need for courts to protect government secrets most often arises when civil suits are brought by private litigants or occasionally by members of Congress. As we have observed, when legal actions are initiated by the executive, usually in prosecutions, the problem for the courts is mitigated because the government can protect its sensitive information by discontinuing the proceeding. However, when the tactical decision goes against abandoning an important prosecution—for example, when proceedings are under the control of an independent special prosecutor—it is the courts that may inherit the problem of balancing the public interest in punishing wrongdoing and the community's need to protect information with important national-security implications. To pursue this balance, the courts have at their disposal, once again, procedures for in camera examination of evidence whose production is sought by defendants. These procedures too seek a middle course between forcing the prosecutor to reveal information that may cripple the nation's capacity to conduct foreign-policy (the fight against terrorism, for example) and allowing an accused criminal to escape prosecution by default through resort to the discovery tactic popularly known as "graymail."

The ability of courts to find this middle ground is suggested by a terse footnote in the report of *United States v. Nixon*: "At the joint suggestion of the Special Prosecutor and counsel for the President, and with the approval of counsel for the defendants, further proceedings in the District Court were held in camera."[32] The Supreme Court, reviewing this part of the lower court's proceeding, commented: "It is elementary that in camera inspection of evidence is always a procedure calling for scrupulous protection against any release or publication of material not found by the court, at that stage, probably admissible in evidence and relevant to the issues of the trial for which it is sought."[33]

Even when the government has chosen to put its secrets at risk by proceeding to prosecute despite the danger of having to disclose sensitive evidence necessary to the defense, the courts have developed ways to limit that risk. Thus, when asked to compel disclosure, they have held that the "government's interest in the security of its files can be protected through an in camera examination of those documents the [defendant] asserts support his claim."[34] Moreover, judges have observed that it is "not . . . difficult to obtain a court reporter and other essential court personnel with the necessary security clearance."[35]

The mechanism for handling the sensitive information likely to be involved in a criminal prosecution is the Classified Information Procedures Act (CIPA).[36] It provides another analogue for foreign-affairs litigation in general if Congress chooses to legislate standards for adjudication that would further reduce the rationale for reliance on the political-question doctrine. Passed in 1980, the CIPA "was designed to establish procedures to harmonize a defendant's right to obtain and present exculpatory material upon his trial and the government's right to protect classified material in the national interest."[37] The act's definition of classified information is broad and makes specific reference to the national defense and foreign relations of the United States.[38] The law seeks to protect secrets by in camera examination but also allows the court to issue protective orders prohibiting the defendant from disclosing any classified information obtained through discovery.[39] As with the FOIA, challenges to the constitutionality of the CIPA have failed.[40]

The principal purpose of the CIPA is to ensure against overbroad discovery of sensitive evidence. Congress's intent, plainly, was to discourage defendants' claiming access to classified information primarily to deter the government from prosecuting.[41] To achieve this balance between a criminal defendant's right to information useful to a vigorous defense and society's interest in protecting its secrets, the law empowers judges to determine in camera the admissibility of evidence sought by a defendant. This puts a broader responsibility on the judge than merely to make a preliminary determination of relevance, which is a necessary but insufficient test for access to classified information through discovery. Rather, the judge must be satisfied that the evidence sought is likely to be helpful to the defense, that if the evidence obtained establishes what the defense hopes, it will actually be exculpatory. In practice, the judges make this examination of the evidence's "helpfulness" in camera and ex parte.[42] At these inquests, the government generally presents the national-security implications of making the evidence available but will also argue that the materials are not *relevant, material,* or *helpful* to the defense's case.[43] For the defense to prevail, the court must be convinced that the evidence meets all three prerequisites. Only then will a judge order discovery.[44]

While the law thus limits the defense's options, it also habitually propels courts into the middle of controversies pitting governmental claims to protect the national interest against private rights asserted by criminal defendants. The final decision on discovery rests squarely with the courts, which must be alert to the fact that the self-proclaimed protector of the national interest is also an interested party in the criminal prosecution. As the D.C. Circuit said in the 1989 *Yunis* decision, "Obviously, the government cannot be permitted to convert any run-of-the-mine [*sic*] criminal case into a CIPA action merely by frivolous claims of privilege."[45]

Judge Gesell of the D.C. District Court, in the 1988 trial of Admiral John Poindexter, the former national security adviser, in connection with his conduct in the Iran-Contra affair, summarized succinctly the CIPA proceedings as follows:

> Under CIPA, the classified information defendant reasonably expects to present or elicit from witnesses during trial proceedings in open court must go through a three-step process before it may be disclosed. First, the defendant is required to notify the Government and the court in writing of any classified information he reasonably expects to present or elicit from witnesses in pretrial or trial proceedings held in open court. Following such notice, the Government may move for a hearing before the Court on the admissibility of the classified information at issue. Once the Court determines the use, relevance or admissibility of the classified information, it then must decide whether the information will be fully disclosed in open court or whether it is appropriate for the information to be presented in an alternative substituted or redacted form. . . .
>
> If following an in camera hearing the Court deems classified information at issue to be inadmissible, the in camera record is to be sealed in the event of a post-trial appeal by the defendant.[46]

The CIPA also imposes strict limits on defendant's eliciting or disclosing classified information at the trial itself, including information not obtained from the government.[47] At the same time, the court has also sought to ensure the congressional objective that the trial judge "fashion creative and fair solutions" for classified-information problems[48] and that it "should not undertake to balance the national-security interests of the government against the rights of the defendant but rather that in the end remedies and sanctions against the government must be designed to make the defendant whole again. . . . [I]n the end, defendant's constitutional rights must control. . . . A way must be found to preserve defendant's constitutional rights that still affords adequate protection for national-security concerns."[49] In the *Poindexter* case, for example, the judge's creative effort included the institution of in camera ex parte proceedings in which the defendant explained his proposed use of classified evidence at hearings from which the prosecution was excluded to prevent premature disclosure of defense tactics.[50]

Not only may courts require ex parte in camera examination of evidence requested by defendants at the discovery stage of a trial, but courts have also held that a trial judge, exceptionally, may bar the press and public from a part of the trial when a motion by the defendant compels the government to reveal sensitive information.[51] It is thus apparent that by analogy, ways and means have been developed and used that mitigate the claim that much evidence in foreign-relations cases is too sensitive to permit courts to take jurisdiction.

A further example of procedures available to courts in sensitive cases is afforded by the in camera hearings used in connection with electronic surveillance. In camera ex parte proceedings are commonly used in granting warrants for wiretaps to gather evidence regarding domestic crime. The magistrate or judge granting the order thus permits the wiretap without alerting the suspect. The use of in camera proceedings in this instance seems obvious, but until *Katz v. United States*,[52] where the Supreme Court ruled that a wiretap constituted a "search" in the constitutional sense, a warrant was not deemed necessary. Thus, there had been no need for special judicial proceedings to determine probable cause. Once wiretaps were recognized as a search, however, probable cause and the rights of the defendant became issues that were subject to in camera resolution. Once again, courts became the balancers of public and private rights and interests. If a confidential informant is used, an in camera examination of the information provided by that source may be made by the court in determining probable cause.[53] The court may also, on its own initiative, ask to examine the fruits of a wiretap in camera to determine whether the tap collected exculpatory information that should be released to the defendant.[54]

Records of wiretapped communications are often kept sealed to protect privacy.[55] Thus, they may be available only in camera, ex parte.[56] The protection of privacy in wiretap cases is thus another area in which the extension of in camera proceedings has been helpful in aiding courts to balance the need for security and the constitutional protection against governmental hunting expeditions as well as the right of defendants to fair and open judicial proceedings. Some of this jurisprudence is likely to be helpful in fashioning a balanced approach to foreign-affairs litigation in general.

A special case of foreign-affairs electronic surveillance is the use of wiretaps against foreign governments or interests, including terrorist organizations. These wiretaps are instituted primarily to protect the national-security, not to prepare a criminal prosecution. Until recently, the executive branch authorized such surveillance without having to obtain a court order. One of the first cases to hold that a warrant is necessary even here also stressed the ability of the court to sit in camera while hearing evidence to determine whether to issue a warrant.[57] Again, the judges concluded that in camera proceedings permit the court to protect Fourth Amendment rights while enabling the executive branch to fulfill its national-security obligations.[58] Judges have also pointed out that "[i]n a field as delicate and sensitive as foreign intelligence gathering . . . there is every reason why the court should proceed in camera and without disclosure to explore the issue of whether the contents of a foreign intelligence surveillance have any relevance to a criminal prosecution plainly unrelated as to subject matter."[59]

The increased readiness of the courts to engage in such balancing was prompted once again not by the judiciary's voluntarism but by mandating legislation. Since 1978, such official eavesdropping has been regulated by the Foreign Intelligence Surveillance Act (FISA).[60] It allows electronic eavesdropping only after the authorities have obtained a judge's order "approving electronic surveillance of a foreign power or an agent of a foreign power for the purpose of obtaining foreign intelligence information."[61] Such approval may be given by any judge with ordinary jurisdiction or by a specially created extra-secure FISA court.[62] To obtain such an order, the government must file an affidavit stating that an adversarial hearing entailing disclosure to the subject of the tap would compromise national-security. The judge will then review the application ex parte, in camera.[63] This enables the district court to "determine the legality of the surveillance without disclosing the contents of the application."[64] On appeal, the confidentiality of the information continues to be protected by in camera ex parte review of the FISA judge's decision to authorize the surveillance.[65]

Since FISA wiretaps are often issued in cases involving international terrorism and applications for an FISA wiretap may include detailed descriptions of intelligence sources and methods,[66] an inordinate level of secrecy is essential. It is surely of broader significance for all foreign-affairs cases that Congress has thought this essential level of secrecy could be achieved in judicial proceedings, albeit ex parte and in camera,[67] and moreover that the national-security agencies have found that premise workable in practice.

There is still another example of the creative role the judiciary can play when it wants, or is legislatively mandated, to balance the concerns of government and private litigant. In the AT&T case, discussed in chapter 5, it was the judges who took the initiative in fashioning the procedures that succeeded in accommodating both interests. The dispute arose when a subcommittee of the House of Representatives issued a subpoena to the American Telephone and Telegraph Company (AT&T) for records of national-security wiretaps placed over a period of pre-FISA years by various security agencies. The Justice Department, seeking to protect the sources and methods of those agencies, sued to enjoin AT&T from complying "on the ground that compliance might lead to public disclosure . . . with adverse effect on national-security."[68] Judge Harold Leventhal, for the D.C. Circuit Court, wrote an opinion that both summarized the need for judicial umpiring and reconciled the diverse constitutionally based interests. His opinion demonstrated the capacity of courts to fashion evidenciary rules that balance but do not compromise the right of Congress to obtain information necessary to legislate effectively against the equally important and constitutionally based right of the executive to protect its sensitive information. In the process of fashioning this pragmatic balance, the court, explicitly and by demonstration, rejected the government's contention that the case called for judicial abstention under the political-question doctrine.[69] In seeking to find an answer to the "problem of accommodating the needs and powers of two coordinate branches in a situation where each claimed absolute authority,"[70] the court did not perceive abstention as constitutionally required or prudentially appropriate.[71] On the contrary, such a conflict created a necessity for judicial inventiveness to permit a settlement conducive to the legitimate interests of both parties.[72] Both Congress's right to know and the executive's claim to protect security-related secrets were deemed entirely legitimate and entitled to judicial protection.[73]

Having demonstrated that the Constitution, by dividing power, requires compromise, the court at first ordered the congressional and executive branches to work out a compromise that would utilize judicial umpires in resolving impasses.[74] When those bilateral negotiations failed, the court imposed its own impasse-breaking procedures on the antagonists. This involved the Justice Department providing the subcommittee with edited accounts of all wiretap requests and a sample of any ten unedited wiretaps selected by the subcommittee, together with the complete backup memoranda. That unedited sample would permit verification of the accuracy of the other, sanitized information being provided. On the basis of this sample, "the Subcommittee would then decide whether to take a claim of inaccuracy—alleging, for example, executive abuse of the 'foreign intelligence' rubric—to the District Court for resolution. If the District Court, upon in camera inspection of the original and edited memoranda and of the staff notes, found significant inaccuracy, it would take remedial action. The specifics of its actions are a matter for sound discretion. Relief might involve, for example, providing the Subcommittee staff access to a larger sample of unedited memoranda to determine whether any previously discovered inaccuracy was isolated or systematic."[75]

To give this court-fashioned procedure a chance, the judges enjoined AT&T from turning over to the subcommittee all the memoranda received from national-security agencies but warned that if in the opinion of the District Court there were serious inaccuracies in the summaries of the memoranda provided to the subcommittee and this "suggested deviousness, the District Court might conclude that the cooperative approach is unfruitful and unmanageable, and that the court should withdraw from its assistance to the executive by dissolving the injunction."[76]

While Judge Leventhal conceded that the procedure he had devised would entail "some delay while the executive and the judicial branches conduct their respective review, this is an inherent corollary of the existence of coordinate branches. The Separation of Powers," he added, "often impairs efficiency, in terms of dispatch and the immediate functioning of government. It is the long-term staying power of government that is enhanced by the mutual accommodation required by the Separation of Powers."[77]

Another instance of courts fashioning an in camera proceeding in litigation initiated by the government is afforded by extradition hearings. The United States ordinarily does not extradite persons for committing a "political offense." Thus, when the government seeks to extradite someone, the person seeking to avoid extradition may ask the judges to determine whether the offense for which he or she is to stand trial abroad is a "political offense." This may require the court to determine difficult issues, such as whether there was a political uprising in progress of the time and place of the offense.[78] That determination, in turn, may depend either upon sensitive evidence or evidence that was gathered through sensitive means. In those circumstances, courts may elect to hear the evidence in camera as a way to balance the legitimate interests and rights of the parties.[79]

Examining these various instances of ex parte and in camera proceedings, some invented by Congress, others by the courts, it becomes apparent that judicial use of such methods has increased. This proliferation has had the active support and confidence of the political branches, as manifest in the enacting and operation of such laws as the amended Freedom of Information Act, the Foreign Intelligence Surveillance Act, and the Classified Information Procedures Act. While these laws with some frequency operate only to facilitate judicial review in narrow categories of cases implicating foreign-affairs, they illustrate a far broader proposition: It is constitutionally and practically possible to create a framework of rules pertaining to evidence that makes it easier for courts to decide foreign-affairs cases while protecting equally the parties' legitimate but adversarial interests in secrecy and disclosure.

These statutes and court rules have not devised a magical, costless system. Courts have deplored the inherent unfairness of in camera proceedings, especially when conducted ex parte.[80] Cases decided in this way necessarily lack precedential weight.[81] In camera review also creates substantial burdens for the district courts and appellate courts, which may have to view hundreds of documents.[82]

On the other hand, the practice has shown that judges can deal with sensitive information and do so with acumen. Courts now regularly dispose of highly complex "foreign" issues and have proven their competence in matters of serious importance to the national interest.[83] Recent history, culminating in the Nixon-tapes litigation, also rebuts lingering concern that adjudication in such areas of great sensitivity could provoke a confrontation between the executive and the judiciary.[84] The cases examined in this section did not generate a single instance of the government's refusing to provide sensitive information in camera when faced with a direct court order issued in accordance with a procedure explicitly mandated by law.[85] The litigation has not crippled governmental security and for the most part has made exercises of extraordinary governmental prerogatives, such as classification and wiretaps, appear more legitimate than hitherto. If anything, these experiments in judicial review may be faulted for having allowed government to purchase this prized legitimation at the cost of few litigious defeats.

THE LESS CONFRONTATIONAL REMEDY:
DECLARATORY JUDGMENTS

Suppose a plaintiff with undoubted standing—for example, Congress by concurrent resolution of both houses authorizing its leadership to act—were to ask the courts to hold unlawful and unconstitutional a military action initiated by the president without a declaration of war and without conforming to the requirements of the War Powers Act. Suppose further that at the time the suit reaches the trial court, large numbers of American military personnel are already engaged in combat. What remedy could the unlucky judge fashion? Even if he or she came to agree with plaintiffs' argument, the judge would surely and justifiably be reluctant to order an injunction compelling the troops to stop fighting and withdraw from the battle theater. To paraphrase Professor Alexander Bickel, the prospect of such an order raises the dark specter not only that such an order would not be obeyed but, perhaps an even darker prospect, that it might be, with potentially disasterous consequences to American military personnel and the nation's interest, as well as the court's legitimacy.[86]

That dark specter no doubt influenced some federal courts to struggle mightily, as we have seen, to find doctrinal defenses against having to take jurisdiction over such cases, most notably during the Vietnam War era. Moreover, those judicial defenses have been invoked by courts even in foreign-relations cases where there was far less at stake. Thus it is clear that if courts are to be asked to assume in foreign-affairs cases their normal responsibility to say what the law is, they must have at hand a remedy with less stark consequences than an order to desist from or to compel action. Foreign relations can and should be conducted in accordance with the law, but not as invoked by the blade of a judicial guillotine.

153

Fortunately, such a remedy already exists. The Supreme Court has been creative in establishing a middle path between denial of a remedy on one hand and immediate relief on the other. In the 1911 decision in *Virginia v. West Virginia*,[87] the Court observed that a "question like the present should be disposed of without undue delay. But a State cannot be expected to move with the celerity of a private business man; it is enough if it proceeds, in the language of the English Chancery, with all deliberate speed."[88]

The most celebrated instance of the Court's using a "deliberate-speed" order—in its accepted sense of *lento ma non troppo*—is in the *Brown II* school-desegregation decision.[89] The judges there recognized the need to balance private against public interests and ordered the authorities to make a start toward the goal of compliance while leaving it to the lower courts to give them the time necessary to carry out the ruling in an effective manner, taking into account the practical problems. Good-faith steps toward compliance at the earliest practicable date, not an immediate and total reversal of policy, was required of the public authorities.

This equitable discretion of courts is codified in the federal Declaratory Judgment Act of 1934,[90] which permits judges to declare the law without at the same time also compelling compliance; that is, without issuing a mandatory injunction.[91] That law's effect is to permit legal issues to be resolved without requiring the losing party to incur damages for noncompliance or to choose between the costs of hurried compliance and noncompliance. The declaratory remedy is particularly suited to cases in which the issues affect a far wider constituency than the specific plaintiff.[92] This is the case in at least some foreign-policy litigation.

In this choice of remedies, both plaintiffs and judges have a role. While it is usual for parties contesting the constitutionality of government action to sue for remedial relief, they have the option to proceed only for declaratory judgment.[93] The choice between proceeding by injunctive or declaratory relief, however, is ultimately not controlled by plaintiffs but by judges.[94] They may opt for declaratory relief even when neither party has requested it[95] and despite one party's clear preference for an injunction.[96]

It is readily apparent, therefore, that the courts face no insuperable dilemma when they decide cases calling into question the constitutionality or legality of foreign-relations initiatives in medias res. They

have at their disposal remedial options that make it possible to recon-
cile pragmatically the obligation to say what the law is with their duty
not to cripple the political branches in their task of defending the
national interest against foreign adversaries. As this study has previously emphasized, relatively few of the cases in which courts have
refused to adjudicate really raised this grave dilemma. For those
that do, however, a solid body of judicial practice shows the way to
a satisfactory resolution.

The declaratory judgment shows respect without abdicating the
court's responsibility to require conformity with law. It is thus well
suited to judicial intervention in some matters having foreign-affairs
implications. In particular, the jurisprudence pertaining to the declaratory judgment demonstrates the capacity of courts to fashion a
remedy that takes into account the political branches' superior ability
to implement policy in conformity with the requirements of law
and the Constitution. In practice, the courts have used this means in
situations of great delicacy to lower the potential for confrontation.
There is no apparent reason why this remedy is not as applicable to
judicial supervision of the rule of law in foreign-affairs as it was to
school integration, legislative districting, or congressional discipli-
nary procedures.[97]

It is therefore apparent that neither the need for secrecy nor that for
the gradual, phased implementation of a reversal of policy need
inhibit courts from saying what the law is in cases affecting foreign-
policy or national-security. In selected areas of litigation, such as
access to information under the FOIA or wiretap warrants against
suspected terrorists or spies, Congress has already demonstrated its
ability to fashion a procedure that relies for its integrity upon the judiciary. The courts in turn have demonstrated that judicial review need
not compromise national-security. It is appropriate on the basis of
this successful experience to extend its lessons to the entire field of
litigation involving foreign affairs, opening the courts to any dispute
where the constitutional requisites of standing and ripeness are met
while placing at the judges' disposal procedures designed to facilitate
an accommodation between the requisites of individual fairness and
collective safety, between the rule of law and an effective foreign-
policy.

Conclusions: Does the Rule of Law Stop
at the Water's Edge?

JUDICIAL REVIEW, as a countermajoritarian device to protect Americans against the arbitrariness of electorally empowered "factions," was the great innovation the founders of American federalism grafted onto more traditional notions of republican virtue previously advanced by Plato, Machiavelli, Montesquieu, and Hume.[1] Jefferson had observed that "an *electoral despotism* was not the government we fought for."[2] Madison too, in *The Federalist No. 10* and elsewhere, warned against reliance on political organs to protect the basic rights and liberties of the citizen. "No man is allowed to be a judge in his own cause," he wrote, "because his interest would certainly bias his judgment, and, not improbably, corrupt his integrity. With equal, nay with greater reason, a body of men, are unfit to be both judges and parties, at the same time."[3] The legislature was that "body of men" that, Madison passionately believed, must never be allowed to usurp the making of "judicial determinations."[4] It was that body that long before there was reason to contemplate the imperial presidency, embodied the feared supremacy of political power over individual or collective rights of the people. Were Madison and Jefferson alive today, they would undoubtedly express the same concern that the presidency not be the judge of its own cause in a clash between political policy and the rule of law.

Sensitive to this historical perspective, many scholars, but few judges, have openly decried the judiciary's tendency to suspend at the water's edge their jealous defense of the power to say what the law is. Professor Richard Falk, for example, has criticized judges' "*ad hoc* subordinations to executive policy"[5] and urged that if the object of judicial deference is to ensure a single coherent American foreign policy, then that objective is far more likely to be secured if the policy is made in accordance with rules "that are themselves not subject to political manipulation."[6] Moreover, as a nation publicly proclaiming its adherence to the rule of law, Falk notes, it is unedifying for America to refuse to subject to that rule the very aspect of its governance that is most important and apparent to the rest of the world.[7]

Professor Michael Tigar too has argued that the deference courts show to the political organs, when it becomes abdication, defeats the basic scheme of the Constitution because when judges speak of "the people" as "the ultimate guardian of principle" in political-question cases, they overlook the fact that "the people" are the "same undifferentiated mass" that "historically, unmistakably and, at times, militantly insisted that when executive power immediately threatens personal liberty, a judicial remedy must be available."[8]

Professor Louis Henkin, while acknowledging that certain foreign-relations questions are assigned by the Constitution to the discretion of the political branches, also rejects the notion that the judiciary can evade responsibility for deciding the appropriate limits to that discretion, particularly when its exercise comes into conflict with other rights or powers rooted in the Constitution or laws enacted in accordance with its strictures.[9] His views echo earlier ones espoused by Professor Louis Jaffe, who argued that while the courts should listen to advice tendered by the political branches on matters of foreign policy and national security, "[t]his should not mean that the court must follow such advice, but that without it the court should not prostrate itself before the fancied needs of diplomacy and foreign policy. The claim of policy should be made concrete in the particular instance. Only so may its weight, its content, and its value be appreciated. The claims of diplomacy are not absolute; to question their compulsion is not treason."[10]

There has been little outright support from the judiciary for such open calls to repudiate the practice of refusing to adjudicate foreign-affairs cases on their merits. While some judges do refuse to apply the doctrine, holding it inapplicable in the specific situation or passing over it in silence, virtually none have hitherto felt able to repudiate it frontally.

On the other side, some judges continue to argue vigorously for the continued validity of judicial abdication in cases implicating foreign policy or national security. These proponents still rely occasionally on the early shards of dicta and more rarely on archaic British precedents that run counter to the American constitutional ethos.

More frequently today, their arguments rely primarily on a theory of constitutionalism—separation of powers—and several prudential reasons.

This study has tried to demonstrate that both constitutional theory and prudential considerations underpinning judicial deference, abstention, and abdication, are simply, but egregiously, wrong. They ignore both the historical theory of the Constitution and the real situational considerations arising from its application to our nation's foreign policy. The prudentialists, moreover, urge the folly of propelling courts to engage in activities—examining national-security "secrets," for example—yet they ignore the numerous analogous instances where judges already engage in judicial review, including those involving important state secrets, and do so with marked success. The prudential considerations supporting judicial reticence appear to lack seriousness once they are exposed to the light of modern judicial practice.

It is possible to see virtue in the vice of incoherence: at least the practice of judicial abstinence is only inconsistently supported and demonstrated by the judicial record. Nevertheless, it is surely jurisprudential defeatism to celebrate conceptual chaos. And that is what we have. Neither abdicationist nor activist judges make a practice of expatiating on their reasons for accepting or rejecting the political-question doctrine in so-called foreign-affairs cases. On the whole, both sides tend to believe that *cela va sans dire*. They mostly classify and assume; they do not explain. And since some judges assume one thing and some the other, since some see a foreign-relations issue that others see as an issue of free speech, incoherence has become the chief, perhaps the only, characteristic of this jurisprudence, which stumbles along between rivers of dicta and mountains of judicial silence whose peaks are magisterial denials of certiorari.

Not since *Baker v. Carr* has the Supreme Court sought to address the political-question doctrine comprehensively. Then it did not succeed. Since then, America has been involved in the Vietnam War, the El Salvador insurrection, the Angolan civil war, a military confrontation with Nicaragua, and two military deployments in the Persian Gulf. We have bombed Libya and Nicaragua, invaded Grenada and Panama. The institutional and instrumental process by which these and other initiatives have been authorized would surely have surprised Madison, Jefferson, and even Hamilton. They would be

158

shocked to find the federal judiciary two hundred years later unable to determine legal challenges to such presidential initiatives by members of Congress and directly affected citizens.

In asserting that courts are competent to—and *should*—decide, this study has sought to show that when courts do take jurisdiction over foreign-affairs cases, the costs to national policy interests are generally far less than the government may have imagined. A judge's fiat to apply the Jones Act to Bermuda, to permit the *New York Times* to publish the Pentagon Papers, or to allow Mr. Kent to travel does not cause the sky to fall. Even a judge's holding that a war has been launched unconstitutionally would almost certainly be in declaratory form, allowing the president time to get congressional approval or to withdraw in gradual, orderly fashion. More to the point, however, when judges do decide the cases brought to challenge a foreign policy, it may safely be assumed, if the past judicial record is prologue, that they would reach out in an effort to agree with the story told by the president's experts. In all but the most egregious instances, they would find a challenged presidential action constitutional and legal. In the German Federal Republic, where judges always decide, there is a clearly discernible pattern of judicial concern for the governmental perspective and respect for the prerogatives of political power in the conduct of foreign relations.

Thus no reasonable foreign-policy manager ought to fear the U.S. courts. Had American judges followed the same jurisprudential path as their German brethren, is it even conceivable that they would have decided that, yes, U.S. aid to Israel does indeed violate RICO or the constitutionally mandated separation of church and state? Pusillanimity and deference, not exaggerated assertiveness, have marked almost every excursion by the American judiciary into foreign-affairs cases. In this they vary not one whit from their German brethren. The costs of judicial review of such cases to presidential discretion has been vastly overstated, not least by the judges themselves.

On the other hand, not to decide has heavy costs, precisely in the area of foreign policy. America's principal shield and sword is not the nuclear bomb but the most powerful idea in today's political marketplace. That idea is the rule of law. To make the law's writ inoperable at the water's edge is nothing less than an exercise in unilateral moral disarmament. It is a strategy urgently in need of judicial review.

❖ *Notes* ❖

CHAPTER ONE
INTRODUCTION

1. *See Worcester v. Georgia*, 31 U.S. (6 Pet.) 515 (1832).

2. *Marbury v. Madison*, 5 U.S. (1 Cranch) 137, 176–78 (1803).

3. Hamilton, *The Federalist No. 78*, in *The Federalist* 522 (J. Cooke ed. 1961).

4. *Id*. at 524.

5. *See* 1978 Digest of United States Practice in International Law, sec. 3 at 80–83; 1973 Digest of United States Practice in International Law, sec. 3 at 11–13.

CHAPTER TWO
HOW ABDICATION CREPT INTO THE JUDICIAL REPERTORY

1. *Baker v. Carr*, 369 U.S. 186, 197 (1962) (reversing lower court's determination that apportionment of congressional districts was a "distribution of political strength for legislative purposes").

2. *Keyes v. School Dist. No. 1*, 413 U.S. 189 (1973) (providing relief to alleviate school-district "gerrymandering of student attendance zones"); *Swann v. Charlotte-Mecklenburg Bd. of Educ.*, 402 U.S. 1 (1971).

3. *Johnson v. Transportation Agency, Santa Clara County*, 480 U.S. 616 (1987) (approving affirmative-action plan by agency that sought to increase gradually the representation of minorities and women within the fire-department staff). *See also United Steelworkers of America v. Weber*, 443 U.S. 193 (1979) (approving collective-bargaining agreement containing affirmative-action program for black steelworkers).

4. *Regents of the University of California v. Bakke*, 438 U.S. 265 (1978) (rejecting regents' establishment of a quota for minority recruitment at the Medical School of the University of California).

5. *See Mitchell v. Laird*, 488 F.2d 611 (D.C. Cir. 1973); *Atlee v. Laird*, 347 F. Supp. 689, 704 (E.D. Pa. 1972) and cases cited therein by Judge Adams, *aff'd sub nom. Atlee v. Richardson*, 411 U.S. 911 (1973).

6. *See Holtzman v. Schlesinger*, 361 F. Supp. 553 (E.D.N.Y.), *rev'd*, 484 F.2d 1307 (2d Cir. 1973), *cert. denied*, 416 U.S. 936 (1974).

7. *See, e.g., Mitchell v. Laird, supra* note 5, at 616 ("In short, we are faced with what has traditionally been called a 'political question' which is beyond the judicial power conferred by Article III of the United States Constitution").

8. *See, e.g., Smith v. Reagan*, 844 F.2d 195 (4th Cir. 1988), *cert. denied*, 488 U.S. 954 (1988); *Americans United for Separation of Church & State v. Reagan*, 786

161

F.2d 194 (3d Cir.), *cert. denied sub nom. American Baptist Churches v. Reagan*, 479 U.S. 914 (1986).

9. *Marbury v. Madison*, 5 U.S. (1 Cranch) 137, 177 (1803).

10. *Brown v. Board of Education*, 347 U.S. 483 (1954) (denouncing the "separate but equal" doctrine announced by *Plessy v. Ferguson*, 163 U.S. 537 (1896) as a "denial of equal protection of the laws").

11. *Miller v. California*, 413 U.S. 15 (1973) (adopting a "forum-community" standard to deny constitutional protection to the mailing of unsolicited sexually explicit material); *Roth v. United States*, 354 U.S. 476 (1957) (removing obscenity from the area of constitutionally protected speech or press).

12. *Roe v. Wade*, 410 U.S. 113 (1973) (formulating a woman's right not to continue a pregnancy).

13. *Bowers v. Hardwick*, 478 U.S. 186 (1986) (state laws criminalizing sodomy, even among consenting adults, do not violate the Constitution).

14. *Furman v. Georgia*, 408 U.S. 238 (1972) (requiring principled means when applying capital punishment).

15. Abridgment of the Congress, Mar. 7, 1800, at 466. For an informative discussion of the Jonathan Robbins case, see Wedgewood, "The Revolutionary Martyrdom of Jonathan Robbins," 100 Yale L.J. 229 (1990).

16. *The Cherokee Nation v. Georgia*, 30 U.S. (5 Pet.) 1, 20 (1831).

17. *Id.* at 30.

18. *Id.*

19. *See, e.g.*, Debate in North Carolina Ratifying Convention, July 29–30, 1788, in 4 *The Founders' Constitution* 601–06, 604 (B. Kurland & R. Lerner eds. 1987).

20. This broad refusal to permit treaties to be litigated as if they were ordinary laws has since been judicially modified. Indeed, one year later, in *Worcester v. Georgia*, 31 U.S. (6 Pet.) 515 (1832), the Supreme Court itself cast doubt on the decision in *Cherokee*. Georgia had arrested, tried, and jailed two missionaries in Cherokee country. The Supreme Court issued a writ of error and reversed the conviction on the ground that such state action violated rights vested by the Cherokee treaties, which were "laws of the United States." The Court thereby decided the very issue it had abjured at its previous session, finding the agreements between the United States and the Indians "treaties" in the constitutional sense and holding Georgia in violation of the rights guaranteed thereunder. For a discussion of these two cases, see L. Jaffe, *Judicial Aspects of Foreign Relations* 18–19 (1933). Subsequently, there have been important cases in which courts also have agreed to resolve conflicts between U.S. treaties and state action. *See Missouri v. Holland*, 252 U.S. 416 (1920). They have also distinguished between self-executing and non-self-executing agreements, making the former enforceable even at the instigation of individuals. *Edwards v. Carter*, 580 F.2d 1055 (D.C. Cir.), *cert. denied*, 436 U.S. 907 (1978).

21. *United States v. Lee*, 106 U.S. 196 (1882).

22. *Id*. at 206.

23. *Id*. at 208.

24. *Id*. at 208–09 (emphasis in original).

25. *Id*. at 209.

26. *United States v. Noriega*, 746 F. Supp. 1506, 1539 (S.D. Fla. 1990).

27. *United States v. Curtiss-Wright Export Corp.*, 299 U.S. 304 (1936).

28. H.R.J. Res. 347, 73rd Cong., 2d Sess., 48 Stat. 811 (1934).

29. *United States v. Curtiss-Wright Export Corp.*, *supra* note 27, at 319–20.

30. Levitan, "The Foreign Relations Power: An Analysis of Mr. Justice Sutherland's Theory," 55 Yale L.J. 467, 473–78 (1946).

31. *See* U.S. Const. art. I, secs. 7, 8; art. II, sec. 2.

32. Hamilton, *The Federalist No. 78*, in *The Federalist* 525 (J. Cooke ed. 1961).

33. *Id*. at 526.

34. *United States v. Verdugo-Urquidez*, 110 S. Ct. 1056 (1990).

35. *United States v. Curtiss-Wright Export Corp.*, *supra* note 27, at 320.

36. *Id.*

37. *Id*. at 315–18.

38. *Cohens v. Virginia*, 19 U.S. (6 Wheat.) 264 (1821).

39. *Id*. at 399–400.

40. *Coleman v. Miller*, 307 U.S. 433 (1939).

41. *Id*. at 454–55.

42. *Baker v. Carr*, *supra* note 1.

43. *Id*. at 211 (citations omitted).

44. *Colegrove v. Green*, 328 U.S. 549 (1946). For cases relying on *Colegrove v. Green*, see *Baker v. Carr*, *supra* note 1, at 208–09.

45. *Luther v. Borden*, 48 U.S. (7 How.) 1, 29 (1849).

46. *Powell v. McCormack*, 395 U.S. 486 (1969).

47. *Barnes v. Kline*, 759 F.2d 21 (D.C. Cir. 1985), *vacated as moot sub nom. Burke v. Barnes*, 479 U.S. 361 (1987).

48. *Id*. at 26–27 (citations omitted).

49. *Id*. at 28 (citing Powell, J. in *Goldwater v. Carter*, 444 U.S. 996 (1979)).

50. *United States v. Munoz-Flores*, 110 S. Ct. 1964 (1990). Here the political-question doctrine was held not to bar judicial review of whether legislation impounding funds of convicted criminals to compensate victims of crime originated in the Senate in violation of the "origination clause" (art. I, sec. 7, cl. 1) of the Constitution, which requires revenue-raising bills to originate in the House of Representatives. The executive had argued that the fact that the House had passed the bill ought to preclude review because it was capable of defending its own constitutional prerogatives and that moreover there were no "judicially manageable standards" by which courts could judge whether a measure was a "revenue raising" one. *Id*. at 1968–71. The Supreme Court rejected all these contentions. *Id*. at 1971.

51. *See, e.g., Coleman v. Miller, supra* note 40, in which the Supreme Court refused to decide how long a congressionally approved constitutional amendment remains open for state ratification and whether a prior defeat of ratification by a state legislature can subsequently be rescinded.

52. *See, e.g., Powell v. McCormack, supra* note 46; *Barnes v. Kline, supra* note 47.

53. *Lowry v. Reagan*, 676 F. Supp. 333 (D.D.C. 1987).

54. *Foster v. Neilson*, 27 U.S. (2 Pet.) 253 (1829).

55. *Id.* at 307.

56. *Id.*

57. *Id.* at 303–04.

58. *Id.* at 308.

59. *Id. See also Garcia v. Lee*, 37 U.S. (12 Pet.) 511, 520 (1838).

60. *See especially Foster v. Neilson, supra* note 54, at 312–13.

61. The *Prize Cases*, 67 U.S. (2 Black) 635 (1862).

62. *Id.* at 670.

63. *Id.* (emphasis in original).

64. *Terlinden v. Ames*, 184 U.S. 270 (1902).

65. *Id.* at 288.

66. *Id.* at 282–85.

67. *Id.* at 285.

68. *Id.*

69. *Id.*

70. Quoted in *id.* at 287.

71. *The Fisheries Case* (United Kingdom v. Norway) 1951 I.C.J. Rep. 116.

72. *Clark v. Allen*, 331 U.S. 503 (1947).

73. Justice Rutledge concurred in part.

74. Treaty of Friendship, Commerce and Consular Rights of 1925, 44 Stat. 2132, art. IV (1925).

75. By 1946, at the time of this litigation, the attorney general had succeeded to the custodian's role. *Clark v. Allen, supra* note 72, at 506.

76. *Id.* at 514.

77. *Id.* at 513.

78. *Id.*

79. *Id.*

80. *Id.* at 513–14.

81. Conversely, there are cases in which the courts do deploy the separation-of-powers rationale of the political-question doctrine without so labeling it, thereby causing the same research difficulty for computer buffs. *Cf. Gilligan v. Morgan*, 413 U.S. 1 (1973).

82. *Sevilla v. Elizalde*, 112 F.2d 29 (D.C. Cir. 1940).

83. 5 Rotuli Par. 375 (House of Lords, 1460).

84. Quoted in *Sevilla v. Elizade, supra* note 82, at 32.

85. *Id.* at 35–36.

86. *Holtzman v. Schlesinger, supra* note 6.

87. 484 F.2d at 1308–09.

88. *Id.* at 1313.

89. *Id.* at 1315.

90. *Crockett v. Reagan*, 720 F.2d 1355 (D.C. Cir. 1983), *cert. denied*, 467 U.S. 1251 (1984).

91. *Id.* at 1356–57.

92. *Id.* at 1357.

93. *Kashani v. Nelson*, 793 F.2d 818, 827 (7th Cir. 1985) (quoting *Harisiades v. Shaughnessy*, 345 U.S. 206, 210 (1953)), *cert. denied*, 479 U.S. 1006 (1986).

94. *Id.* at 819–25.

95. *Id.* at 823.

96. *Smith v. Reagan, supra* note 8.

97. 22 U.S.C. sec. 1732 (1982).

98. *Smith v. Reagan, supra* note 8, at 198.

99. *Id.* at 199.

100. *Id.* at 201.

101. *Belk v. United States*, 858 F.2d 706 (Fed. Cir. 1988).

102. *Id.* at 710.

103. *Id.* at 709.

104. *Eveland v. Director of C.I.A.*, 843 F.2d 46 (1st Cir. 1988).

105. Although it was unclear against which officials the action was brought, the plaintiff made service upon the following persons, and the court deemed them the only defendants: Richard Helms, William E. Colby, Kermit Roosevelt, Sr., Archibald B. Roosevelt, Henry Kissinger, Robert McFarlane, James J. Angleton, and George P. Shultz. *Id.* at 47.

106. *Id.* at 49.

107. *Id.* at 50–51.

108. *Id.* at 50.

109. Generally a court will not disturb an agency's determinations "unless they are arbitrary, capricious, or manifestly contrary" to the powers delegated to the agency by Congress. *Chevron U.S.A. Inc. v. Natural Resources Defense Council, Inc.*, 467 U.S. 837, 844 (1984).

110. *Eveland v. Director of C.I.A.*, *supra* note 104, at 48.

111. *Antolok v. United States*, 873 F.2d 369 (D.C. Cir. 1989).

112. *Id.* at 373–79.

113. *Id.* at 379.

CHAPTER THREE
TWO PRINCIPLED THEORIES OF CONSTITUTIONALISM

1. A. Bickel, *The Least Dangerous Branch* 111–98 (1962).

2. *Id.* at 184.

3. W. Blackstone, 1 *Commentaries* 250 (T. Cooley ed., 3d ed. 1884).

4. *Id.*

5. Hamilton, *The Federalist No. 75*, in *The Federalist* 505–06 (J. Cooke ed. 1961).

6. D. Richards, *Foundations of American Constitutionalism* 74–75 (1989) (citations omitted).

7. *The Prize Cases*, 67 U.S. (2 Black) 670 (1862) (emphasis in original).

8. *Id.* at 690.

9. *Id.* at 695.

10. *Id.* at 697 (emphasis added).

11. *Johnson v. Eisentrager*, 339 U.S. 763 (1950).

12. *In re Yamashita*, 327 U.S. 1 (1946).

13. *Johnson v. Eisentrager, supra* note 11, at 789.

14. *Id.*

15. *Id.* at 795.

16. *Id.* at 797–98.

17. *Reid v. Covert*, 354 U.S. 1 (1957).

18. *Id.* at 17. It is instructive to compare Black and Douglas's separate concurring opinion in *Z. & F. Assets Realization Corp. v. Hull*, 311 U.S. 470 (1941) in which they insist that in a matter pitting a citizen's alleged monetary interest against an executive exercise of legislatively delegated discretion, the Court's duty is to avoid a "square clash between the executive and judicial branches" because the former "is the ultimate arbiter of momentous questions of public policies affecting this nation's relations with the other countries of the world." *Id.* at 493.

19. *Baker v. Carr*, 369 U.S. 186, 211 (1962) (reversing lower court's determination that apportionment of congressional districts was a "distribution of political strength for legislative purposes").

20. *Goldwater v. Carter*, 444 U.S. 996 (1979).

21. U.S. Const. art. VI.

22. *Goldwater v. Carter, supra* note 20, at 1004.

23. *Id.* at 997.

24. *Id.* at 1006.

25. *Id.*

26. *Id.* at 996.

27. *Goldwater v. Carter*, 617 F.2d 697 (D.C. Cir. 1979).

28. *Goldwater v. Carter*, 481 F. Supp. 949 (D.C. Cir. 1979).

29. *Goldwater v. Carter, supra* note 20, at 1002.

30. *Id.* at 1006.

31. *Id.* at 1006–07 (citations omitted).

32. *Baker v. Carr, supra* note 19.

33. *Id.* at 217.

34. *Id.* For a further illumination of Justice Brennan's views, which, however, did not command the support of a majority of the Court's justices, see his dissent in *Goldwater v. Carter, supra* note 20, at 1006.

35. L. Jaffe, *Judicial Aspects of Foreign Relations* 14 (1933).

36. *Z. & F. Assets Realization Corp. v. Hull*, 114 F.2d 464, 468 (D.C. Cir. 1940), *aff'd*, 311 U.S. 470 (1941). To similar effect, see *Logan v. Secretary of State*, 553 F.2d 107 (D.C. Cir. 1976); *Freiberg v. Muskie*, 651 F.2d 608 (8th Cir. 1981). These cases seek to compel a change in U.S. government strategy respecting pursuit of plaintiffs' claims against a foreign government. Each of these could readily have been resolved on the merits by a judicial finding that the State Department was acting within its authorized ambit of discretion.

37. *Sneaker Circus, Inc. v. Carter*, 566 F.2d 396 (2d Cir. 1977).

38. *Id*. at 401 (citation omitted).

39. *Durand v. Hollins*, 8 Fed. Cas. 111 (C.C.S.D.N.Y. 1860) (No. 4,186).

40. *Id*. at 111.

41. *Id*. at 112.

42. *Id*.

43. *Id*.

44. *Farmer v. Rountree*, 252 F.2d 490 (6th Cir.), *cert. denied*, 357 U.S. 906 (1958).

45. *Id*. at 491.

46. *Conyers v. Reagan*, 578 F. Supp. 324 (D.D.C. 1984).

47. *Conyers v. Reagan*, 765 F.2d 1124 (D.C. Cir. 1985).

48. *Dickson v. Ford*, 521 F.2d 234 (5th Cir. 1975), *cert. denied*, 424 U.S. 954 (1976).

49. *Id*. at 235.

50. *Id*. at 236, *citing Oetjen v. Central Leather Co.*, 246 U.S. 297, 302 (1918).

51. *See Americans United for Separation of Church & State v. Reagan*, 786 F.2d 194 (3d Cir.), *cert. denied sub nom. American Baptist Churches v. Reagan*, 479 U.S. 914 (1986).

52. *Tel-Oren v. Libyan Arab Republic*, 726 F.2d 774 (D.C. Cir. 1984), *cert. denied*, 470 U.S. 1003 (1985).

53. *Id*. at 804.

54. *United States v. Uhl*, 137 F.2d 903 (2d Cir. 1943).

55. *Id*. at 906.

56. *Dole v. Carter*, 569 F.2d 1109, 1110 (10th Cir. 1977).

57. *United States v. Baker*, 24 Fed. Cas. 962 (C.C.S.D.N.Y. 1861) (No. 14, 501).

58. Madison, *Letters of Helvedius*, No. 1 of Aug. 24, 1793, in 6 *The Writings of James Madison* 145 (G. Hunt ed. 1906).

59. *Lowry v. Reagan*, 676 F. Supp. 333 (D.D.C. 1987).

60. 50 U.S.C. sec. 1543(a)(l) (1988).

61. 50 U.S.C. sec. 1544(b) (1988).

62. *Lowry v. Reagan*, *supra* note 59, at 337–39.

63. *Id*. at 339.

64. *Id*.

65. *Id*. The separate concurring opinion of Justice Powell in *Goldwater v. Carter, supra* note 20, at 997, admittedly lends support to this requirement on grounds of "ripeness," although he specifically rejects a conceptual link between this ripeness requirement, which goes to the question of standing, and the political-question doctrine. *Id*. Ripeness is also employed in the separate concurring opinion by Judge Ginsburg in *Sanchez-Espinoza v. Reagan*, 770 F.2d 202 (D.C. Cir. 1985), in which he states that "no gauntlet has been thrown down here by a majority of the Members of Congress" and that if Congress does not act specifically to confront the president, the judiciary certainly should not do so. *Id*. at 211.

66. *Lowry v. Reagan*, No. 87-5426 (D.C. Cir. Oct. 17, 1988).

67. *Commonwealth of Massachusetts v. Laird*, 400 U.S. 886 (1970).

68. *Id*. at 893, 897–98.

Chapter Four
Prudential Reasons for Judical Abdication

1. *See* chapter 5, *infra*.

2. *Foster v. Neilson*, 27 U.S. (2 Pet.) 307–09 (1829).

3. *Williams v. The Suffolk Ins. Co.*, 38 U.S. (3 Pet.) 415, 420 (1839). *See also Pearcy v. Stranahan*, 205 U.S. 257 (1906).

4. *Williams v. The Suffolk Ins. Co.*, at 420.

5. *Jones v. United States*, 137 U.S. 202 (1890).

6. *Id*. at 217.

7. *Id*. at 216.

8. *See Lehigh Valley R. Co. v. State of Russia*, 21 F.2d 396 (2d Cir.), *cert. denied*, 275 U.S. 571 (1927); *The Maret*, 145 F.2d 431 (3d Cir. 1944).

9. *See Republic of Panama v. Republic National Bank*, 681 F. Supp. 1066 (S.D.N.Y. 1988); *Republic of Panama v. Citizens & Southern Int'l Bank*, 682 F. Supp. 1544 (S.D. Fla. 1988).

10. *Baker v. Carr*, 369 U.S. 186, 217 (1962).

11. *Oetjin v. Central Leather Co.*, 246 U.S. 297, 302 (1918).

12. *Id*. at 304.

13. *Compania Espanola de Navegacion Maritima, S.A. v. The Navemar*, 303 U.S. 68, 74 (1938). *See also Sullivan v. State of Sao Paulo*, 122 F.2d 355 (2d Cir. 1941).

14. *See Mitchell v. Laird*, 488 F.2d 616 (D.C. Cir. 1973).

15. *Id*.

16. *Holtzman v. Schlesinger*, 361 F. Supp. 553 (E.D.N.Y.), *rev'd*, 484 F.2d 1307 (2d Cir. 1973), *cert. denied*, 416 U.S. 936 (1974).

17. 484 F.2d at 1310. *See also Smith v. Reagan*, 844 F.2d 195 (4th Cir. 1988), *cert. denied*, 488 U.S. 954 (1988).

18. *Baker v. Carr, supra* note 10, at 217.

19. *Occidental of Umm al Qaywayn, Inc. v. A Certain Cargo of Petroleum*, 577 F.2d 1196, 1198 (5th Cir. 1978), *cert. denied sub nom. Occidental of Umm al Qaywayn, Inc. v. Cities Serv. Oil Co.*, 442 U.S. 928 (1979).

20. *Id.* at 1203–04.

21. *Id.* at 1204–05.

22. *Banco Nacional de Cuba v. Sabbatino*, 376 U.S. 398 (1964).

23. *Id.* at 428 (citation omitted).

24. *Id.* at 431.

25. *Id.* at 434.

26. *See Korematsu v. United States*, 323 U.S. 214 (1944). *Compare Korematsu v. United States (Korematsu II)*, 584 F. Supp. 1406 (N.D. Cal. 1984).

27. *United States v. Belmont*, 301 U.S. 324 (1937).

28. *Id.* at 328.

29. *Id.* at 330.

30. *Id.* at 331.

31. *Id.* at 332.

32. *United States v. Pink*, 315 U.S. 203 (1942).

33. *Id.* at 212.

34. *Id.* at 211.

35. *Id.* at 214.

36. *Id.* at 217.

37. *Id.* at 222–23.

38. *Id.* at 227.

39. *Id.*

40. *Id.* H.R.J. Res. 315, 53 Stat. 1199 (1939).

41. *Id.* at 228–29.

42. *Id.* at 228.

43. *Id.* at 229.

44. *Baker v. Carr, supra* note 10.

45. *United States v. Pink, supra* note 32, at 240.

46. *Id.* at 242.

47. *Harisiades v. Shaughnessy*, 342 U.S. 580 (1952).

48. *Id.* at 588–89 (citation omitted).

49. *Id.* at 600.

50. *Id.*

51. *Chicago & Southern Air Lines v. Waterman Steamship Corp.*, 333 U.S. 103 (1948).

52. *Id.* at 106.

53. *Id.* at 109–10.

54. *Id.* at 111.

55. *Id.*

56. *Id.* at 116.

57. *See Crockett v. Reagan*, 720 F.2d 1355, 1357 (D.C. Cir. 1983) (J. Bork, concurring), *cert. denied*, 467 U.S. 1251 (1984); *Holtzman v. Schlesinger, supra* note 16, at 1315.

58. *See Prize Cases*, 67 U.S. (2 Black) 670 (1862); *see also Holtzman v. Schlesinger, supra* note 16, at 1313.

59. *Mitchell v. Laird, supra* note 14.

60. *Id.* at 615.

61. *Id.* at 616.

62. *Id.*

63. *Id.*

64. For a more conventional case holding that Congress may choose any of several means to consent to presidential warmaking and that this choice is insulated from judicial review by the political-question doctrine, *see Orlando v. Laird*, 443 F.2d 1039 (2d Cir.), *cert. denied*, 404 U.S. 869 (1971).

65. A. Bickel, *The Least Dangerous Branch* 184 1962).

66. *United States v. Lee*, 106 U.S. 209 (1882).

67. *See, e.g., Kent v. Dulles*, 357 U.S. 116 (1958).

68. *See I.N.S. v. Chadha*, 462 U.S. 944 (1983).

69. *See, e.g., Greer v. United States*, 378 F.2d 931, 933 (5th Cir. 1967).

70. *See* Tigar, "Judicial Power, the 'Political Question Doctrine,' and Foreign Relations," 17 U.C.L.A. L. Rev. 1135, 1149–52 (1970). For mootness, see *Conyers v. Reagan*, 765 F.2d 1124 (D.C. Cir. 1985).

71. *See Lockerty v. Phillips*, 319 U.S. 182 (1943); *Yakus v. United States*, 321 U.S. 414 (1944).

72. *Mitchell v. Laird, supra* note 14, at 616.

73. *The Cherokee Nation v. Georgia*, 30 U.S. (5 Pet.) 1, 20 (1831).

74. *Worcester v. Georgia*, 31 U.S. (6 Pet.) 515 (1832).

75. C. Warren, 1 *The Supreme Court in United States History* 759 (rev. ed. 1926), *citing* H. Greeley, 1 *The American Conflict* 106 (1864).

76. *See, e.g.,* Leuchtenburg, "The Origins of Franklin D. Roosevelt's 'Court-Packing' Plan," 1966 Sup. Ct. Rev. 347; Leuchtenburg, "FDR's Court-Packing Plan: A Second Life, a Second Death," 1985 Duke L.J. 673.

77. *See, e.g.,* Pollack, "The Supreme Court Under Fire," 6 J. Pub. L. 428, 428–31 (1957) (discussing populist efforts to impeach Earl Warren); Burbank, "Alternative Career Resolution: An Essay on the Removal of Federal Judges," 76 Ky. L.J. 643, 645–46 (1987–88) (same).

CHAPTER FIVE
WHEN JUDGES REFUSE TO ABDICATE

1. *The Paquete Habana*, 175 U.S. 677, 700 (1900).

2. *Ware v. Hylton*, 3 U.S. (3 Dall.) 199 (1796).

3. *Id.* at 281 (emphasis in original). In this case, John Marshall made his

only appearance as counsel before the Supreme Court, on behalf of the losing party. L. Henkin, *Foreign Affairs and the Constitution* 392 n.65 (1972).

4. *Foster v. Neilson*, 27 U.S. (2 Pet.) 253 (1829).

5. *Id* at 307.

6. *Mitchell v. Harmony*, 54 U.S. (13 How.) 115 (1851).

7. *Id.* at 133.

8. *Id.* at 134.

9. *Id.*

10. *Id.* at 135.

11. *Id.*

12. *Youngstown Sheet & Tube Co. v. Sawyer*, 343 U.S. 579 (1952).

13. *Id.* at 634–55.

14. "Presidential powers are not fixed but fluctuate, depending upon their disjunction or conjunction with those of Congress." *Id.* at 635.

15. *Id.* at 635 n.2.

16. *Id.* at 635.

17. *Id.* at 638.

18. *Id.* at 640.

19. *Id.* at 642 (citation omitted).

20. *Id.* at 643–44 (emphasis in original).

21. *Id.* at 646.

22. *Id.* at 647 (emphasis added). Jackson was responding to the argument that as attorney general, he had advanced assertions of inherent presidential power in foreign-relations and national-security affairs.

23. "Regardless of the general reference to 'inherent powers,' the citations were instances of congressional authorization." *Id.* at 649 n.17.

24. *Id.* at 652.

25. *Id.* at 655 (citation omitted).

26. *Id.* at 596.

27. *Ramirez de Arellano v. Weinberger*, 724 F.2d 143 (D.C. Cir. 1983), *rev'd*, 745 F.2d 1500 (D.C. Cir. 1984), *vacated*, 471 U.S. 1113 (1985), *on remand*, 788 F.2d 762 (D.C. Cir. 1986).

28. Judges Bork, Scalia, and Starr dissented on the grounds that there was no standing (given the separation-of-powers issues raised by the proper deference due the political branches of the government). 745 F.2d at 1550–74. Judge Tamm dissented under a strict political-question approach. *Id.* at 1545–50.

29. *Id.* at 1515; *see also id.* at 1542 ("While separation of powers concerns may outweigh judicial adjudication in the typical case involving a foreign act of state, the prudential balance may shift decidedly when United States citizens assert constitutional violations by United States officials").

30. 724 F.2d at 147 ("The district court's concern about interfering with our foreign policy of providing assistance to threatened governments of Central

America is a valid one"); *see also id.* at 148 ("The issuance of an injunction is discretionary, and where that remedy will intrude into the conduct of foreign affairs it should be granted only on an extraordinarily strong showing").

31. In November 1985, all U.S. military personnel departed, and all U.S.-owned facilities were removed from plaintiffs' land. *See* 788 F.2d at 764 ("Upon consideration of these recent developments, we are persuaded that dismissal of the complaint should be upheld on the narrow ground that the controversy has now become too attenuated to justify the extraordinary relief sought through equity's intervention").

32. *Id.*

33. *Dames & Moore v. Regan*, 453 U.S. 654 (1981).

34. Exec. Order No. 12,170, 3 C.F.R sec. 457 (1980).

35. *See* 31 C.F.R secs. 535.203(e), 535.504(a), and 535.805 (1980).

36. Declaration of the Government of the Democratic and Popular Republic of Algeria Concerning the Settlement of Claims by the Government of the United States of America and the Government of the Islamic Republic of Iran (Jan. 19, 1981).

37. Exec. Order Nos. 12,276–12,285, 46 Fed. Reg. 7,913–7,932 (Jan. 23, 1981).

38. Exec. Order No. 12,294, 46 Fed. Reg. 14,111 (Feb. 26, 1981).

39. *See United States v. Belmont*, 301 U.S. 324 (1937); *United States v. Pink*, 315 U.S. 203 (1942).

40. *Youngstown Sheet & Tube Co. v. Sawyer*, *supra* note 12.

41. Pub. L. No. 95-223, 91 Stat. 1626. Codified at 50 U.S.C. secs. 1701–1706 (1988).

42. *Dames & Moore v. Regan*, *supra* note 33, at 668.

43. *Id.* at 669–74.

44. *Id.* at 668.

45. *Oetjen v. Central Leather Co.*, 246 U.S. 297, 302 (1918).

46. *Guaranty Trust Co. v. United States*, 304 U.S. 126 (1938).

47. *Id.* at 138–41.

48. For a discussion of the ensuing three cases, this study draws on T. Franck, *The Power of Legitimacy Among Nations* 131–32 (1990).

49. *Salimoff & Co. v. Standard Oil Co.*, 262 N.Y. 220, 186 N.E. 679 (1933).

50. *Id.* at 224, 186 N.E. at 681.

51. *Id.* at 227, 186 N.E. at 682.

52. *Id.* at 228, 186 N.E. at 683.

53. *Upright v. Mercury Bus. Mach. Co.*, 13 A.D.2d 36, 213 N.Y.S.2d 417 (1961).

54. *Id.* at 38, 213 N.Y.S.2d at 419.

55. *Id.* at 39, 213 N.Y.S.2d at 420.

56. *Id.* at 41, 213 N.Y.S.2d at 422.

57. *Id.*

58. *Morgan Guaranty Trust Co. v. Republic of Palau*, 639 F. Supp. 706, 713 (S.D.N.Y. 1986).

59. *Id.* at 714. *See, similarly, Iran-Handicraft & Carpet Export Center v. Marjan Int'l Corp.*, 655 F. Supp. 1275 (S.D.N.Y. 1987); but *see contra, Republic of Panama v. Republic National Bank*, 681 F. Supp. 1066 (S.D.N.Y. 1988).

60. *Tastar Chem. Co. v. United States*, 116 F. 726 (C.C.S.D.N.Y. 1902).

61. *Id.* at 729.

62. *Id.* at 728.

63. *Id.* at 729–30.

64. *Vermilya-Brown Co. v. Connell*, 335 U.S. 377 (1948).

65. *See* Fair Labor Standards Act of 1938, Pub. L. No. 75-718, sec. 3(c), 52 Stat. 1060, 1060 (1938).

66. *Vermilya-Brown Co. v. Connell, supra* note 64, at 380.

67. *Id.*

68. *Id.* at 383–90.

69. *Id.* at 401. Jackson is joined in the dissent by Chief Justice Vinson and Justices Frankfurter and Burton.

70. *Id.* at 409.

71. *Algonquin SNG, Inc. v. Federal Energy Admin.*, 518 F.2d 1051 (D.C. Cir. 1975), *rev'd*, 426 U.S. 548 (1976). The Supreme Court reversed, holding that the Trade Expansion Act of 1962 granted the FEA a measure of discretion in determining the method used to adjust imports and that nothing in the statutory language restricted the adjustment of imports to encompass only quantitative methods as opposed to monetary methods that effect such adjustments.

72. *Id.* at 1053.

73. *Id.* at 1063.

74. *Id.* at 1062.

75. *Id.* at 1061. *See also United States v. Yoshida Int'l, Inc.*, 526 F.2d 560, 583 (C.C.P.A. 1975) ("The declaration of a national emergency is not a talisman enabling the President to rewrite the tariff schedules").

76. Only two judges joined Justice Rehnquist in the judgment of the Court, two (Douglas and Powell) joining in the result but not in the reasoning and four dissenting.

77. *First National City Bank v. Banco National de Cuba*, 406 U.S. 759 (1972).

78. *Id.* at 764.

79. *Id.* at 766.

80. *Id.* at 772 (Douglas, J.), 788–89 (Brennan, J.).

81. *Id.* at 773.

82. *Dames & Moore v. Regan, supra* note 33.

83. *Id.* at 666–67.

84. *Id.* at 668–69 (citations omitted).

85. *Id.* at 675–80.

86. *Id.* at 680, citing especially the International Claims Settlement Act of 1949, Pub. L. No. 81-455, 64 Stat. 12 (codified as amended at 22 U.S.C. sec. 1621 *et seq.* (1988)).

87. *Id.* at 682.

88. *Id.* at 686 (quoting *Youngstown Sheet & Tube Co. v. Sawyer, supra* note 12, at 610–11 (Frankfurter, J.)).

89. *United States v. Sperry Corp.*, 110 S. Ct. 387 (1989).

90. *Id.* at 393–97.

91. Convention for the Unification of Certain Rules Relating to International Transportation by Air, Oct. 12, 1929, 49 Stat. 3000, T.S. No. 876 (1934).

92. Bretton Woods Agreement Act of 1976, Pub. L. No. 94-564, 90 Stat. 2660.

93. *Trans World Airlines, Inc. v. Franklin Mint Corp.*, 466 U.S. 243, 253–57 (1984).

94. *Id.* at 254.

95. *Id.* at 259–60.

96. *Id.* at 260.

97. *Id.* at 276 n.5.

98. *Id.*

99. *Chandler v. Director of Public Prosecutions*, (1962) 3 All E.R. 142 (H.L.).

100. *Id.* at 153–59.

101. *Id.* at 159.

102. *See Washington Post Co. v. United States Dep't of State*, 840 F.2d 26, 35 (D.C. Cir. 1988), *vacated on other grounds*, 898 F.2d 793 (D.C. Cir. 1990). In *Washington Post*, the court reversed the district court's decision to deny discovery of Department of State (DOS) documents regarding citizenship of certain officials in the Iranian government. The case was remanded for appropriate fact-finding so that the court could review the DOS determination per congressional language calling upon the courts to review agency withholding claims de novo. Only Judge Bork, in a dissenting opinion, suggested the applicability of the political-question doctrine. *Id.* at 40–45.

103. *Id.* at 36–37.

104. *Commonwealth of Massachusetts v. Laird*, 451 F.2d 26 (1st Cir. 1971).

105. *Id.* at 30.

106. *Id.* at 31.

107. *Id.*

108. *Id.* at 29.

109. *Berk v. Laird*, 429 F.2d 302 (2d Cir. 1970).

110. *Mitchell v. Harmony, supra* note 6.

111. *In re Yamashita*, 327 U.S. 1 (1946).

112. *See id.* at 7.

113. *Id.* at 8.

114. *Id.*

115. *Id.*

116. *Id.*

117. *Id.*

118. *Id.* at 9–25.

119. *Id.* at 25.

120. *New York Times Co. v. United States,* 403 U.S. 713 (1971).

121. *Id.* at 732–33 (White, J. concurring).

122. *Id.* at 714 (per curiam).

123. *United States v. Progressive, Inc.,* 467 F. Supp. 990 (W.D. Wis. 1979).

124. For example, during the December 1989 U.S. invasion of Panama, it was announced by White House Press Secretary Marlin Fitzwater that a woman, Captain Linda L. Bray, had led a U.S. attack in a "fiercely resisted assault" on "an important military objective" (a guard-dog kennel) that had been "heavily defended" and in which three Panamanian security-force members had been killed. "It was an important military operation," he said. "A woman led it, and she did an outstanding job." This analysis from the White House stimulated a wide discussion, drawing in members of Congress and women's-rights advocates and raised serious constitutional issues about the military rules prohibiting the deployment of women in combat, which has implications for their promotion through the ranks. Shortly thereafter, news reports claimed that Captain Bray had led no such assault and that no Panamanians had been killed in the reported circumstances. Responding, Fitzwater acknowledged that he had "taken the figures on the dead Panamanians from newspaper accounts." "Report of Woman's Role Is Called Into Question," N.Y. Times, Jan. 8, 1990, at B8.

125. *Zweibon v. Mitchell,* 516 F.2d 594 (D.C. Cir. 1975).

126. *Id.* at 607.

127. *Zweibon v. Mitchell,* 363 F. Supp. 936, 943 (D.D.C. 1973).

128. *Zweibon v. Mitchell, supra* note 125, at 619–20.

129. *Id.* at 621–23.

130. *Id.* at 624.

131. *Id.* at 626.

132. *Id.* at 627, *citing United States v. Robel,* 389 U.S. 258, 263 (1967).

133. *Finzer v. Barry,* 798 F.2d 1450 (D.C. Cir. 1986), *aff'd in part, rev'd in part,* 485 U.S. 312 (1988).

134. *Id.* at 1452.

135. *Id.* at 1453.

136. *Id.*

137. *Id.* at 1459.

138. *Id.*

139. *Id.*

140. *Id.* at 1460 (citation omitted).

141. *Id.* at 1462.

142. *Id.* at 1463.

143. *Quinn v. Robinson,* 783 F.2d 776 (9th Cir. 1986).

144. *Id.* at 787.

145. *Id.* at 788.

146. *Planned Parenthood Fed. v. Agency for Int'l Dev.,* 838 F.2d 649 (2d Cir. 1988).

147. *Id.* at 655–56.

148. *Id.* (citations omitted).

149. *Cf. Diggs v. Richardson,* 555 F.2d 848 (D.C. Cir. 1976).

150. *Power Authority of New York v. Federal Power Com'n,* 247 F.2d 538 (D.C. Cir.), *vacated,* 355 U.S. 64 (1957).

151. *Natural Resources Defense Council, Inc. v. Nuclear Reg. Com'n,* 647 F.2d 1345 (D.C. Cir. 1981).

152. *See* Atomic Energy Act of 1954, Pub. L. No. 83-703, 68 Stat. 919 (codified as amended at 42 U.S.C. secs. 2011 *et. seq.* (1988)); Nuclear Non-Proliferation Act of 1978, Pub. L. No. 95-242, 92 Stat. 120 (codified at 22 U.S.C. secs. 3201 *et. seq.* (1988)).

153. It does not. *Chang v. United States,* 859 F.2d 893 (Fed. Cir. 1988).

154. *Haitian Refugee Center v. Gracey,* 809 F.2d 794, 798 (D.C. Cir. 1987).

155. The plaintiff's nonrefoulement claim was based on article 33 of the United Nations Convention Relating to the Status of Refugees, 19 U.S.T. 6223, T.I.A.S. No. 6577.

156. *Harisiades v. Shaughnessy,* 342 U.S. 580 (1952).

157. *Narenji v. Civiletti,* 617 F.2d 745 (D.C. Cir. 1979), *cert. denied sub nom. Confederation of Iranian Students v. Civiletti,* 446 U.S. 957 (1980).

158. *Id.* at 747–48. ("To reach a contrary conclusion the District Court undertook to evaluate the policy reasons upon which the regulation is based. In doing this the court went beyond an acceptable judicial role. Certainly in a case such as the one presented here it is not the business of courts to pass judgment on the decisions of the President in the field of foreign policy"). *Id.* at 748.

159. *Jean v. Nelson,* 727 F.2d 957 (11th Cir. 1984), *aff'd,* 472 U.S. 846 (1985).

160. *Id.* at 971.

161. *Id.* at 976 ("The discretionary decisions of executive officials in the immigration area are therefore subject to judicial review, but the scope of that review is extremely limited").

162. *Id.* at 977.

163. *Abourezk v. Reagan,* 785 F.2d 1043 (D.C. Cir. 1986), *aff'd,* 484 U.S. 1 (1987).

164. *Kleindienst v. Mandel,* 408 U.S. 753 (1972).

165. *Id.* at 766.

166. *See* Immigration and Nationality Act of 1952, 66 Stat. 182 (codified at 8 U.S.C. secs. 1182(a)(28)(D) and (d)(3)(A) (1988)).

167. *Kleindienst v. Mandel, supra* note 164, at 757.

168. *Id.* at 758–59, 769. Evidence was adduced that limits placed on prior waivers had not been respected by the plaintiff. The Court's adjudication also determined that the applicant had been rejected not on the initiative of the State Department but by the Immigration and Naturalization Service in opposition to State Department advice. *Id.* at 759.

169. *Id.* at 769.

170. *See Perkins v. Elg,* 307 U.S. 325, 350 (1939) (recognizing discretion of secretary of state to deny issuance of a passport).

171. *Kent v. Dulles,* 357 U.S. 116 (1958).

172. *See* Act of July 3, 1926, Pub. L. No. 69-493, sec. 1, 44 Stat. 887 (codified as amended at 22 U.S.C. sec. 211a); Immigration and Nationality Act of 1952, Pub. L. No. 82-414, sec. 215, 66 Stat. 163 (codified at 8 U.S.C. sec. 1185).

173. Act of July 3, 1926, sec. 1 (*quoted in Kent v. Dulles, supra* note 171, at 123).

174. *Kent v. Dulles, id.* at 124–25.

175. *Id.* at 125.

176. *Id.*

177. *Id.* at 128.

178. *Id.* at 129.

179. *Id.*

180. *Panama Refining Co. v. Ryan,* 293 U.S. 388, 420–30 (1935).

181. *United States v. Verdugo-Urquidez,* 110 S. Ct. 1065 (1990).

182. *Id.* at 1066.

183. *I.N.S. v. Chadha,* 462 U.S. 919 (1983).

184. *See* Franck and Bob, "The Return of Humpty Dumpty: Foreign Relations Law After the Chadha Case," 79 Am. J. Int'l L. 912 (1985).

185. *I.N.S. v. Chadha, supra* note 183, at 940.

186. *Baker v. Carr,* 369 U.S. 186, 217 (1962).

187. *I.N.S. v. Chadha, supra* note 183, at 941, citing the brief for petitioner in No. 80-1270, p. 48.

188. *Id.* at 941–42 (emphasis added).

189. *Id.* at 942–43.

190. *Dames & Moore v. Regan, supra* note 33 and accompanying text.

191. *I.N.S. v. Chadha, supra* note 183, at 942 n.13.

192. *Id.* at 944.

193. *Id.* at 944–59.

194. For a critique of the *Chadha* decision, *see* Franck and Bob, *supra* note 184.

195. *Goldwater v. Carter,* 444 U.S. 996 (1979).

196. *United States v. American Telephone & Telegraph Co.,* 567 F.2d 121 (D.C. Cir 1977).

197. *Id.* at 126.

198. *Id.* at 127.

199. *Id.* at 128 (footnotes omitted).

200. *Id.* at 134. *See also Romer v. Carlucci*, 847 F.2d 445 (8th Cir. 1988) (Defense Department cannot avoid judicial review of a decision to emplace MX missiles on sites in Colorado by characterizing this decision as a political question if it is challenged as having been made in violation of environmental-impact-statement requirements).

201. *United States v. American Telephone & Telegraph Co.*, 551 F.2d 384, 395 (D.C. Cir. 1976).

202. *United States v. American Telephone & Telegraph Co.*, *supra* note 196, at 131–33.

203. *Id.* at 132.

204. *Edwards v. Carter*, 580 F.2d 1055 (D.C. Cir.), *cert. denied*, 436 U.S. 907 (1978).

205. Judge MacKinnon's is a dissenting opinion, but as to the applicability of the political-question doctrine, his views clearly interpret what the majority did. *Id.* at 1064–66.

206. *Id.* at 1066 (citations omitted). To the same effect, *see Adams v. Vance*, 570 F.2d 950 (D.C. Cir. 1977); *United States v. Decker*, 600 F.2d 733, 737 (9th Cir.), *cert. denied*, 444 U.S. 855 (1979); *British Caledonian Airways Ltd. v. Bond*, 665 F.2d 1153, 1162 (D.C. Cir. 1981) ("We also reject the proposition that the determination in this case of whether the FAA Administrator has acted consistently with this nation's treaty obligations is a question that is constitutionally committed to the executive branch of the government"). *See also Stuart v. United States*, 813 F.2d 243, 247 (9th Cir. 1987) where the applicability of the doctrine is specifically rejected in a case involving interpretation of a tax treaty. It may be significant that the government, on appeal, did not persist in its contention on this point. *See Stuart v. United States*, 489 U.S. 353 (1989).

207. *South African Airways v. Dole*, 817 F.2d 119 (D.C. Cir.), *cert. denied*, 484 U.S. 896 (1987).

208. *Sneaker Circus, Inc. v. Carter*, 566 F.2d 396 (2d Cir. 1977).

209. *Id.* at 402.

210. *Japan Whaling Ass'n v. American Cetacean Soc.*, 478 U.S. 221 (1986).

211. 16 U.S.C. sec. 1821(e)(2) (1988).

212. 62 Stat. 1716, T.I.A.S. No. 1849 (entered into force Nov. 10, 1948).

213. *Japan Whaling Ass'n v. American Cetacean Soc.*, *supra* note 210, at 227–28.

214. *Baker v. Carr*, *supra* note 186, at 217.

215. *Japan Whaling Ass'n v. American Cetacean Soc.*, *supra* note 210, at 230.

216. *Id.*

217. *Id.* at 240–41.

218. *Id.* at 244–50.

219. *Lowry v. Reagan*, 676 F. Supp. 333 (D.D.C. 1987).

220. *Sanchez-Espinoza v. Reagan*, 568 F. Supp. 596 (D.D.C. 1984).

221. *Sanchez-Espinoza v. Reagan*, 770 F.2d 202, 206 (D.C. Cir. 1985). Rather the same approach, rejecting the doctrine and deciding in procedural and substantive merits, was employed by the D.C. Circuit in *Committee of United States Citizens in Nicaragua v. Reagan*, 859 F.2d 929 (D.C. Cir. 1988). The plaintiffs in that case had sought injunctive and declaratory relief regarding funding of Contras on the grounds that such funding violated the UN Charter, customary international law, the Administrative Procedure Act (APA), and the First and Fifth amendments. The court consciously limited the application of the doctrine, stating: "Given the care with which the political question doctrine should be applied and given the variety of claims encompassed by the present case, we find the trial court's blanket invocation of the political question doctrine to be inappropriate." *Id.* at 933.

222. *I.N.S. v. Chadha, supra* note 183, at 942.

223. *See* R. Falk, *Role of Domestic Courts in the International Legal Order* 11–13 n.20 (1964); Tigar, "Judicial Power, the 'Political Question Doctrine,' and Foreign Relations," 17 U.C.L.A. L. Rev. 1135, 1178–79 (1970); Henkin, "Is There a 'Political Question' Doctrine?" 85 Yale L.J. 597 (1976); L. Jaffe, *Judicial Aspects of Foreign Relations* 78 (1933).

224. "The courts, when a case or controversy arises, can always 'ascertain whether the will of Congress has been obeyed.' *Yakus v. United States.*" *I.N.S. v. Chadha, supra* note 183, at 953 n.16 (citation omitted).

Chapter Six
Mandated Adjudication

1. *Hudson v. Guestier*, 8 U.S. (4 Cranch) 293, 293–94 (1808). *See also American Banana Co. v. United Fruit Co.*, 213 U.S. 347 (1909).

2. Dellapenna, "Deciphering the Act of State Doctrine," 35 Vill. L. Rev. 1, 39 (1990). *See also W.S. Kirkpatrick & Co. v. Environmental Tectonics Corp., Int'l*, 110 S. Ct. 701, 704 (1990).

3. *Alfred Dunhill of London, Inc. v. Cuba*, 425 U.S. 682, 705 n.18, 726–28 (1976).

4. *Doe v. Braden*, 57 U.S. (16 How.) 635, 657–59 (1853).

5. *Alfred Dunhill of London, Inc. v. Cuba, supra* note 3, at 715; *First Nat'l City Bank v. Banco Nacional de Cuba*, 406 U.S. 759, 773–76 (1972).

6. *Banco Nacional de Cuba v. Sabbatino*, 376 U.S. 398 (1964).

7. 193 F. Supp. 375 (S.D.N.Y. 1961).

8. 307 F.2d 845 (2d Cir. 1962).

9. *Banco Nacional de Cuba v. Sabbatino, supra* note 6, at 423.

10. *Id.* at 428.

11. *Mannington Mills, Inc. v. Congoleum Corp.*, 595 F.2d 1287, 1292 (3d Cir. 1979). This is quoted with approval in *Tel-Oren v. Libyan Arab Republic*, 726 F.2d 774, 802 (D.C. Cir. 1984).

12. Pub. L. No. 88-633, sec. 301(d)(2), 78 Stat. 1009, 1013 (1964) (codified at 22 U.S.C. sec. 2370(e)(2) (1988)).

13. 22 U.S.C. sec. 2370(e)(2) (1988).

14. 110 Cong. Rec. 18,944 (daily ed. Aug. 14, 1964).

15. Dellapenna, *supra* note 2, at 110–11.

16. *See Banco Nacional de Cuba v. Farr*, 383 F.2d 166, 173–83 (2d Cir. 1967), *cert. denied*, 390 U.S. 956 (1968).

17. Comment, "Foreign Expropriation Cases in the United States: Conflicting Legislation and Judicial Policies," 17 U.S.F.L. Rev. 117 (1982); Dellapenna, *supra* note 2, at 111–21.

18. *W.S. Kirkpatrick & Co. v. Environmental Tectonics Corp., Int'l, supra* note 2. *See also Liu v. Republic of China*, 892 F.2d 1419 (9th Cir. 1989), *cert. dismissed*, 111 S. Ct. 27 (1990).

19. 110 Cong. Rec. 18,946 (daily ed. Aug. 14, 1964).

20. *The Schooner Exchange v. M'Faddon*, 11 U.S. (7 Cranch) 116 (1812).

21. *Ex Parte Peru*, 318 U.S. 578, 589 (1943).

22. *The Schooner Exchange v. M'Faddon, supra* note 20, at 137.

23. 1 *Restatement (Third) Foreign Relations Law of the United States* 391 (1987) (hereafter, *Restatement*). *See also Berizzi Bros. Co. v. Steamship Pesaro*, 271 U.S. 562 (1926).

24. *Cf.* International Convention for the Unification of Certain Rules Relating to the Immunity of State-Owned Vessels, Apr. 10, 1926, 176 L.N.T.S. 199; Hackworth, 2 *Digest of International Law* 463 (1941); European Convention on State Immunity, May 16, 1972, Eur. T.S. No. 74.

25. 26 Dept. of State Bull. 984 (1952).

26. *Define Jurisdiction of U.S. Courts in Suits Against Foreign States*, S. Rep. No. 1310, 94th Cong., 2d Sess. 10 (1976).

27. *Id.*

28. *Restatement, supra* note 23, at 393, and supporting citations therein.

29. *Rich v. Naviera Vacuba, S.A.*, 295 F.2d 24 (4th Cir. 1961); *Spacil v. Crowe*, 489 F.2d 614 (5th Cir. 1974).

30. Pub. L. No. 94-583, 90 Stat. 2891 (1976) (codified at 28 U.S.C. secs. 1330, 1332(a)(2)–(4), 1391(f), 1441(d), 1602–11 (1988)).

31. *Verlinden B.V. v. Central Bank of Nigeria*, 461 U.S. 480 (1983).

32. *Define Jurisdiction, supra* note 26, at 12.

Chapter Seven
Abolsihing Judicial Abdication

1. Bachof, "The West German Constitutional Judge Between Law and Politics," 11 Texas L.J. 403, 405 (1977).

2. *Id.* at 409.

3. D. Kommers, *The Constitutional Jurisprudence of the Federal Republic of Germany* 163 (1989).

4. *Id.* For example, state governments may ask for advisory opinions.

5. Quoted in *id.* at 168.

6. Note the clarity with which the German Basic Law resolves this problem of "standing," which in U.S. jurisprudence is closely related to the political-question doctrine and remains substantially unresolved. *See* T. Franck and M. Glennon, *Foreign Relations and National Security Law* 799–855 (1987) and cases noted therein. This permits the German courts to resolve disputes between legislators and the government that in the United States would usually fester and go unresolved. Moreover, it makes for government accountability, which is substantially absent in the U.S. system. For example, in a 1986 case before the Constitutional Court brought by the Parliamentary Green Party, the judiciary held that the agreement of the Federal Republic to the stationing in Germany of U.S. Pershing 2 missiles need not take the form of a treaty, which, under the Basic Law, would have required authorizing legislation. *Pershing 2 (#2) Case*, No. 1, 68 B Verf GE 1 (1986). Article 59(2)(1) of the Basic Law sets forth the requirement regarding enactment of legislation giving effect to treaties. *See also*, for an account of the pleadings and legal maneuouvers in this case, W. Heide, W. Schreiber, and Gotthard Wohrmann, *Die Nachrustung vor dem Bundesverfassungsgericht* (1986). Although the court once again granted the government wide latitude in the choice of means to pursue its foreign-relations policy, the judges expressed no doubt about their jurisdiction. They took responsibility for deciding whether the government was constitutionally authorized to make international commitments by lesser means than treaties. There is no sense in the German decisions that the judges should protect the balance of power by a policy of abstention. If by interpreting the Constitution they can resolve political struggle, they appear perfectly willing to do so.

7. *Case Concerning the Constitutionality of the Law of 24 May 1955 Implementing the Agreement of Paris of 23 October 1954 on the Status of the Saar*, No. 15, 4 B. Verf GE 157, 163–64 (1956). Translations of this and other parts of the decisions of the Constitutional Court are those of the author and are somewhat freely adapted from the German to convey their intended meaning rather than their literal structure.

8. *Id.* at 164–65.

9. *Id.* at 165–66.

10. *Id.* at 166.

11. *Id.*

12. *Id.* It should be noted that the agreement was subsequently rejected by the Saar in a plebescite and that the status of the Saar state in the German Federal Republic is now indistinguishable from that of the other states. For a

discussion of the status of the Saar, see the forthcoming entry *Saar Territory*, by Professor Fritz Munch, in 12 *Encyclopaedia of International Law*, The Max Planck Institute for Foreign Policy and Public International Law, 1990 (Heidelberg).

13. *The Inter-German Basic Treaty Case*, No. 1, 36 B. Verf GE 1 (1973).

14. *Id.*

15. *Id.*

16. *The Eastern Agreements Case*, No. 16, 40 B. Verf GE 141 (1975).

17. Arts. 14 and 16 of the Basic Law. *Id.* at 177.

18. *The Rudolph Hess Case*, No. 23, 55 B Verf GE 349 (1980).

19. *Id.* at 354.

20. *Id.*

21. *Id.* at 366.

22. *Id.*

23. *See Smith v. Reagan*, 844 F.2d 195 (4th Cir. 1988), *cert. denied*, 488 U.S. 954 (1988) and accompanying text.

24. For a discussion of this case, see Bockstaff and Koch, *The Tabatabai Case: The Immunity of Special Envoys and the Limits of Judicial Review*, 25 Ger. Yb. Int'l L. 539 (1982).

25. *The Tabatabai Case*, Fed. Ct. of Just., Third Crim. Div., Order of 27 Feb. 1984, BGH St 1984. This English translation was provided by E. A. Michos-Ederer and Markus Ederer (mimeo).

26. *Id.*

27. *The Extradition Case*, No. 14, 59 B Verf GE 280 (1982); *See also* R. Bernhardt, *Bundesverfassungsgericht und Volkerrechtliche Vertrage*, in Drath, Friesenhahn, et al., 2 *Bundesverfassungsgericht und Grundgesetz* 154 (1976).

28. Judgment of B Verf GE of Sept. 29, 1990, 2 Bv R 1247/90 DVBl. 15 Nov. 1990, 1223.

29. *The Citizenship Case*, No. 7, 77 B Verf GE 137 (1988).

30. *Id.* at 145.

31. *Id.* at 146–47.

32. *See* R. Hofmann, *Staatsangehorigkeit im getoilten Deutschland*, 49 ZaoRV 257 (1989).

33. *The Citizenship Case, supra* note 29, at 150–53.

34. *Id.* at 155.

35. *Id.* at 156.

36. *Id.* at 159.

37. *Id.* at 161.

38. *Id.*

39. *Id.* at 162.

40. *Id.* at 163.

41. *Id.* at 167.

42. *The Asylum Case*, 16 Eur. Grundr. Zeitschr. 19/20, 444 (12 Dec. 1989).

43. For the German jurists' clear perception of the American political question, see H. Simon, *Kerfassungsgerichtbarkeit*, in Benda, Maihofer, and Vogel, *Handbuch des Verfassungsrechts* 1252 (1983).

44. *Supra* note 29.

45. A stated purpose of the Foreign Sovereign Immunities Act, Act of October 21, 1976, Pub. L. No. 94-583, 90 Stat. 2891 (codified at scattered sections of 28 U.S.C.) was to get the Department of State out of what had hitherto been the inappropriate business of starting findings of fact and law in the context of specific disputes more appropriately left to the courts. H.R. Rep. No. 1487, 94th Cong., 2d Sess. 7, *reprinted in* 1976 U.S. Code Cong. & Admin. News 6604, 6605–06.

46. *Inter-German Basic Treaty Case, supra* note 13, at 14.

47. *The Schleyer Kidnapping Case,* 46 B Verf GE 160 (1977).

48. *The Pershing 2 and Cruise Missile Case I,* No. 3, 66 B Verf GE 39 (1983). *See also The Pershing 2 and Cruise Missile Case II,* No. 1, 68 B Verf GE 1 (1984).

49. *Id.* at 60.

50. *Id.*

51. *Id.* at 61.

52. *Id.*

53. *Id.*

54. *Baker v. Carr,* 369 U.S. 186, 197 (1962).

55. *The Pershing 2 and Cruise Missile Case I* and *The Pershing 2 and Cruise Missile Case II, supra* note 48, at 62–63. The same view was taken in similar circumstances by the Supreme Court of Canada, which also decided in favor of the government but rejected that part of its argument based on nonjusticiability. *Operation Dismantle Inc. v. Canada,* 59 N.R. 1 (1985). In that case, plaintiffs, using a "right-to-life" provision of the Canadian Charter of Rights, challenged the cabinet's agreement to allow U.S. tests of cruise missiles over Canadian territory. As Chief Justice Dickson explained, "To succeed at trial, the appellants would have to demonstrate, *inter alia*, that the testing of the cruise missile would cause an increase in the risk of nuclear war. It is precisely this link between the cabinet decision to permit the testing of the cruise and the increased risk of nuclear war which, in my opinion, they cannot establish." *Id.* at 10. At the same time, however, the chief justice had "no doubt that disputes of a political or foreign policy nature may be properly cognizable by the courts." *Id.* at 19. Justice Wilson, concurring, emphasized that "if what we are being asked to do is decide whether any particular act of the Executive violates the rights of the citizen, then it is not only appropriate that we answer the question; it is our obligation under the Charter to do so." *Id.* at 36.

56. *The Chemical Weapons Case,* No. 8, 77 B Verf GE 170 (1987).

57. *The Rudolph Hess Case, supra* note 538.

58. *Id.* at 368.

59. *Id.*

60. *Id.*

61. *Case Concerning the Constitutionality of the Law of 24 May 1955 Implementing the Agreement of Paris of 23 October 1954 on the Status of the Saar, supra* note 7, at 168.

62. *Id.* at 169.

63. *Id.*

64. *Id.* at 170.

65. *Id.*

66. *Id.*

67. *Id.* at 174.

68. *Id.*

69. "Spielraum für die politische Gestaltung." *The Inter-German Basic Treaty Case, supra* note 13.

70. *Id.*

71. *The Rudolph Hess Case, supra* note 18.

72. *Id.*

73. *Id.*

74. *Id.* at 365.

75. *Id.* at 366.

76. *Id.*

77. *Id.* at 367.

78. *Id.*

79. Arts. 14 and 16 of the Basic Law. *Id.* at 177–78.

80. *Id.* at 178.

81. *Id.* at 178–79.

82. *Operation Dismantle v. The Queen* (1985) 1 S.C.R. 441.

83. *Id.* at 459. *See also* the extensive treatment (and thoughtful rejection) of the U.K. act of state doctrine and the U.S. political-question doctrine by Wilson, J. *Id.* at 463–72.

Chapter Eight
A Rule of Evidence in Place of the Political-Question Doctrine

1. *United States v. Kendall*, 26 F. Cas. 702, 747–48 (C.C.D.C. 1837) (No. 15,517), *aff'd*, 37 U.S. (12 Pet.) 524 (1838).

2. *Id.* at 753.

3. *Kendall v. United States*, 37 U.S. (12 Pet.) 524 (1838).

4. *The Constitution of the United States of America* 480 (E. Corwin, ed. 1953).

5. *Kendall v. United States, supra* note 3, at 610.

6. L. Henkin, *Constitutionalism, Democracy, and Foreign Affairs* 72 (1990).

7. *Commonwealth of Massachusetts v. Laird*, 400 U.S. 886, 893 (1970).

8. *I.N.S. v. Chadha*, 462 U.S.919, 941 (1983).

9. Henkin, "Is There a 'Political Question' Doctrine?" 85 Yale L.J. 597 (1976). Henkin asserts, rightly, that the political-question doctrine, properly understood, asserts nothing that is not firmly established in courts' ordinary rules of statutory and constitutional construction.

10. War Powers Resolution, 50 U.S.C. secs. 1541–48, sec. 2(c) (1976).

11. *Id.* at secs. 3, 4(a)(1).

12. *Sterling v. Constantin,* 287 U.S. 378 (1932).

13. *Id.* at 398.

14. *Id.*

15. *Id.*

16. *Id.* at 399.

17. *Id.*

18. *Id.* at 399–400, *citing Martin v. Mott,* 25 U.S. (12 Wheat.) 19, 29–30 (1827).

19. *Id.* at 400.

20. *Id.*

21. *Fiallo v. Bell,* 430 U.S. 787 (1977).

22. Immigration and Nationality Act of 1952, 66 Stat. 182, as amended, 8 U.S.C. secs. 1101(b)(1)(D), 1101(b)(2).

23. *Fiallo v. Levi,* 406 F. Supp. 162, 166 (E.D.N.Y. 1975).

24. *Fiallo v. Bell, supra* note 21, at 796 (*quoting Mathews v. Diaz,* 426 U.S. 67, 81–82 (1976)).

25. *Harisiades v. Shaughnessy,* 342 U.S. 580, 596–97 (1952).

26. That the Constitution may call on the courts to intervene even in alien exclusion cases is stated explicitly in *Fong Yue Ting v. United States,* 149 U.S. 698, 713 (1893).

27. *Fiallo v. Bell, supra* note 21, at 796.

28. *Id.* at 795–96 n.6.

29. *Id.*

30. *See Mathews v. Diaz,* 426 U.S. 67, 81–82 (1976).

31. *Fiallo v. Bell, supra* note 21, at 798.

32. *See Case Concerning the Constitutionality of the Law of 24 May 1955 Implementing the Agreement of Paris of 23 October 1954 on the Status of the Saar,* No. 15, 4 B Verf GE 157, 163–64 (1956). Translations of this and other parts of the decisions of the Constitutional Court are those of the author and are somewhat freely adapted from the German in order to convey their intended meaning rather than their literal structure. *The Rudolph Hess Case,* No. 23, 55 B Verf GE 349 (1980); for a discussion of this case, see Bockstaff and Koch, *The Tabatabai Case: The Immunity of Special Envoys and the Limits of Judicial Review,* 25 Ger. Yb. Int'l L. 539 (1982); *The Extradition Case,* No. 14, 59 B Verf GE 280 (1982). *See also* R. Bernhardt, *Bundesverfassungsgericht und Volkerrechtliche Vertrage,* in Drath, Friesenhahn, et al., 2 *Bundesverfassungsgericht und Grundgesetz* 154 (1976); *The Citizenship Case,* No. 7, 77 B Verf GE 137 (1988).

33. *Fiallo v. Bell, supra* note 21, at 805.

34. *Id.*

35. L. Henkin, *supra* note 6, at 84.

36. *Fiallo v. Bell, supra* note 21, at 808–09.

Chapter Nine
The Special Cases

1. *See* Annotation, *Exclusion of Public from State Criminal Trial In Order to Avoid Intimidation of Witness,* 55 A.L.R. 4th 1196, 1199 (1987); Fed. R. Crim. P. 16(d), which provides a procedure through which discovery may be undertaken subject to a protective order; and Fed. R. Crim. P. 14, which provides for in camera inspection of the defendant's statements or confessions that the government introduces as evidence at trial. *But see Globe Newspaper Co. v. Superior Ct.,* 457 U.S. 596, 602–04 (1982); *Press-Enterprise Co. v. Superior Court of Cal.,* 478 U.S. 1, 12–14 (1986); *see also Gannett Co. v. DePasquale,* 443 U.S. 368 (1979).

2. *See* T. Franck and E. Weisband, *Secrecy and Foreign Policy* (1974).

3. 5 U.S.C. sec. 552(b).

4. The executive order currently in effect is Executive Order 12,356.

5. *EPA v. Mink,* 410 U.S. 73 (1973).

6. *Id.* at 82.

7. *See Washington Post Co. v. United States Dep't of State,* 840 F.2d 26, 32–35 (D.C. Cir. 1988), *vacated on other grounds,* 898 F.2d 793 (D.C. Cir. 1990), which examines the legislative history of the 1974 amendments.

8. *Ingle v. Department of Justice,* 698 F.2d 259, 264–65 (6th Cir. 1983).

9. *Halkin v. Helms,* 598 F.2d 1 (D.C. Cir. 1978).

10. The NSA is primarily responsible for cryptology and interception of communications.

11. *Halkin v. Helms, supra* note 9, at 7.

12. *Hayden v. National Security Agency,* 452 F. Supp. 247, 249 (D.D.C. 1978), *aff'd,* 608 F.2d 1321 (D.C. Cir. 1979), *cert. denied,* 446 U.S. 937 (1980).

13. *Id.* at 250.

14. *See, e.g., Phillippi v. Central Intelligence Agency,* 546 F.2d 1009, 1012 (D.C. Cir. 1976).

15. In *Bennett v. Department of Defense,* 419 F. Supp. 663, 666 (S.D.N.Y. 1976), the department submitted affidavits detailing "clandestine intelligence operations and . . . individual sources of information."

16. *See, e.g., Simmons v. Department of Justice,* 796 F.2d 709, 710 (4th Cir. 1986).

17. *Doyle v. Federal Bureau of Investigation,* 722 F.2d 554, 556 (9th Cir. 1983).

18. *Ollestad v. Kelley,* 573 F.2d 1109, 1110 (9th Cir. 1978).

19. "[I]ndexes serve not only the stated purpose of providing a justification for a claimed exemption, but also serve as mechanisms that allow a plaintiff to argue more effectively against specific agency claims." Note, "In Camera Inspection of National Security Files Under the Freedom of Information Act," 26 Kansas L. Rev. 617, 619 (1978).

20. *Holy Spirit Assoc. for the Unification of World Christianity v. Central Intelligence Agency*, 636 F.2d 838 (D.C. Cir. 1980), vacated as moot 455 U.S. 997 (1982). Although the appellate court mandated disclosure, the Unification Church subsequently withdrew its request for the documents, and the Supreme Court vacated the judgment.

21. *Ellsberg v. Mitchell*, 709 F.2d 51, 59 (D.C. Cir. 1983), *cert. denied*, 465 U.S. 1038 (1984). *See also Salisbury v. United States*, 690 F.2d 966, 971–73 (D.C. Cir. 1982) in which the appellate court upheld a summary-judgment motion made by the NSA and acknowledged that the agency has a large measure of discretion over classification decisions.

22. *Halperin v. National Security Council*, 452 F. Supp. 47, 49 (D.D.C. 1978), *aff'd*, 612 F.2d 586 (D.C. Cir. 1980).

23. *See Hrones v. Central Intelligence Agency*, 685 F.2d 13, 18 (1st Cir. 1982), *Ray v. Turner*, 587 F.2d 1187, 1195 (D.C. Cir. 1978).

24. Note, "National Security Information Disclosure Under the FOIA: The Need for Effective Judicial Enforcement," 25 B.C.L. Rev. 611, 633 (1984).

25. The leading example is President Richard Nixon's submitting to the subpoena of Watergate tapes rather than precipitating a constitutional crisis. *See United States v. Nixon*, 418 U.S. 683 (1974).

26. *Patterson v. Federal Bureau of Investigation*, 893 F.2d 595, 600 (3d Cir.) (emphasis in original), *cert. denied*, 111 S. Ct. 48 (1990).

27. *Lame v. United States Dep't of Justice*, 654 F.2d 917, 922 (3d Cir. 1981).

28. *See* Note, *supra* note 24, at 632.

29. *Jaffe v. Central Intelligence Agency*, 516 F. Supp. 576, 581–83 (D.D.C. 1981).

30. *Stern v. Richardson*, 367 F. Supp. 1316, 1319 (D.D.C. 1973). Note, however, that the FBI did not use either exemption (b)(1) or (b)(3). *Id.* at 1318–19.

31. *See, e.g.*, the "just compensation for inventors" cases where provision is made for in camera procedures. *Halpern v. United States*, 258 F.2d 36 (2d Cir. 1958). *See also* the use of special masters and issuance of protective orders to guard the confidentiality of privileged trade and manufacturing information held by a regulatory agency but sought by a plaintiff in a products-liability suit. *In re "Agent Orange" Product Liability Litigation*, 96 F.R.D. 578 (E.D.N.Y. 1983).

32. *United States v. Nixon, supra* note 25, at 688 n.6.

33. *Id.* at 714.

34. *United States v. Brown*, 539 F.2d 467, 470 (5th Cir. 1976); *see also United States v. Zolin*, 109 S. Ct. 2619 (1989).

35. *Halpern v. United States, supra* note 31, at 43.

36. Classified Information Procedures Act, Pub. L. 96–456, 94 Stat. 2025 (1980) (codified as amended at 18 U.S.C. app. secs. 1 *et. seq.* (1988)).

37. *United States v. Wilson*, 571 F. Supp. 1422, 1426 (S.D.N.Y. 1983).

38. In section 1 of the act, classified information is defined as "any information or material that has been determined by the United States Government pursuant to an Executive order, statute, or regulation, to require protection against unauthorized disclosure for reasons of national security." 18 U.S.C. app. sec. 1(a) (1988). Section 1(b) defines *national security* as the "national defense and foreign relations of the United States." *Id.* at sec. 1(b).

39. 18 U.S.C. app. sec. 3 (1988).

40. *United States v. Jolliff*, 548 F. Supp. 229, 232 (D. Md. 1981).

41. Sen. Rep. No. 823, 96th Cong., 2d Sess. 2, *reprinted in* 1980 U.S. Code Cong. & Admin. News 4294, 4295.

42. *United States v. Yunis*, 867 F.2d 617, 619 (D.C. Cir. 1989).

43. *Id.* at 619–21.

44. *Id.* at 623.

45. *Id.*

46. *United States v. Poindexter*, 698 F. Supp. 316, 317–18 (D.D.C. 1988).

47. *See* 18 U.S.C. app. secs. 5(a),(b); 6(a),(b) (1988).

48. Sen. Rep. No. 823, *supra* note 41, at 7, *reprinted in* 1980 U.S. Code Cong. & Admin. News at 4301.

49. *United States v. Poindexter, supra* note 46, at 320–21.

50. *Id.* at 321. *See also United States v. North*, 708 F. Supp. 399 (D.D.C. 1988).

51. *United States v. Bell*, 464 F.2d 667, 670 (2d Cir. 1972). The motion of defendant Bell asked for the suppression of evidence seized when he was searched as a "selectee" under an antihijacking program. In the closed portion of the trial, the government gave evidence to defend the reasonableness of its secret profile for identifying selectees for search.

52. *Katz v. United States*, 389 U.S. 347 (1967). This decision overruled *Olmstead v. United States*, 277 U.S. 438 (1928), which had held that a wiretap did not constitute a Fourth Amendment search.

53. *United States v. De Los Santos*, 819 F.2d 94, 96–97 (5th Cir.), *cert. denied*, 484 U.S. 978 (1987). Although the court did not base its decision entirely on the in camera hearing, the information divulged there was helpful in making the determination.

54. *United States v. Willis*, 578 F. Supp. 361, 364–65 (N.D. Ohio 1984).

55. *United States v. Cianfrani*, 573 F.2d 835, 855–60 (3d Cir. 1978).

56. *See McQuade v. Michael Gassner Mechanical & Elec. Contractors*, 587 F. Supp. 1183, 1190 (D. Conn. 1984).

57. *Zweibon v. Mitchell*, 516 F.2d 594, 624 (D.C. Cir. 1975).

58. *United States v. American Telephone & Telegraph Co.*, 567 F.2d 121, 131–32 (D.C. Cir. 1977).

59. *United States v. Lemonakis*, 485 F.2d 941, 963 (D.C. Cir. 1973), *cert. denied*, 415 U.S. 989 (1974). *See also United States v. Ajlouny*, 629 F.2d 830, 838–39 (2d Cir. 1980), *cert. denied*, 449 U.S. 1111 (1981).

60. Foreign Intelligence Surveillance Act, Pub. L. No. 95-511, 92 Stat. 1783 (1978) (codified at 50 U.S.C. secs. 1801 *et seq.* (1988)).

61. *Id.* at sec. 1802(b).

62. *Id.* at sec. 1803.

63. *Id.* at sec. 1806(b); *see also In re Grand Jury Proceedings*, 856 F.2d 685, 687 (4th Cir. 1988).

64. *United States v. Badia*, 827 F.2d 1458, 1464 (11th Cir. 1987), *cert. denied*, 485 U.S. 937 (1988).

65. *Id.*

66. *See United States v. Duggan*, 743 F.2d 59, 67 (2d Cir. 1984).

67. *See United States v. Belfield*, 692 F.2d 141, 146 (D.C. Cir. 1982).

68. *United States v. American Telephone & Telegraph Co.*, *supra* note 58, at 122–23.

69. *Id.* at 125–27.

70. *Id.* at 123.

71. *Id.* at 126–27.

72. *Id.* at 126.

73. *Id.* at 128 (citations omitted).

74. The court ordered the parties to try to negotiate a compromise in which the district court might play an umpiring role regarding access to sensitive information. *United States v. American Telephone & Telegraph Co.*, 551 F.2d 384, 395 (D.C. Cir. 1976). The parties were unable to work out such an agreed solution. *United States v. American Telephone & Telegraph Co.*, *supra* note 58.

75. *Id.* at 132.

76. *Id.*

77. *Id.* at 133 (citations omitted).

78. *See Quinn v. Robertson*, 783 F.2d 776, 788 (9th Cir.), *cert. denied*, 479 U.S. 882 (1986).

79. *Id.* at 788; *Eain v. Wilkes*, 641 F.2d 504, 515 (7th Cir.), *cert. denied*, 454 U.S. 894 (1981).

80. *Military Audit Project v. Bush*, 418 F. Supp. 876, 878–80 (D.D.C. 1976).

81. Note, "In Camera Inspections Under the Freedom of Information Act," 41 U. Chi. L. Rev. 557, 560 (1974).

82. *Id.* at 560. This problem can be somewhat minimized by requiring the provider of the information to develop an index.

83. *Ray v. Turner*, *supra* note 23, at 1211.

84. *But see* Note, "National Security and the Amended Freedom of Information Act," 85 Yale L.J. 401, 415 (1976) (alleging that the FOIA would exacerbate executive and judicial differences).

85. These procedures, as we have seen, are designed to protect sensitive evidence. While the chapter has focused on in camera procedures, these have also been supplemented by other methods. Another procedure intended to allay fear of disclosure is the use of special masters in such cases. *In re United States Dep't of Defense*, 848 F.2d 232, 234–38 (D.C. Cir. 1988). In this case the district court's appointment of a special master was approved. Such a special master is someone who holds or has recently held a security clearance. Congress could also empower the court to require security clearances for court personnel involved in the case. Note, "FOIA Exemption 3 and the CIA: An Approach to End the Confusion and Controversy," 68 Minn. L. Rev. 1231, 1258 (1984).

86. A. Bickel, *The Least Dangerous Branch* 184 (1962).

87. *Virginia v. West Virginia*, 222 U.S. 17 (1911).

88. *Id.* at 19–20.

89. *Brown v. Board of Education*, 349 U.S. 294 (1955).

90. Pub. L. No. 73-343, 48 Stat. 955 (1934) (codified as amended at 28 U.S.C. secs. 2201, 2202 (1988)).

91. *See* Note, "Declaratory Judgment and Matured Causes of Action," 53 Col. L. Rev. 1130, 1131–33 (1953).

92. *President v. Vance*, 627 F.2d 353, 364 n.76 (D.C. Cir. 1980) (declaratory judgment appropriate when it will clarify legal issues or "terminate and afford relief from the uncertainty, insecurity, and controversy giving rise to the proceeding" (citation omitted)).

93. *See, e.g., National Organization for the Reform of Marijuana Laws v. United States Dep't of State*, 452 F. Supp. 1226, 1228 (D.D.C. 1978).

94. Note, "Declaratory Judgment and Matured Causes of Action," *supra* note 91, at 1130–31.

95. *Interdynamics, Inc. v. Wolf*, 698 F.2d 157, 165 (3d Cir. 1982).

96. *National Organization for the Reform of Marijuana Laws v. United States Dep't of State*, *supra* note 93, at 1235.

97. *See Baker v. Carr*, 369 U.S. 186, 194–95 (1962). For instances of declaratory judgments directed to Congress, see *Powell v. McCormack*, 395 U.S. 486, 517–18, 550 (1969). *See also Democratic Party of the United States v. National Conservative Political Action Committee*, 578 F. Supp. 797, 802 (E.D. Pa. 1983).

CHAPTER TEN
CONCLUSIONS

1. *See* D. Richards, *Foundations of American Constitutionalism* 32–130 (1989).

2. T. Jefferson, *Notes on the State of Virginia* 120 (1784).

3. Madison, *The Federalist No. 10*, in *The Federalist* 59 (J. Cooke ed. 1961).

4. *Id*.

5. R. Falk, *Role of Domestic Courts in the International Legal Order* 11 (1964).

6. *Id*. at n.20.

7. *Id*. at 11–13.

8. Tigar, "Judicial Power, the 'Political Question Doctrine,' and Foreign Relations," 17 U.C.L.A. L. Rev. 1135, 1178–79 (1970).

9. *See* Henkin, "Is There a 'Political Question' Doctrine?" 85 Yale L.J. 597 (1976).

10. L. Jaffe, *Judicial Aspects of Foreign Relations* 78 (1933).

❖ Index ❖